Advance Praise for *Under the Dome*

"America's 'front door to democracy' is wide open today thanks to the passion and persistence of many champions during the challenging and twisting course navigated to realize the construction of the Capitol Visitor Center. Having been part of this journey, I found that Alan Hantman's account in *Under the Dome* is both accurate and refreshingly transparent as he chronicles his stewardship of the Capitol and this historic expansion."—Rebecca W. Rimel, former president, The Pew Charitable Trusts

"Hantman's insider understanding reveals how America balanced security and the imperative of free public access to America's 'temple of democracy,' our Capitol, through the tumultuous times of the 1998 shooting of two Capitol Police officers, the 9/11 and anthrax attacks, and finally the building of the Capitol Visitor Center, which now provides a safe and welcoming entry to this sacred space."—Jane Louise Campbell, president and CEO, US Capitol Historical Society

"I witnessed the challenging path of politics and critics the 10th Architect of the Capitol navigated to design and build an addition that has transformed the Capitol from a building once hostile to visitors into a stately center of learning and comfort, welcoming millions each year. *Under the Dome* faithfully documents the largest expansion of the Capitol in its history, and it does so in an accessible and entertaining way."—John Mica, former US Representative

"*Under the Dome* is based on the unique perspective of a professional who served our nation well. It makes evident why public service is so important while illustrating the challenges public servants face in striving to accomplish major initiatives at the heart of our government."—Jeff Trandahl, former clerk, US House of Representatives

"At its dedication ceremony, I was honored to bless those who invested years of their lives under difficult circumstances to bring the multilayered dream of the Capitol Visitor Center to fruition. The crafted architecture described in *Under the Dome* opened new dimensions of freedom and accessibility to the People's House for generations to come."—Daniel P. Coughlin, former chaplain, US House of Representatives

"I witnessed firsthand Hantman's talent as an architect and committed historic preservationist when he served as the 10th Architect of the Capitol and member of the Advisory Council on Historic Preservation. *Under the Dome* tells the incredible story of how he applied these talents to the design and construction of the largest expansion of the Capitol in its history. This is compelling reading for anyone who has ever visited, or wanted to visit, our nation's Capitol."—Reid J. Nelson, Washington, DC

D1451819

UNDER THE DOME

Other Titles of Interest from Georgetown University Press

Between Freedom and Equality: The History of an African American Family in Washington, DC
Barbara Boyle Torrey and Clara Myrick Green

DC Jazz: Stories of Jazz Music in Washington, DC
Maurice Jackson and Blair A. Ruble, Editors

A Georgetown Life: The Reminiscences of Britannia Wellington Peter Kennon of Tudor Place
Grant S. Quertermous, Editor

Georgetown's Second Founder: Fr. Giovanni Grassi's News on the Present Condition of the Republic of the United States of North America
Giovanni Grassi, Translated and Introduced by Roberto Severino

George Washington's Final Battle: The Epic Struggle to Build a Capital City and a Nation
Robert P. Watson

Spy Sites of Washington, DC: A Guide to the Capital Region's Secret History
Robert Wallace and H. Keith Melton, with Henry R. Schlesinger

Under THE Dome

POLITICS, CRISIS, *and* ARCHITECTURE *at the* UNITED STATES CAPITOL

Alan M. Hantman, FAIA

10TH ARCHITECT *of the* CAPITOL

Foreword by Former Senate Majority Leader Harry M. Reid Jr.

GEORGETOWN UNIVERSITY PRESS / WASHINGTON, DC

The publisher is not responsible for third-party websites or their content.
URL links were active at time of publication.

Library of Congress Cataloging-in-Publication Data

Names: Hantman, Alan M., author. | Reid, Harry, 1939-2021, writer of foreword.
Title: Under the dome : politics, crisis, and architecture at the United States Capitol /
Alan M. Hantman, FAIA ; foreword by former Senate Majority Leader Harry Reid Jr.
Description: Washington, DC : Georgetown University Press, [2024] | Includes bibliographical references and index.
Identifiers: LCCN 2023021876 (print) | LCCN 2023021877 (ebook) | ISBN 9781647124243 (paperback) | ISBN 9781647124250 (ebook)
Subjects: LCSH: United States Capitol (Washington, D.C.) | United States Capitol Visitor Center (Washington, D.C.) | Architecture—Washington (D.C.)—History. | Washington (D.C.)—Buildings, structures, etc.
Classification: LCC F204.C2 H23 2024 (print) | LCC F204.C2 (ebook) | DDC 725/.1109753—dc23/eng/20230524
LC record available at https://lccn.loc.gov/2023021876
LC ebook record available at https://lccn.loc.gov/2023021877

∞ This paper meets the requirements of ANSI/NISO Z39.48-1992 (Permanence of Paper).

25 24   9 8 7 6 5 4 3 2 First printing

Printed in the United States of America

Cover design by Erin Kirk
Interior design by Classic City Composition

DEDICATION

To my parents, Sam and Adele Hantman, who never had the opportunity to walk Capitol corridors with me and hear their footsteps echo off its historic walls; and to my wife and life partner, Rosalyn, who has walked together with me every step of our fifty-nine-year journey.

CONTENTS

Foreword

As I reflect on my thirty-four years of congressional service, I recall with solemnity my work with Alan Hantman, the 10th Architect of the Capitol (AOC), from February 1997 until February 2007.

New members of Congress spend years learning the floor plan of the massive US Capitol structures; I didn't have to. When I first came to Washington, DC, in 1961 to attend George Washington Law School, I served as a member of the US Capitol Police. During my 3:00 p.m. to 11:00 p.m. shift, I spent much of my time walking around the Capitol. Because of this, I know every nook and cranny of this immense building.

Knowing the Capitol building in addition to the three House office buildings and the three Senate office buildings was most helpful to me in all of my work, including my work with Alan Hantman when he served as the AOC.

Alan Hantman's book *Under the Dome: Politics, Crisis, and Architecture at the United States Capitol* is a much-needed new, vibrant book on the modern Capitol. His book clearly shows the wide latitude of the AOC's oversight of the Capitol campus.

The AOC is responsible for more than 18.4 million square feet of office space, 570 acres of grounds, 30 buildings, and thousands of works of art.

My work with Alan Hantman came at a pivotal point in the management of the US Capitol. When I arrived in Washington, DC, in 1961, the Capitol grounds were open to visitors. The only security was a Capitol Police guard at the few entrances that existed to the Capitol building at the time. The police on duty were seated at a desk at the entrances for members of Congress, staff, and public.

The murders of Capitol Police Special Agent John Gibson and Capitol Police Officer Jacob J. "J.J." Chestnut by a mentally ill gunman in 1998 changed the freedom of movement in and around the Capitol forever. Their murders were the impetus for major security upgrades across Capitol Hill. These tragic events caused an immediate focus on the security of having convenient entrances to all Capitol buildings for members of Congress, staff, and visitors.

The result was a bipartisan congressional approval of a very large appropriation to construct a safe, secure entrance to the Capitol which became known as the Capitol Visitor Center. This huge project was impeded by the 9/11 terrorist attacks at the New York World Trade Center, the Pentagon, and United Flight 93, which killed almost three thousand. Occurring near the same time was the anthrax poisoning attack in the Hart Senate Office Building. Through all of this, AOC Alan Hantman continued the major construction of the Capitol Visitor Center. Upon entering the visitor center, one would experience the new central gathering place for visitors coming to see the Capitol: Emancipation Hall, named to recognize the enslaved laborers who helped construct the US Capitol.

Under the Dome is an exemplary display of the birth, growth, and future of these iconic grounds and buildings.

—Former Senate Majority Leader
Harry M. Reid Jr. (1939–2021), May 2021

UNDER THE DOME

Introduction

Shafts of light creep their way around the rotunda's stone walls in sync with the earth's rotation around the sun. The intensity changes with the seasons; the angle of the sun's rays penetrate most deeply into the circular chamber when the dog days of summer come to the nation's Capitol.

Thirty-six windows ring the rotunda's circumference behind the cast iron peristyle of columns designed in 1855 by the 4th Architect of the Capitol, Thomas Ustick Walter. This monumental colonnade provides a visually stable base to carry the nine-million-pound dome, curving upward to the nineteen-foot-tall *Statue of Freedom* crowning its summit. These noble Corinthian columns mime the weight-bearing stone columns of antiquity, but they are hollow, fabricated of cast iron. These purely decorative elements are themselves supported on concealed iron brackets, not bearing any of the tremendous weight of the great dome rising above.

This beautiful band of illusions functions only as fireplace flues for member rooms below and as rain-leaders to siphon away the waters of Washington's storms. The dome's design masks the fact that it is built of fish-scaled, overlapping cast iron plates, not the classically inspired stone and tile composition it appears to be. The full weight of the dome and its peristyle are in reality carried by the ninety-six-foot-diameter inner foundation wall, built in the 1820s by the 3rd Architect of the Capitol, Charles Bulfinch.

The domed US Capitol building is recognized around the world as America's most iconic symbol, the forum for our representative democracy, the physical stage for our quadrennial transfer of executive power. Perfect in its geometry, the dome is more than a classic crown on a historic building: it is a symbol of unity, of cohesiveness, inspiring respect in those who applaud our democracy. Under the dome, portrayed on the 180-foot-high rotunda ceiling, is Constantino Brumidi's *Apotheosis of Washington*, depicting our first president flanked by mythological figures representing Liberty, Victory, and the original thirteen colonies. Inscribed above Washington is a banner proclaiming *E pluribus unum*, "out of many, one."

As the 10th Architect of the Capitol, I was honored to serve from 1997 to 2007 as head of the 2,300-member legislative branch agency dedicated to preserving and upgrading this magnificent structure, and all the buildings and grounds of Capitol Hill. I came to know and love every corner of this dynamic and complex ecosystem. The Architect of the Capitol is an officer of Congress entrusted with 18 million square feet of space across 30 buildings, more than 500 acres of grounds, and thousands of irreplaceable works of art.

Architect of the Capitol is also the name of a legislative branch agency with an annual budget exceeding $500 million. Staff members work around the clock in support of Congress, the Supreme Court, and the Library of Congress and as responsible stewards preserving Capitol Hill's heritage assets on behalf of all Americans. As architect, I was in charge of a talented team in the design and construction of new facilities, the renovation and reconstruction of

Figure I.1. Rotunda sunlight. Courtesy of Alan M. Hantman

others, preventive maintenance and repairs, support services for Congress, and building and grounds operations. I testified at more than fifty public hearings before House and Senate oversight committees in support of these stewardship responsibilities and the work of the Capitol Police Board—each hearing a unique challenge.

Anyone who spends time on Capitol Hill soon recognizes that beneath that awe-inspiring dome, behind the Capitol's monumental sandstone and marble façade, dynamic currents of power push and pull those within its walls in waves, counter-currents, and irresistible undertows of dogma and political expediency. Years, even decades, can pass before an urgent need develops a critical mass that finally ripens into a priority—for this need to come

so sharply into focus that it can no longer be ignored or kicked down the road to await resolution by unknown successors.

The crystallization of such a need occurred in an instant in 1998, when a single disturbed man, Russell E. Weston Jr., walked into the Capitol, pistol in hand. He immediately murdered Officer J.J. Chestnut and in an exchange of gunfire shot and killed Detective John Gibson. Weston had come in search of a powerful "ruby satellite system" he believed was hidden within the "great safe" in the Senate, just waiting for him to find so that he could be transported back in time to when he would be "no longer deceased."[1]

This tragedy brought into painful focus the critical need for major security upgrades across Capi-

Figure I.2. Aerial view of Capitol campus, looking east. Courtesy of Architect of the Capitol

tol Hill, catapulting long-pending plans onto Congress's front burner. At its core was a new Capitol Visitor Center (CVC) to safely screen, respectfully welcome, and provide visitors with educational opportunities as they move into the physical heart of the US Capitol. A divided Congress had long resisted such calls, avoiding the risk of expending appropriated funds on a project that watchdogs and political foes would inevitably consider a nonessential political perk.

Under the Dome describes the design and construction of the Capitol Visitor Center, the balancing of security and preservation with safe and open public access, and the issues, people, and competing government committees and processes that impacted the project—all combined with historic perspective, architectural detail, personal observations, and congressional interactions.

Our intent was always to respect the historic Capitol building while keeping visitors and the Congress safe. The quality and proportions of its public spaces, its exhibits and visitor orientation program, and the transition from the underground center into the Capitol building were designed to be seamless and historically compatible.

The visitor center project faced many hurdles, including being caught in the crosshairs of partisan bickering, budget battles, national crises, and Capitol Christmas tree lightings gone wrong. Despite the complexity of this process and controversial media coverage as the visitor center scope and schedule continued to morph, newspaper editorials ultimately recognized the design as "Superb."[2] It received unanimous bipartisan support from the eighteen-member Capitol Preservation Commission, with the Congress appropriating essential funding over time. Positive design reviews soon gave way to criticism of both the Architect of the Capitol and Congress due to cost increases and elongated schedules caused by major post-9/11 scope increases and multiple security-based redesigns over the course of construction. In the face of this, I remain enormously proud of the major contribution our team made in fulfilling our stewardship responsibilities campus-wide while the visitor center expanded the Capitol building by 70 percent, the largest increment of growth since it was originally conceived in 1793.

To a visitor's eye, the Capitol appears to be a model of unity, but in truth it is more of a physical container within which conflicting philosophies

Figure I.3. East–west rotunda axis. Courtesy of Jeffrey Schwarz Photography

clash, where hidden prejudices battle. Looking at the Capitol from afar, one sees two symmetrical sections of the building—the House of Representatives on the south and the Senate on the north. The government established by the founding fathers in the Constitution fully intended to create basic legal and philosophical differences between those two bodies. What can't easily be conceptualized is the invisible east–west axis running through the centerline of the dome, a dividing line scrupulously maintained between the two houses of Congress, effectively cutting the Capitol in half.

Early in my tenure I began to understand just how tenaciously members of each chamber guard each square foot, each physical prerogative within their respective half of the people's house. I had always seen the building as a single entity, a unified whole, and did not understand that the members of Congress saw it as fundamentally split, divided at its core. Each half is divided into one hundred distinct companies in the Senate, and 435 in the House, each purporting to represent their constituencies in support of our Constitution and our democracy. But just as the thirty-six columns at the base of the dome are hollow, architectural decorations only appearing to support the magnificent nine-million-pound construction above, many members place political survival over the Constitution they have sworn to uphold, or to any true commitment to *E pluribus unum*. Like the hollow columns, their commitment to unity, to working together in the best interests of the nation, is, too often, an illusion.

During my ten-year term, the country saw three presidential inaugurations, a presidential impeachment, the shooting of two US Capitol Police officers, the attacks on 9/11 and the anthrax attacks in the Hart Senate Office Building, as well as sacred Congressional Gold Medal ceremonies, lying-in-state and lying-in-honor memorial services, and hundreds of public events and milestones marked within the walls or on the grounds of this, our national stage. I was honored to witness Presidents Bill Clinton and George W. Bush walking these Capitol corridors and stairs, out through the western doors to their inaugural stands to be greeted by hundreds of thousands of Americans on the National Mall celebrating the orderly transfer of power.

On January 6, 2021, the eyes of the country and the world were drawn to the US Capitol building for another reason, to witness a mob of thousands swarming down Pennsylvania Avenue from the White House to the Capitol, attacking the Congress convened there to count the 2020 presidential electoral votes already certified by each of the fifty states.

It was gut-wrenching to gape helplessly as mobs of terrorists overpowered thin police lines, helpless behind flimsy bicycle racks. To see insurrectionists defile Capitol grounds, erecting a gallows and noose in the spot where each holiday season the Architect of the Capitol erects and decorates a congressional Christmas tree, where thousands come together to commemorate our nation's heroes on Memorial Day, and where we celebrate our independence at July Fourth concerts.

We all watched as thousands of rioters stormed the Capitol, climbing inaugural stands built by the architect for the swearing-in ceremony of our new president, ripping off speakers and throwing them at police below. Dozens scaled Frederick Law Olmsted's historic 1880s marble terraces to launch a coordinated attack on police officers desperately protecting the central west front door just outside the Architect of the Capitol offices, crushing and bloodying an officer crying out for help, dragging others into the crowd to be kicked and beaten with a crutch, a hockey stick, with long poles flying American flags, all used as weapons to overpower police. Insurgents breached the Capitol at more than eight points, smashing in windows and doors.

We were shaken as cameras from all angles captured images of these insurrectionists freely marauding through vaulted Senate corridors graced with Constantino Brumidi's historic murals, halls we restored and maintained. They invaded the Speaker's offices in their rampage, breaking through the outer door of a conference room with terrified staff members huddled beneath a table within. Hundreds defiled Statuary Hall, flying White nationalist and Confederate flags, then entered the Capitol Rotunda crowned with Constantino Brumidi's majestic fresco, the *Apotheosis of Washington*, 180 feet above. This fresco celebrates our first president, who refused calls by some that he become our king, willingly stepping down, first as commander of our armies, and then again after completing his elected terms of office.

A police officer died as a result of the attack, four others soon died by suicide, 140 more were injured. I visualized the Capitol crypt, with its Doric sandstone columns encircling the white compass rose, the point of origin for the city's quadrants, and the poignant, care-worn bust of Abraham Lincoln, weeping as he watched rampaging terrorists overpower the police, screaming and pushing their way through this sacred chamber as they hunted congressional leaders and the vice president to capture, beat, or kill.

For generations in our free and democratic society, we have debated how to balance security needs against the contrasting imperative of free public access. For a decade I served with the sergeants at arms of the House and the Senate as a member of the three-person Capitol Police Board, responding to earlier attacks on the Capitol, repeatedly wrestling with this insoluble security versus access dilemma as Congress authorized increasingly tighter security provisions, an increasingly larger Capitol Police force, and enhanced paths of communications and decision-making that had clearly broken down.

These efforts were all prelude to the January 6 insurrection and the interruption of the constitutionally mandated counting of the ballots, presenting "lessons learned" opportunities. In retrospect, through all our security planning sessions with multiple federal security agencies, through all our congressional hearings before House and Senate committees, the specter of thousands of insurrectionists advancing on the Capitol had never been raised. The appalling January 6 attack has brought this debate to ever greater heights, with many calling for major increases in physical security measures that would continue to severely limit access to the people's house.

It is impossible to predict what a new normalcy will look like in Washington, DC, and on Capitol Hill. Impossible to predict what new measures Congress will authorize over the months and years to come, as officials continue to investigate and call for strengthened security. Going forward, it is clear that to protect our country, we must not only reevaluate current security provisions but must also work together to foster respect for our Constitution, for truth, for our precious but fragile democratic institutions, and against the twin pandemics of mistrust and hate sweeping our deeply polarized political parties and our nation.

In 1993 our nation celebrated the two-hundredth anniversary of the ceremonial laying of the Capitol building's first cornerstone. This kicked off the ten-year celebration of the Capitol's bicentennial, during which, according to William C. Allen, architectural historian in the Office of the Architect of the Capitol, "numerous projects and programs were undertaken to give the American people a better understanding of this great building and the ideals that it stands for. One of the projects was a comprehensive history of the Capitol's design and construction."[3]

Allen is the author of *History of the United States Capitol: A Chronicle of Design, Construction, and Politics*, a definitive book written largely under my oversight. I strongly supported this important effort and wrote in its foreword:

> Within the general story of the Capitol's development lies the history of the office I am honored to hold. . . . In reading about the history of the Capitol I am struck by the fact that for more than 200 years it has been a work in progress. Construction of the building that George Washington approved was begun in 1793 but was soon altered by an architectural metamorphosis dictated by changing circumstance, fashion, and fortune. Furthermore, as the nation grew so did the Congress and the Capitol. Change and growth seem to be the threads that bind the Capitol's history together.[4]

Bill Allen's research has been invaluable in placing the metamorphosis of the Capitol building into his well-chronicled historical context, a context that I build upon with my own decade-long slice of history lived within our Temple of Liberty.

Notes

1. "Weston's Trial May Never Happen," *Roll Call*, July 19, 1999, 27.
2. "Superb," *Roll Call*, October 19, 2000.
3. Alan M. Hantman, foreword, in Allen, *History of the United States Capitol*, xii.
4. Hantman.

ONE

A Building of Permanence

In 1790 President George Washington recognized that it was essential the Congress of our newborn nation be housed in a substantial structure—a dignified and stately building constructed of enduring materials to demonstrate to nations abroad that the United States was a cohesive nation worthy of respect. He anticipated this would also defeat the efforts of politicians and wealthy citizens of New York and Philadelphia who craved the US Capitol for their cities.

The Residence Act of 1790 determined that a federal city was to be carved out of the states of Maryland and Virginia on ten square miles of land straddling the banks of the Potomac River. A board of commissioners was appointed to oversee the creation of major buildings to accommodate the new government, and Washington appointed Pierre "Peter" Charles L'Enfant, a young French American military engineer who had served under his command during the Revolutionary War, to prepare a master plan for the new city.[1]

L'Enfant laid out a rectilinear grid of north–south and east–west streets overlain by a strong pattern of intersecting diagonal avenues, "covering about eleven square miles[;] the city on paper was three square miles larger than London and ten square miles larger than Philadelphia."[2] It was an ambitious plan for a national capital, meant to foster a stronger sense of connection among the individual states of the young Union. L'Enfant was also asked to design the President's House and the Congress House, which Secretary of State Thomas Jefferson soon renamed the Capitol. Historian William C.

Allen writes, "Instead of a mere House for Congress, the nation would have a capitol, a place of national purposes, a place with symbolic roots in the Roman Republic and steeped in its virtues of citizenship and ancient examples of self-government."[3]

In 1791 the board of commissioners planned to sell city lots to raise construction funds for the Capitol and the President's House, and they told L'Enfant to publish his city plan in advance so buyers could decide which lots to purchase. He refused and began construction of the Capitol building on Jenkins Hill without sharing any of his plans. He also had the recklessness to have his workers rip down a large brick residence under construction by Daniel Carroll because it encroached into what L'Enfant planned would become New Jersey Avenue.

The site had been owned by Carroll's family for generations, and he was clearly enraged: "Learning of L'Enfant's folly, Washington said that his actions 'astonish me beyond measure.'"[4] Secretary Jefferson wrote to L'Enfant on February 27, 1792, ending his services, and a week later suggested the commissioners advertise for plans for the Capitol. Designs in this open competition were to be submitted by July 15, 1792, with the award to be five hundred dollars and a building lot in the new city.

President Washington selected the winner of this competition, Dr. William Thornton, considered the 1st Architect of the Capitol. The architect was initially a consulting architect, reporting to the commissioners, until Congress formally established the office of Architect of the Capitol in 1876 with an open-ended term of office. Eight others followed

Thornton in the first two hundred years of the Capitol's history.

In 1990 the 101st Congress elected not to allow the 9th Architect of the Capitol, George White, to continue as a lifetime appointee by passing legislation, to go into effect in 1995, establishing a ten-year term for the architect and stipulating that a bicameral, bipartisan congressional commission would recommend a minimum of three candidates for the president to consider. For the first time, the Senate would review and approve whomever the president chose to nominate. White, who had served for almost twenty-five years, was eligible to reapply, but he chose instead to leave office. At seventy-five, he "had little support on the House side. He had cultivated close ties to senators and seemed to lavish attention on the Senate, miffing House members."[5]

The American Institute of Architects (AIA) recommended a list of eleven candidates to the search committee, and my ten years of experience as vice president of architecture, planning, construction, and historic preservation at Rockefeller Center Management Corporation qualified me to become one of the candidates. All candidates were urged to seek supporting recommendations from influential advocates. As an officer at Rockefeller Center, I found it made sense to start with my boss, David Rockefeller, who graciously wrote to Senate Majority Leader Robert Dole on my behalf. After additional contacts and interviews, my New Jersey senators, Bill Bradley and Frank Lautenberg, wrote to Democratic Leader Senator Tom Daschle, and my congressman wrote to Senate Rules Committee Chair John Warner. Then, we all waited.

Two months before George White's retirement, an AIA letter dated August 8, 1995, arrived saying that the selection process was finally moving forward, and requiring that twenty-seven copies of candidate biographies be sent to the search committee by early September to allow for an orderly transition. But interviews were delayed until the following year since the two houses of Congress could not agree on the selection process itself or on basic candidate qualifications. In the interim, George's deputy architect, William L. "Bill" Ensign, himself a candidate, served as acting Architect of the Capitol.

A shortlist of five candidates was finally announced and interviews scheduled with search committee senior staff for June 1996. I rode the Amtrak train to Washington, arriving at Union Station on a cloudless evening. As I exited the terminal, there in the distance, framed through an arch of the station's colonnade, was the brightly lit Capitol Dome etched into the sky, an image that remains with me still.

Senior Staff Power

The interview room sat beneath the rotunda level on the Senate side of the Capitol. I was graciously escorted in, noting six people seated on the long side of a large rectangular table and two others at each of the shorter ends. I stood by the lone chair centered on the unpopulated side. "If I had known I would be so badly outnumbered," I heard myself say, "I would have brought reinforcements."[6]

It was a strange thing to say at a critical interview in the US Capitol, but, because half of the assembled interviewers were young staffers, I didn't feel intimidated. This was my first experience with the level of power and authority staff exercise in all aspects of congressional decision-making. They would determine whether I proceeded to the next step in the interview process or whether my candidacy would end that day.

They asked about my experience at Rockefeller Center and my attitude toward privatization of functions and staff, at the time a hot issue on Capitol Hill. They wanted to know about my professional experience in architecture, engineering, historic preservation, and facilities management. Ten years of experience at Rockefeller Center had earned me a perspective that few architects could have developed.

There were many parallels between the physical realities at the Capitol and Rockefeller Center. Both were national historic landmarks of more than fifteen million square feet, were major tourist attractions with millions of annual visitors, had security issues and dedicated police forces, and required constant attention to facilities management issues, and both had a serious commitment to service excellence. The interview went well, and five weeks later I was asked to meet with actual decision-making members of Congress on July 10 and 11, 1996.

The Capitol was a ten-minute walk from Union Station beneath wonderfully mature, fully leafed pin oaks lining Delaware Avenue, so lush that only fragmented views of the dome peaked through their dense canopies. I was enveloped in the Hill's aura as I entered the Senate north door, passed through a security checkpoint, and wound my way toward a 3:00 p.m. interview with Senator John Warner, visitor map and pass in hand.

Warner was still in the prime of his distinguished career. He had served in World War II and the Korean War, and as secretary of the navy under President Nixon, he had negotiated the US-Soviet Incidents at Sea agreement. Queen Elizabeth II named him "an honorary Knight Commander for his work strengthening the American-British military alliance."[7] To some, however, he was known as the sixth husband of actress Elizabeth Taylor.

The Capitol's main north–south corridor flowed off into the distance, its width decreasing as I walked, vivid colors giving way to monotones, daylight supplanted by dim wall sconces. The building's spine tracked southward from the 1850s Thomas U. Walter expansion, through the bare stone surfaces of Benjamin Latrobe's original Capitol wing, to the circular crypt beneath the Capitol Rotunda above. Three rings of squat sandstone columns encircled the white stone compass rose marking the center of the crypt and the Capitol itself. As L'Enfant had planned, this was the point of origin for many of Washington's major avenues shaping the city's core.

A right turn, down a few steps, another right turn, and I arrived punctually at room S-151. A low-burning fire lent a warmth to the room as Senator Warner welcomed me to the Capitol and ushered me to a comfortable chair facing him. Standing beyond the fire's glow were senior staff representatives of Senators Strom Thurmond (R-SC), Trent Lott (R-MS), Mark Hatfield (R-OR), and other Senate Rules Committee members.

"You have a very impressive résumé," said Warner, then a three-term senator from Virginia. "I have the responsibility of selecting three candidates to be sent to the president."[8]

He explained that concerns for the stewardship of the Capitol building, its iconic dome, and other national treasures on Capitol Hill rarely appear on the radar screens of members of Congress. Such concerns only consciously register with the submission of the architect's annual budget requesting funds for repairs, maintenance, security, and expansion of the congressional portfolio of buildings and grounds. He said many requests are excised by appropriators, kicking them down the road for future Congresses to deal with. Available funds are usually allocated to congressional constituencies more powerful than the architect.

"There won't be enough money to do all that needs to be done to preserve our buildings," Warner said. "How would you deal with that reality?"[9]

"New York City has faced the same problem for decades with its roads, bridges, and other infrastructure," I responded. "With no glory in scraping off rust, repainting and performing basic maintenance, available money is used for more visible and newsworthy projects. The infrastructure is left to fall apart. If I find major problems at the Capitol, I'll stand on the table and yell."[10]

The senator smiled and continued on to other issues facing the next architect, placing a lot of emphasis on the deficit-plagued Senate restaurant, then under the architect's purview. The warmth, civility, and very presence of this larger-than-life Senate stalwart made our upbeat half-hour interview pass all too quickly. I immediately felt a positive connection.

I awaited my next interview along with two other candidates in the reception room of Senator Wendell Ford (D-KY), the ranking minority member of the Senate Rules Committee. He entered the room, focused on me, and said aloud, "He even looks artsy, doesn't he," and to me, "Come on in!"

Ford spoke of the upcoming Senate office moves, an outgrowth of the last election, and the need for temporary holding offices as renovations proceeded in thirteen offices. He also discussed the money-losing Senate restaurant and told me the food was bad and "everything had salsa on it." I thought it was strange that he and Warner spent so much interview time on a minor part of the architect's responsibilities. It was clearly an issue close to their hearts and stomachs, and they considered the deficit an embarrassment, especially with the heavy pressure for deep budget cuts being pushed by House leadership. The Rules Committee was determined to keep its fingerprints off the Senate restaurant by making it the architect's dilemma.

Two months later, the interview process hit an unexpected obstacle when Senate Majority Leader Robert Dole declared his candidacy for president and stepped down from his leadership post. As Dole's replacement, "Senate Republicans . . . overwhelmingly chose Sen. Trent Lott (R-MS). . . . Staunchly conservative and fiercely competitive, Lott . . . is also an experienced legislative craftsman who, like Dole, can cut deals across partisan and ideological lines when he wants to."[11]

Kicking the Tires

On September 9, 1996, I received a call asking me to travel to Washington the following day to meet with the new majority leader at the Capitol at 3:00 p.m. Senate Majority Leader Trent Lott had not been an active member of the search committee but now wanted to personally "kick the tires" of the primary choice the committee was ready to recommend to President Bill Clinton.

My train arrived early at Union Station, leaving time for a leisurely walk to the Capitol along Delaware Avenue. Directions from the reception desk guided me through richly decorated historic halls and up a flight of ornate stairs to the imposing carved wooden doors of the majority leader's second-floor suite. As I sat alone in the reception area enjoying the artwork and decorative treatments, an endless parade of supplicants passed by on their way to the new leader's inner sanctum.

I was soon joined by Tom Anderson, who had worked for a dozen years as Lott's administrative assistant when the senator was House Republican whip. Tom was later appointed ambassador to the eastern Caribbean and ran unsuccessfully for Congress in a 1989 Mississippi special election before rejoining Senator Lott as his chief of staff. More recently, Anderson served as an on-call adviser. He regaled me with tales of his years as ambassador, his private plane, the ambassador's residence, and the beautiful Caribbean weather. He also peppered me with questions such as, "What about loyalty?"

"I worked with Mike McCambridge for eighteen years, the last ten at Rockefeller Center," I told him about my boss. "I always protected his flanks, made sure he wasn't surprised. Integrity is critical to me. When I give my word, you can take it to the bank."

"That's important," Tom replied. "People around here have to rely on each other's word. "What's your weakest point?" he asked. I was feeling pretty comfortable so I offered, "My backhand in racquetball, and my short game in golf. I would also like to be more computer literate. I can't think of anything else."

"That's okay," Tom said. "You thought of more than I could."

We talked for almost two hours as I described my experiences at Rockefeller Center, the challenges we faced, the renovations we accomplished, and the parallels I saw with Capitol Hill. Finally, just before 5:00 p.m., the line of visitors walking past us slowed to a trickle and finally stopped. Leader Lott emerged and apologized for keeping me waiting.

"Senator Lott," I said, as he led us into his office, "you don't have to worry about a thing. Tom and I have it all worked out."

"How's that?" he responded.

"We've agreed that Tom should be Architect of the Capitol, and I should be the ambassador to Antigua, Barbados, and all those wonderful islands."[12]

He smiled, gestured to a comfortable seating arrangement in front of a warm working fireplace, and excused himself to freshen up from his meetings. Tom reiterated that loyalty was important to Senator Lott. I didn't quite know how to take that piece of information. I was certainly loyal to my family, friends, community, and country, but I also understood that the architect was to operate in a bipartisan, bicameral way in support of the entire Congress.

Before I could respond, Lott rejoined us, apologized again, and thanked me for coming to see him on such short notice. He acknowledged that the selection process had been going on for quite some time but said that he wanted to "kind of kick the tires on this guy from New York City." The senator said he was a southern boy and northerners could sometimes be suspect. He spoke in a friendly, disarming manner asking about my experience and my commitment to protecting this historic Capitol of ours. The interview didn't last long. He asked Tom to hang back before escorting me out and saying, "You're not so bad for a guy from New York."

Loyalty would come up consistently throughout my ten-year term. My conversation with Tom Anderson let me know that as far as Trent Lott was concerned, this was at least as important as any advanced degree or professional experience. A person wise about Capitol Hill later pointed out that my two hours with Tom had been the real interview. Lott was relying on his trusted adviser—along with staff support—to evaluate me and make a recommendation. This reinforced the sense of staff power I experienced during my first interview. Without the approval of Tom and the staff, my candidacy would have crashed.

Nominations and Oath of Office

Once Lott cleared my nomination, Senator Warner sent a letter recommending three potential candidates to President Clinton, with me as its primary choice "by a substantial margin."[13] This kicked off a four-month process of White House deliberations, with teams of FBI agents interviewing my neighbors and previous employers to corroborate back-

ground information and determine if I was trustworthy, of upstanding character, and a loyal citizen. After a year-and-a-half-long search, the president accepted the search committee's recommendation.

THE WHITE HOUSE
Office of the Press Secretary
for Immediate Release
January 6, 1997
PRESIDENT CLINTON NAMES ALAN MICHAEL HANTMAN TO BE THE ARCHITECT OF THE CAPITOL.
The President announced today his intent to nominate Alan Michael Hantman to be the Architect of the Capitol. . . . The Architect of the Capitol (AOC) is responsible for the upkeep, preservation, and changes to all congressional office buildings, the Library of Congress, the Supreme Court, the Federal Judiciary Building, the Capitol Power Plant, the Capitol Police Headquarters, and the Taft Memorial. The AOC has been assigned a wide range of duties by Congress including service on numerous governing or advisory bodies, such as the Advisory Council on Historic Preservation and the Washington Metropolitan Transit Authority. The face and nature of Capitol Hill, the Botanic Gardens and, in fact, all of the District of Columbia are therefore impacted by this position.[14]

This was wonderful news, but there still needed to be a confirmation hearing by the Senate Rules and Administration Committee, followed by a vote of the full Senate and a formal swearing-in. Since Warner was certain enough that all would go well, he retained me as a consultant to the Joint Congressional Committee overseeing President Clinton's second inauguration on January 20, 1997, including seating arrangements for twenty-seven thousand guests at the Capitol's West Front and the inspection of the presidential stands' construction.

As I rode Amtrak back to New York from inaugural duties in DC, I thought about the reality of becoming Architect of the Capitol and the life changes this would bring, from selling our house and relocating to Washington, to Rosalyn's resignation as an officer at Columbia University after eleven years of creativity and commitment. I marveled at the concept of being entrusted with the awesome responsibility of becoming the steward of the greatest symbol of our democracy. Whatever actions are taken, or words spoken, by politicians of either party, there looming in the background, as the touchstone of legitimacy for this endless flow of words, was the pristine dome of the Capitol. I was honored that my name was to be associated with the preservation of this national icon.

During my conversations with Warner, he described the energy and commitment he felt when he served as secretary of the navy from 1972 to 1974. "I couldn't wait to get to work each morning," he said. "I'd bound up the steps two at a time to get to my desk, I wouldn't wait for the elevator."[15] He smiled and said he hoped I would feel this energy as well. What a strong, clear-eyed example to emulate!

Confirmation Hearing

My Senate confirmation hearing before the Rules and Administration Committee was an opportunity for a cross section of members to voice areas of concern. Senator Robert Torricelli (D-NJ) suggested that cars be banned from the East Front Plaza, and Senator Kay Bailey Hutchison (R-TX) lambasted "the recently built meeting rooms on the 'C' level of the Capitol building. . . . They are worthy of any Holiday Inn in America, but not worthy of the United States Congress." She said, "Our generation has a responsibility to maintain the quality that our forefathers and foremothers gave us."[16]

Warner was joined in his questioning by Senators Mitch McConnell (R-KY), Wendell Ford, Ted Stevens (R-AK), Trent Lott, and Rick Santorum (R-PA). They went through a laundry list of Capitol complex complaints, focusing on the conflicting requirements of security and visitor accessibility. This whole experience gave me a taste of how divergent the views held by members of Congress could be, preparing me for the compromises that would be essential on issues large and small.

The full Senate then voted unanimously to confirm me as architect. I was told this was unusual for a nonpolitical professional who did not have a history of making significant campaign contributions.

In the Old Supreme Court Chamber

All that remained was to be formally sworn into office, with the oath to be administered by Chief Justice William Rehnquist in the Old Supreme Court Chamber of the Capitol.

During Washington's early years, the people of the city filled this fifty-foot by seventy-foot chamber dimly lit by smoky oil lamps mounted around the room. Minimal rays of natural light streamed in through three windows partially shielded behind the court's bench. The people came to hear arguments of the most distinguished attorneys and orators of the day and the judgments passed down from the bench. With few forms of public entertainment in this still remote capital city, this chamber became a major focus of community interest and social interaction.

They heard the nine sitting justices deliberate about landmark cases from 1810 through 1860, cases that fundamentally impacted the fabric of our nation. In 1860 when the Senate moved to its new chambers in the north wing of the expanded Capitol, the court moved upstairs to the now vacant Old Senate Chamber. In 1935 the Supreme Court finally moved to its own imposing classical building, designed by noted architect Cass Gilbert, directly across First Street from the Capitol (chapter 9).[17]

This historic chamber was used as a law library, as offices for the Joint Committee on Atomic Energy, and ultimately relegated to become a furniture storage room. George White finally received necessary funding in 1975 to restore the chamber to its original grandeur, including restoration of its graceful umbrella vaulted ceiling.

Figure 1.1. Old Supreme Court Chamber. Courtesy of Architect of the Capitol

For my swearing-in, the court lamps once again glowed and voices again filled this noble space as members and officers of the Congress, friends, and family filled the room. I stood in the well with Chief Justice Rehnquist before the court's bench, a wooden balustrade separating us from the rest of the chamber.

With my right hand raised to shoulder level, palm facing forward, I held the Bible my father had given me more than twenty-five years earlier in my left hand. For my twenty-seventh birthday, he had asked if there was something in particular I might like. I requested and gladly received his gift of this Bible.

I particularly cherish the blessing he inscribed on the inside cover of the Pentateuch: "May the Lord bless you and guard you. May he cause his countenance to shine upon you and bring you peace."

I held his Bible and blessing in my hand and in my heart. My father, Sam Hantman, had died two years before my confirmation. He had known I was a candidate for the position and was enormously proud of that. He worked in the Bronx Central Station Post Office for thirty years, taking the night shift to earn a 10 percent premium in salary, additional money vital for the support of our family. His night owl schedule left us few quiet moments together. Our

Figure 1.2. Chief Justice Rehnquist administers the oath. Courtesy of Architect of the Capitol

most memorable conversations took place when he returned home at 4:30 a.m. and I was still awake studying for an exam or completing a term paper.

My father had spoken with great pride about traveling to Capitol Hill to meet with members of the Eighty-Fifth and Eighty-Sixth Congresses in his capacity as an officer of the New York City branch of the American Postal Workers Union. I visualize him meeting with members of Congress, intent on his responsibility to effectively represent his fellow employees. My mother had passed away almost forty years earlier at the age of only fifty-two, and I regret I never had the opportunity to design and build the house I promised her. But in those long-ago years, she too had been proud of her young architect.

Though I could not share the important milestone of my swearing-in with my parents, the smiles of Rosalyn, our three daughters, sons-in-law, grand-children, family, and friends filled the historic chamber.

Chief Justice Rehnquist read the oath in phrases, waiting as I repeated each in turn:

> I do solemnly swear that I will support and defend
> the Constitution of the United States against all
>   enemies,
> foreign and domestic,
> and that I will bear true faith and
> allegiance to the same;
> that I take this obligation freely,
> without any mental reservation or purpose of
>   evasion;
> and that I will well and faithfully discharge the du-
>   ties of the office
> on which I am about to enter,
> so help me God.[18]

NIGHT SOUNDS

President Washington's vision of permanence, a Capitol built of enduring brick and stone, is still a reality after more than 230 years.

Sounds in the building vary greatly depending on the hour of day or night, the cacophony of daylight yielding to nighttime footsteps reverberating off stone walls, stone and tile floors, gracefully arched plaster ceilings.

There is a unique spirit to the Capitol. A historical presence radiates from its walls with the faded echoes of representatives, senators, and presidents who walked those corridors, crossed the decorative Minton floor tiles, their rich geometric and floral patterns deeply dished, details erased by generations long gone.

While not of the House nor of the Senate, but an officer of Congress as a whole, I present an image of life within the Capitol, of its ever-changing cast of players who tread its halls, inhabit its forums, and shape our democracy.

This ceremony launched me on my ten-year term of office, following in the footsteps of the Architects of the Capitol who had gone before, William Thornton, Benjamin Latrobe, Thomas Ustick Walter, George White, and five others. I understood that one hundred senators and 435 members of the House now constituted my conclave of bosses, and I welcomed this challenge at the heart of our nation.

Notes

1. 1 Stat. 130, July 16, 1790.
2. Allan Greenberg, *George Washington, Architect* (London: Andreas Papadakis, 1999, 212), quoted in Allen, *History of the United States Capitol*, 9–10.
3. Allen, 10.
4. Washington to Jefferson, January 18, 1792, Padovar, National Capitol, 88, quoted in Allen, 11.
5. Mary Jacoby, "Averting Fight, White to Retire: Lauded as 'Only Real Architect This Century,'" *Roll Call*, February 20, 1995.
6. Alan M. Hantman, personal notes.
7. Neil H. Simon, "Queen to Name John Warner Honorary Knight," *Richmond Times-Dispatch*, February 19, 2009.
8. Hantman, personal notes, July 10, 1996.
9. Hantman, personal notes, July 10, 1996.
10. Hantman, personal notes, July 10, 1996.
11. Helen Dewar, "Senate GOP Chooses Trent Lott to Take Dole's Place as Leader," *Washington Post*, June 13, 1996.
12. Hantman, personal notes.
13. Letter to the president from Chairman John Warner, September 18, 1996.
14. Office of the Press Secretary, "President Clinton Names Alan Michael Hantman to Be the Architect of the Capitol," press release, January 6, 1997.
15. Hantman, personal notes.
16. Juliet Eilperin, "Senators Ask New Architect to Nix Cars on East Front, Hantman Becomes Tenth to Hold Post," *Roll Call*, January 30, 1997.
17. US Senate, Supreme Court Chamber, 1810–1860, S. Pub. 106-12.
18. Oath of Office, United States Senate, 1884.

TWO

The Capitol's Architects

L'Enfant's City Plan

In George Washington's new federal city, the Capitol was to be built on Jenkins Hill, from which many of Pierre L'Enfant's diagonal avenues radiated, tying the city together. The avenues were named for states of the Union, including New Jersey, Maryland, and Delaware. Pennsylvania Avenue would visually connect the new Capitol building to the President's House, which was to be the point of origin for New York, Vermont, and Connecticut Avenues. Even though, as William C. Allen writes in his *History of the United States Capitol*, "L'Enfant's city plan also included sites for fountains; a national church; squares for states to improve with statues, columns, or obelisks; and unassigned squares that might later be used for colleges and academies," the Capitol was the focal point, crowning the crest of its hill, visible from all facets of the city.[1]

Washington believed the Capitol should be as permanent as any European national building and evoke a sense of importance, of respect. It could not be built of wood, nor could it look like just another provincial courthouse. Only the solidity of brick and stone could express the intent and strength of the words, the concepts embedded in the nation's new Constitution. Secretary of State Thomas Jefferson's design competition was meant to ensure this goal was achieved.[2]

A Winning Design: Dr. William Thornton, 1st Architect of the Capitol

Many designs for the Capitol building were submitted in 1792, but the designers were thinking small, and no concept measured up to the president's vision. Their proposals had no grandeur, no nobility. In 1793 Washington was delighted by a late submission by a physician and architect named William Thornton, from the West Indies island of Tortola. In a letter to the city's commissioners, the president commended this new presentation for its "grandeur, simplicity and beauty."[3]

Thornton's design captured a sense of permanence and respect by drawing from the proportions and sophistication of ancient classical architecture, a legitimacy Washington and Jefferson wanted for the Capitol building. It was to be built of brick and stone, with columns, noble capitals, pediments, entablatures, and a well-proportioned low-stepped dome modeled after Rome's ancient Pantheon. This classically conceived proposal had not been Thornton's first design. Thornton, according to Allen, "took his design to Philadelphia in the last days of 1792 and was told to give it to Jefferson for the President's consideration. Before sending it along . . . he soon learned about the failed entries and the administration's evolving thoughts about the Capitol. Prudently, Thornton put aside his 'Tortola scheme,' and at once began a new design, one that 'would be more suited to the situation.'"[4]

Thornton's new design accommodated separate but equal wings for the Senate and the House,

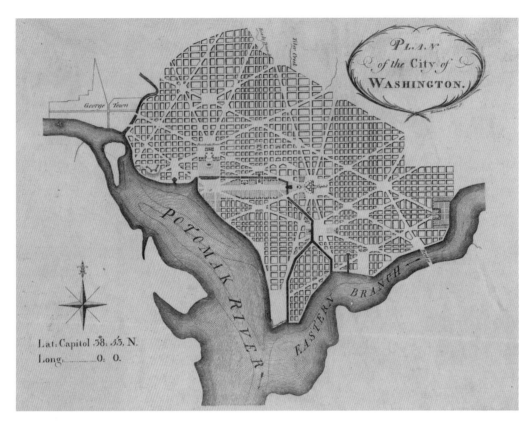

Figure 2.1. L'Enfant's Plan of the City of Washington, 1792. Courtesy of Library of Congress

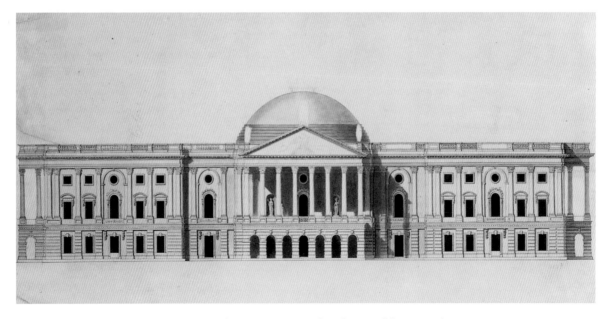

Figure 2.2. William Thornton's winning design. Courtesy of Architect of the Capitol

Figure 2.3. Capitol building burned by the British in 1814. Courtesy of Architect of the Capitol

a symmetry that has been maintained over two centuries as the Capitol expanded. After Thornton's design was selected, he was chosen to serve as a commissioner, overseeing construction of the Capitol. By 1800, due to inadequate funding and a lack of skilled labor, only the northern wing was ready for occupancy by not only the Senate but also the House of Representatives, the Supreme Court, the Library of Congress, and the courts of the District of Columbia.

Benjamin Henry Latrobe, 2nd Architect of the Capitol

In 1803 President Thomas Jefferson, who fortunately possessed refined design sensibilities, brought on a professional architect, Benjamin Henry Latrobe, to continue work on the Capitol as surveyor of public buildings, in effect becoming the 2nd Architect of the Capitol. Latrobe made major changes to the interior design, and by 1811, in collaboration with Jefferson, he had completed the southern wing for the House of Representatives. Thornton was openly critical of these changes, which ultimately resulted in a libel suit he lost to Latrobe. The cost of the impending War of 1812 caused construction to halt, and Latrobe left Washington. In 1815 he was recalled

under James Madison's presidency to reconstruct the Capitol, burned by the British during their invasion of the fledgling city. Latrobe referred to the burned building as "a melancholy spectacle."

In 1817 Latrobe was maligned by Congress for extravagant spending and schedule issues and resigned. He had reported to the commissioner of public buildings, Colonel Samuel Lane, who made him the scapegoat in front of President James Monroe for issues that were beyond his control, including funding by Congress that was so piecemeal he had difficulty hiring and maintaining an adequate workforce of artisans and laborers. When Latrobe left, the House and Senate wings had almost been completed, and he had prepared plans for the central section. Major changes have been made to his work over the years, yet his creativity can still be appreciated in the beautiful masonry vaulted old Supreme Court Chamber and the corncob columns he designed to support its vaulted vestibule.

Charles Bulfinch, 3rd Architect of the Capitol

In 1818 Monroe selected Charles Bulfinch as the 3rd Architect of the Capitol. Bulfinch is believed to be the first American-born professional architect. Through his work in Boston as the city's architect-administrator and as chair of the Board of Selectmen, he understood the politics and deference needed to accomplish public building projects. During his twelve years in office, he moved forward relatively easily in contrast to the previous twenty-five years of delays and acrimony under the first two architects. Bulfinch completed the north and south

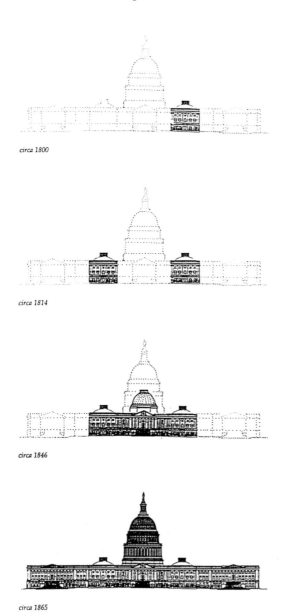

circa 1800

circa 1814

circa 1846

circa 1865

Figure 2.4. Growth of the Capitol over time. Courtesy of CRTKL

wings in accordance with Latrobe's plans, but he ran into a presidential roadblock when it came to the design of the dome.

He ended up building an almost unrecognizable version of Thornton's original low-profile design that some called an ungainly and disproportionate upside-down kettle. Bulfinch knew it was an unhappy perversion of the design so admired by Washington in 1793, but he found it impossible to disagree with the dictates of President James Monroe, who preferred a higher dome that could be seen from greater distances. As architect, Bulfinch was the target of the resulting design criticism, and "wrote philosophically, 'Architects expect criticism and must learn to bear it patiently.'"[5]

Due to congressional budget constraints, he had to build the dome of copper-sheathed wood rather than the more expensive brick and stone he preferred. With the Capitol finally complete in 1829, thirty-eight years after Washington had begun his planning, Bulfinch's eleven and a half years of service was terminated with five days' notice, and he returned to Boston. For the next two decades, the Capitol was under the care of the commissioner of public buildings.

Thomas Ustick Walter, 4th Architect of the Capitol

By 1851 seven new states (Arkansas, Michigan, Florida, Texas, Iowa, Wisconsin, and California) had been admitted to the Union, and membership of the House and Senate had grown from 138 members in 1800 to 292 for the Thirty-First Congress of 1849–51. An expansion of the Capitol was needed to accommodate these increased numbers, and more than a dozen architects entered the design competition. Congress narrowed the field to five architects, dividing the five-hundred-dollar prize among them and leaving selection of the winner to President Millard Fillmore.

Thomas U. Walter of Philadelphia proposed expanding the Capitol to the east by replicating its existing configuration to form an enclosing square. While the House of Representatives preferred this approach, the Senate favored a plan by Robert Mills to add northern and southern wings, greatly lengthening the building from 400 feet to more than 750. Fillmore, his aim on compromise, selected Walter, the House's preferred architect, but had him build the Senate's preferred north and south extensions.

Walter's new Senate and House wings tripled the Capitol's area and almost doubled the length of the building. He recognized that not only was Bulfinch's wood and copper dome subject to fire but the newly elongated base changed the building's proportions and made Monroe's "upside-down kettle" seem even more ungainly. In 1854 he took the initiative of designing a monumental, proportionately balanced dome and hung his seven-foot-long conceptual drawing in his office where it would be seen by visiting members of Congress. Congressman Alfred Greenwood of Arkansas was among its detractors, saying he opposed "useless expenditures" such as this. The first vote yielded a seventy-seventy tie, broken only by the committee chair's "aye."

Within ten weeks, most members had become so captivated by the stateliness and power of the design that, on the second vote, the full Congress provided an initial hundred-thousand-dollar appropriation to begin building the new dome to replace Bulfinch's leaky twenty-five-year-old ungainly one.

In the coming years, when further appropriations were requested, a number of members blamed the architect and chief engineer for not making clear that the $100,000 was only an initial funding and not the dome's ultimate cost. Walter's iconic dome ended up costing $1,047,000, but it has stood for more than 150 years as the most recognizable worldwide symbol of the United States, its value to our nation incalculable. Walter continued to serve at the Capitol under "five presidents; five secretaries of the interior; five secretaries of war, including Jefferson Davis who later became President of the Confederacy; two supervising army engineers; and countless committee chairmen, senators and representatives."[6]

Political infighting prevented many of these relationships from being cordial or constructive as Walter strove to design and construct the new extensions and his magnificent fireproof cast iron dome. Work was suspended through the Civil War when the Capitol was used as a military barracks, hospital, and bakery. After fourteen years of service, he resigned at the end of the war under political fire, having transformed the awkward building of 1829 into the majestic Capitol we see rising today from the crest of Jenkins Hill. According to William C. Allen, for this "lasting legacy of honor to his country, Walter left the city without so much as a handshake or a word of farewell at the train station."[7]

Edward Clark, 5th Architect of the Capitol

President Andrew Johnson appointed Edward Clark to succeed Walter in 1865. Clark had come to Washington in 1851 as Walter's apprentice and soon became his main assistant. Clark was the first of several internal personnel promoted over the years to architect without consideration of qualified outside competition. He oversaw the completion of Walter's work on the Capitol's north and south porticoes and on Brumidi's *Apotheosis of Washington* in the rotunda. In 1866 the building was tightly hemmed in between A Streets North and South, which were lined with shabby restaurants, saloons, and private housing. It cried out for breathing room to allow this magnificent monument to be viewed and appreciated from all angles.

Commissioner French had made proposals to expand the Capitol grounds as early as 1854, and proposals were also made by others in the Senate as construction proceeded, with the House consistently voting against it. Some members from western states hoped the government would soon move west to the physical center of the expanding nation, where miles of open land were there for the taking, and objected to purchasing land adjacent to the Capitol. One of Clark's lasting legacies is in his 1865 annual report, where he supports the expansion and improvement of the Capitol grounds. Again in 1868 he proposed extending the grounds even farther to tie them more closely to the Mall and the President's House. He proposed separating leisure carriage roadways from street traffic, similar to New York's Central Park, designed by Frederick Law Olmsted.

Finally, in 1872, President Ulysses S. Grant signed legislation that expanded the grounds to fifty-eight acres by absorbing A Streets North and South and purchasing the private blocks up to B Streets North and South. Clark hired landscape architect Frederick Law Olmsted with congressional support, an important recognition that the Architect of the Capitol could supervise the work of expert consultants without needing to be expert in all issues related to the Capitol. Clark stated, "Not having any practice or pretentions to skill as landscape gardener, I earnestly recommend that a first-class artist in this line may be employed to plan, plant, and lay out the grounds."[8]

Working with Clark, Olmsted developed and implemented a naturalistic treatment for his 1874 General Plan for the US Capitol grounds (fig. 7.3). His majestic West Front marble terraces created a pedestal for the greatly enlarged Capitol, eliminating the visual sense that the building was insecurely teetering on the brink of Jenkins Hill.

Clark also recommended that a separate Library of Congress building was needed to house its rapidly growing collection, which was increasingly taking up space in the Capitol. The library's wonderfully exuberant Thomas Jefferson Building, designed in the Beaux-Arts style by John L. Smithmeyer, Paul J. Peltz, and Edward Pearce Casey, was begun in 1889 and opened in 1897 across from the Capitol on First Street Southeast. This was the beginning of a Capitol Hill campus, now numbering a dozen and a half legislative and judiciary buildings.

During Clark's thirty-seven-year tenure, he proved to be an able administrator by bringing in outside experts to install the first elevator in 1874, modern plumbing and drainage in 1893, and building-wide electrical wiring in 1897. It was during his tenure that Congress formally gave the Architect of the

Capitol all responsibilities previously held by the commissioner of public buildings at the Capitol. Clark worked well with his staff of twelve employees, was agreeable and well liked. This, along with his recognized design sensibilities, led Congress to ask him to also review and approve designs for municipal architecture in the District of Columbia and to an extended tenure as Architect of the Capitol, remaining in office until his death in 1902.

6th and 7th Architects of the Capitol

For the next half century, the office was filled by two administrators who were promoted from within rather than by professional architects. Elliott Woods had worked under Clark since 1885 and became acting Architect of the Capitol when Clark became ill in 1898. Woods was supported by Joseph Cannon (R-IL), chair of the House Committee on Appropriations, who petitioned the president on his behalf. The American Institute of Architects opposed his promotion because a City Beautiful plan, based on the McMillan Plan of 1902, was under development to guide the orderly development of the city's entire monumental core. Many believed that only an experienced professional architect could implement the Capitol Hill portion of the McMillan Plan, which included a separate Supreme Court building and new Senate and House office buildings.

Woods, appointed by President Theodore Roosevelt, rose to the needs of the position, retaining the prestigious architectural firm of Carrère and Hastings to design the Cannon House Office Building and the Russell Senate Office Building. He earned professional respect for the advice he provided to many other architects on how to work with Congress and how to foster congressional support for important Washington projects. Toward the end of his career, his actions vindicated him and he was voted in as a member of the AIA.[9]

Woods died of heart failure in 1923, after twenty-one years of service, and was replaced by the 7th Architect, David Lynn, his chief assistant and a close friend. Lynn was appointed in 1923 by President Calvin Coolidge and served for thirty-one years. He was not a professional architect, but he assured that the House Longworth Building and the Supreme Court Building complemented the Capitol by bringing in architects who worked in the neoclassical style, Allied Architects of Washington and Cass Gilbert of New York. As had Woods and Clark before him, Lynn supported the implementation of the McMillan Plan, aimed at reestablishing landscaped parks and the Mall area between the Capitol and the Washington Monument.

Lynn wanted to create the tree-lined promenade envisioned in L'Enfant's 1791 plan, and to do so, he moved the US Botanic Garden off the National Mall, building new conservatories, and using the Bartholdi Fountain from the 1876 Centennial Exposition in Philadelphia as the southern focal point of a new park. The Baltimore and Ohio Railroad station was also removed from the Mall to a site north of the Capitol, where it became the classically designed Union Station, the city's monumental point of arrival for all trains.

When Lynn retired at age eighty-one, after thirty-one years of service, he had increased the agency's staff to more than nine hundred to fulfill the greatly increased managerial and custodial missions brought by the major changes to Capitol Hill.[10]

J. George Stewart, 8th Architect of the Capitol

The string of appointments from within ended with J. George Stewart, a politician who had served one term, representing Delaware, in the Seventy-Fourth Congress, and in other nonelected government positions after he lost a bid for reelection. With the support of Speaker of the House Joe Martin (R-MA), he was appointed architect by President Dwight Eisenhower in 1954, even though he was not an architect and had no experience working within the architect's agency. Stewart carried out David Lynn's plans for the construction of the Senate Dirksen Building and the controversial plans for the expansion of the Capitol's East Front championed by Sam Rayburn, the powerful Speaker of the House of Representatives.

The Capitol's east façade had been the site of important presidential swearing-in ceremonies going back to Andrew Jackson in 1829, and landmark speeches by Abraham Lincoln and Franklin Roosevelt. The rationale for building the expansion included the need to cover the deteriorating sandstone wall at the center of the building with a more permanent marble façade thirty-two feet to the east, which would provide almost one hundred new rooms for the Congress. Thomas U. Walter had proposed a similar solution in 1863 since the dome's non-load-bearing cast iron peristyle of columns was cantilevered out over the east portico, giving the visual impression that the dome was inadequately supported at its base. Yet despite this historic pedigree, the press and the public pushed back against it, demonstrating the historic preservation movement's growing strength.

Speaker Rayburn supported an exact "archaeological reproduction" of the East Front, and Stewart followed his direction, selecting Georgia special white marble for the façade. President Eisenhower laid the cornerstone on July 4, 1959, with the trowel used by George Washington in 1793 during the Masonic ceremony laying the Capitol's first cornerstone.

Stewart, under the Speaker's direction, oversaw the design of a third House office building and remodeled the two existing House buildings to improve House member accommodations and provide more committee rooms. House appropriators supported the Speaker's request for $2 million "and any additional money 'as may be necessary' to begin construction."[11] The Philadelphia architectural firm of Harbeson, Hough, Livingston and Larson was retained, and in 1958, $8 million in excavation and foundation work was begun without significant congressional debate or any public presentation of the building's design.

In October 1959, four years after Rayburn's initial funding request, Stewart presented the final design as a fait accompli, solicited bids, and five months later, awarded the construction contract. The massive H-shaped building provided three room suites, supporting amenities, and impressive views of the Capitol building popular with members. Problematically, the overall design lacked any sense of human scale and is still panned by architectural critics. The historians who wrote a 1993 overview of the city's architecture, *Buildings of the District of Columbia*, referred to it as Washington's "most maligned public building," calling it "a bombastic architectural expression of raw, arrogant, and uncontrolled power that dominates through sheer size rather than coexisting amicably with its neighbors."[12]

The building's scope of work had grown to include 1.2 million square feet of parking garages for 1,600 cars, a subway and connecting tunnels, furniture and furnishings, and grounds work. The $2 million initial appropriation morphed into a final cost of more than $135 million, including a remodeling of the existing Cannon and Longworth Buildings. The Rayburn Building, named for the Speaker who died in 1962 during its construction, was first occupied in 1965. Stewart was heavily criticized, and there were calls for reforming the agency and placing the architect under the US Commission of Fine Arts or National Capitol Planning Commission.

With the support of Speaker John W. McCormick, Representative (later President) Gerald Ford, and Senator Lyndon Johnson, Stewart continued with his work until his death in 1970. He increased the staff to two thousand employees and expanded the Capitol Power Plant, planned the James Madison Memorial Building for the Library of Congress, and proposed an eighty-eight-foot extension to the deteriorating West Front to be used for offices, meeting rooms, and restaurant and visitor facilities. This proposal was even more controversial than the East Front Capitol expansion, marring the reputation of his successor.

George M. White, 9th Architect of the Capitol

After Stewart's death, the search for a new architect once again included an ex-member of Congress and nonprofessional and led to a bit of tongue-in-cheek legislation being introduced in the House: "resolving that 'the Architect of the Capitol shall be an architect, or, in the alternative, the physician of the Capitol shall not be a physician.'" The AIA drew up a list of candidates, with one of its vice presidents, George M. White, as its top recommendation. White was an architect, engineer, attorney, and a Republican endorsed by his state of Ohio's Republican senators.

When White was appointed by President Richard Nixon in 1971, the selection was a welcome departure from the practice of sacrificing professionalism to insider party service. White worked to improve the public's perceptions of the architect's office and built its staff to 2,500, including more than seventy professionals, who supported daily operations and maintenance of Capitol Hill buildings and grounds, planned and designed necessary improvements, and supported all events and ceremonies throughout the Capitol complex, including joint sessions, Congressional Gold Medal presentations, and presidential inaugurations.

White provided continuity to the work his predecessor initiated by constructing the library's James Madison Building. After studying Congress's space needs, White also reversed his original stance favoring West Front restoration and supported the controversial expansion project inherited from Stewart. Powerful opposition from the public and the growing historic preservation movement during the first half of White's tenure, however, undercut Congress's support for the expansion in favor of a full restoration of the West Front.

White accepted this decision and replaced 40 percent of the damaged sandstone, including the original cornice, with Indiana limestone blocks. He set more than a thousand stainless steel tie rods to stabilize the two-hundred-year-old masonry arches and vaults. He applied a special stone consolidant and painted the façade to blend with the northern and southern Capitol wings. In 1987 White received an AIA preservation award upon completion of the project. He also completed meticulous repairs and restorations of the Old Supreme Court Chamber, the Old Senate Chamber, National Statuary Hall, the *Apotheosis of Washington* (the fresco at the top of the rotunda), and the *Statue of Freedom* crowning the dome.

Early in his tenure, White was asked about the overcrowded work environment caused by Senate staff growth from 2,500 in 1958 to 7,000 in 1972. White found that the average area per person was less than half that of the minimum government standard, leading Congress to authorize an extension of the Dirksen Senate Office Building that would double its capacity. White retained the firm of John Carl Warnecke, designers of the executive office building across from the White House and President Kennedy's grave at Arlington National Cemetery, and initiated the design and construction of what was to become the Hart Senate Office Building, the Senate's third.

To avoid the criticism Stewart had received, White invited six architects, as well as the chair of the Commission of Fine Arts, J. Carter Brown, to review and comment on Warnecke's proposed design at a public hearing. The uniformly positive feedback led to Senate approval in August 1974.

White was criticized for the delayed schedule and increased budget that grew from the initial $47 million estimate to a final cost of $137 million. This continued even though White pointed out that the Senate had greatly increased the size and scope of the project, with a 76 percent rate of inflation over the course of the project compounding the budget increase. What was originally conceived as an expansion and duplication of the classically inspired Dirksen Building evolved into the modern, million-square-foot Hart Senate Office Building. Sitting senators declined offices in the building, fearing charges of expending large amounts of appropriated funds for their own benefit. In 1982 the 50 lowest-ranking senators became the grateful inhabitants of the 4,000-to-6,000-square-foot, flexibly designed suites in this major nonclassical office building.

Importantly, Architect White recognized that Capitol Hill's growth—of the House, Senate, Judiciary, and Library of Congress—had been haphazard and that the future could not be guided by the broad concepts of the 1902 McMillan Plan or L'Enfant's plan of 1791. A comprehensive strategy for future growth was needed as a "framework for rational decision making." His 1975 appropriation included funding to begin a planning process, allowing White to bring together a team of experts in architecture, landscape architecture, urban planning, ecology, civil engineering, transportation, economics, and historic preservation. Based on an in-depth analysis of space needs, movement problems, and visual considerations, the team produced the 1981 "Master Plan for Future Development of the Capitol Grounds and Related Areas," which recommended that the federal government not encroach upon the historic neighborhood to the east; Senate growth be accommodated on the sites north of the existing Russell, Dirksen, and Hart Senate Office Buildings; the House's growth should be along South Capitol Street; and, most controversially, the Supreme Court be moved off the Hill to its own campus. The court did not receive this last proposal well, and it never went anywhere.

The Mood on Capitol Hill

By 1990 George White had served as architect for almost twenty years, and House members believed he was treating the Senate preferentially. Under White, the agency was also seen as hindering the advancement of women and minorities. Senator Barbara Mikulski (D-MD) saw this as cause to request White's resignation. For whatever reason, Congress was not going to let White get closer to Edward Clark's thirty-seven-year record than the two decades he had already served. Legislation was passed that set the architect's term at ten years, with a new selection process to be implemented beginning in 1995. White was entitled to reapply for his position.

During the next five years, White selected the site for the Thurgood Marshall Federal Judiciary Building, the first major building that was part of the 1981 Master Plan. This building completed the framing of Columbus Circle by filling the gap immediately to the east of Union Station. White was authorized to use creative financing to lease the site to a competitively selected architect-developer team that would design, develop, and finance the construction of this six-hundred-thousand-square-foot, $101 million building. White then leased the finished building to be used by the judiciary "for thirty years, at which time it would revert to the government at no cost. Rents on the space would be used to amortize the privately raised debt."

A jury selected Boston Properties as the developer with the design team of Edward Larrabee Barnes and John M. Y. Yee & Partners. Chief Justice William H. Rehnquist approved the design in 1989. White's private financing arrangement produced a handsome modern building that was completed in 1992. Its entrance was through an inviting five-story glass atrium, its granite façade echoing the scale and movement of the classically conceived Union Station.

The 1981 Master Plan also recognized that the Capitol's current visitor facilities were not sufficient to welcome and serve the three million people who journeyed there each year, and it recommended that the underutilized Union Station serve as the visitor center site. Mass transit would move both visitors and staff from this arrival point to Capitol Hill, cutting down on parking needs. But issues related to security and the convenience of staff parking assured that this proposal would never receive traction. Instead, White was authorized in 1994 to prepare a plan and estimate for a visitor center on Capitol grounds.

As 1995 approached, White determined that he did not have enough political support to be reappointed and decided not to reapply for his position. The visitor center design remained unfunded, and the project was left to his successor. With his retirement, both chambers of Congress agreed to restructure the architect's office as a contracting agency. According to Allen, House and Senate appropriators "endorsed a proposal to privatize the office of the Architect and slash its workforce by more than 80 percent, and use the emptied offices to offset space demands throughout the Capitol."[13]

The debate about downsizing government agencies and outsourcing work to the private sector began with Ronald Reagan's 1985 State of the Union, in which he said, "overall government program spending will be frozen at the current level. It must not be one dime higher than fiscal year 1985."[14] This long-simmering House-Senate dispute yielded a series of recommendations transmitted by Speaker Newt Gingrich to Senator John W. Warner (R-VA), chair of the Architect of the Capitol search committee.

In a letter to Warner, Gingrich called for the new architect to have "a demonstrated commitment to sensible downsizing, privatizing, contracting out and consolidating." He also called for splitting control and operations of the Capitol in half by eliminating the architect's office of the superintendent of the Capitol. Instead, the superintendent of the House office buildings would have responsibility for control and operations of the House half of the Capitol building, with the Senate's half given to the superintendent of Senate office buildings. Gingrich concluded his letter: "It is my hope that the House and Senate can come to an agreement on future operation and structure of the Office of the Architect before we begin interviewing candidates to permanently fill the Architect position."[1] The appropriators proposed cutting the architect's 2,500-person workforce to between 50 and 400 people.

Capitol Hill is essentially an interconnected city, with the architect's team providing essential services to 100 senators, 435 representatives, tens of thousands of congressional staffers, and millions of visitors who make the pilgrimage to the Hill each year. Architect of the Capitol staff members work largely behind the scenes, their efforts not generally noted or understood by senators and representatives or by congressional staff who expect building maintenance and support services across the Capitol Hill campus to somehow be provided day and night. It would be a daunting challenge to eliminate 85 to 95 percent of the architect's staff and privatize all agency functions, especially while continuing to support comprehensive security needs for all parts of the campus, including members' individual offices.

The Senate moved the architect selection process forward without resolving the issues of privatization, downsizing, or splitting operations of the Capitol building in half. Once George White announced his retirement, these concerns were left for the next architect to address, part of a pattern begun early in the Capitol's history of pushing major decisions and spending issues down the road.

10th Architect of the Capitol and Continuity

The 1990 legislative bill that led to George White's retirement called for a joint Senate-House search committee and subjected this presidential appointment to the advice and consent of the Senate. As the selection process dragged on with the House and Senate debating the responsibilities of the architect and the qualifications required, William L. Ensign, White's assistant architect and himself a candidate, served as acting architect from November 1995 until February 1997. During this period, the architect's staff shrank by three hundred positions to 2,200, with Ensign not permitted to fill any vacancies.

Once appointed as the 10th Architect, the baton of continuity was passed to me as it had been to each of my predecessors. I worked to improve existing operations and maintenance efforts across Capitol Hill while continuing to enhance and move the projects they had initiated forward. This included repairing and restoring the Capitol Dome, Capitol grounds, and the US Botanic Garden Conservatory, renovating the library's Thomas Jefferson Building,

upgrading the Capitol Power Plant, and planning for a United States Capitol Visitor Center.

I soon found that the party in power controls all aspects of life in its chamber, while members of both parties jointly guard their chamber's prerogatives from the congressional chamber at the other end of the building. I also learned that whatever I attempted to achieve that involved design, construction, and oversight would be fraught with debate, criticism, and the political rhetoric expected in Washington, DC.

Historically, as the Capitol grew and evolved through the vision of this succession of architects, the quality and nature of its finishes changed with each addition. The differences initiated over the centuries by my predecessors become obvious as one walks the corridors leading from the northern 1850s Senate wing toward the central crypt and the core

Figure 2.5. Senate wing transition corridor. Courtesy of Alan M. Hantman

of the original 1800s building. The corridor narrows; the tile and stone floors have become dished and polished by the footfalls of generations past. Sharp echoes reverberate off hard surfaces, and natural rays of sunshine are replaced by artificial blurs of light soaking into solid stone walls and floors.

Transitions from the 1850s House and Senate wings to the core of the original building are marked by pronounced archways that framed the Capitol's original entry doors, highlighting continuous growth of the building over time. Similarly, William Thornton's low-profile dome was never built, his concept evolving instead into the iconic symbol of America we know today. I followed the unbroken pattern of building symmetry established by these early architects with the design of the Capitol's ninth and largest increment of growth, the Capitol Visitor Center. This project, opened to the public in 2008, increased the area of the Capitol by 70 percent while maintaining physical equality between the House and Senate.

"For over two hundred years," Allen wrote, "the Capitol's story has been populated by naysayers and critics who have cast long shadows over the work. . . . History has proven that builders on Capitol Hill must expect in-depth oversight, changes, and significant criticism, and this no doubt will continue forever."[16]

Along with Congress's criticism and second-guessing, however, comes the opportunity to create a lasting legacy, to contribute to the flow of history at the heart of our nation's democracy despite its imperfections.

Notes

1. Allen, *History of the United States Capitol*, 9.
2. Allen, 13.
3. Washington to the Commissioners, January 31, 1793, quoted in Allen, 19.
4. Allen, 19–20.
5. Allen, 146.
6. Allen, 335.
7. Allen, 335.
8. Allen, 345.
9. Bushong, *Uncle Sam's Architects*, 31–39.
10. Bushong, 40–42.
11. Allen, *History of the United States Capitol*, 433.
12. Scott and Lee, *Buildings of the District of Columbia*, 136–37.
13. Marcia Gelbert, "Architect's Office to Be Privatized under Republican Proposal," *The Hill*, February 8, 1995.
14. Transcript of President Ronald Reagan's State of the Union address, February 6, 1985, CNN.com, January 31, 2005.
15. Speaker Newt Gingrich letter to Senator John Warner, March 28, 1996.
16. Allen, *Controversies in the Construction History*.

THREE

State of the Union

President Clinton's Address

On my first official day in office, February 4, 1997, I welcomed the president of the United States to the Capitol. William Jefferson Clinton had won a second term, defeating Republican Robert Dole in the 1996 election. He was to deliver the first State of the Union address of his new term, and the House and Senate Sergeants at Arms Bill Livingood and Greg Casey, respectively, and I had the honor of escorting him to the House Chamber for this joint session of Congress.

A cold winter night in suits and ties, we, the three-member Capitol Police Board, waited at the open carriageway beneath the monumental rotunda stair. A squad of motorcycles rumbled by, followed by black SUVs leading a heavily armored limousine. The president's limo drew to a weighty stop and was instantly surrounded by a covey of Secret Service officers. Long seconds passed in silence as the guard at the rear door awaited instructions.

A signal was given, the door opened, and Clinton unfolded his six-foot-two-inch frame out of the car. He and Hillary Clinton climbed the half dozen steps to the landing outside East Front 100, a meeting room straddling the east–west axis of the Capitol. Too small to be divided between the House and the Senate, this room was assigned to the architect as neutral territory where the president and other visiting dignitaries could be welcomed.

As the president entered, Livingood said: "Mr. President, may I introduce the new Architect of the Capitol, Alan Hantman." Clinton had nominated

me, but we had not previously met. I thanked him for his trust, and he congratulated me, wished me good luck, and introduced me to First Lady Hillary Clinton. We chatted as the rest of their entourage filed into the holding room to prepare for the joint session.

The president, as head of the executive branch, is treated as a guest at the Capitol, the home of the legislative branch. As officials of Congress, we escorted the president and his entourage to the House sergeant at arms suite to await the call for his House Chamber entrance.

Clinton was relaxed and affable as we walked the hallways side by side, with statues from the National Statuary Hall Collection punctuating our path. We discussed the design of the Capitol and how the quality of finishes changes from one distinct section to another. The First Lady and her party were escorted separately to the House Chamber Gallery to be seated just before the president was formally announced.

At the appointed time, Bill, Greg, and I escorted Clinton to the chamber entrance where Livingood formally intoned, "Mr. Speaker, the president of the United States." (Bill later confided that he had inked that traditional sentence on his bare hand just in case he forgot it in the pressure of the moment.) We slowly led the president down the chamber's center aisle, followed by the members of the entire United States Senate, who were also welcomed as guests of the House of Representatives.

We inched through the press of congresspeople reaching out to be recognized by the president,

Figure 3.1. Escorting President Clinton to State of the Union address. Courtesy of White House Communications Agency

trying to get close enough to shake his hand. Passing groupings of Cabinet members, the Supreme Court, the joint chiefs of staff, and foreign dignitaries, we finally arrived at the base of the rostrum. Clinton mounted the steps, greeted Vice President Al Gore, shook hands with Speaker Newt Gingrich, and presented them with copies of his address.

As the Speaker formally introduced the president and called the joint session of the 105th Congress to order, the sergeants at arms and I took our seats to the left of the rostrum, joining Gary Cisco, the secretary of the Senate. I was seated just twenty-five feet from the president of the United States as he began his address to a worldwide audience: "I come before you tonight with a challenge as great as any in our peacetime history—and a plan of action to meet that challenge, to prepare our people for the bold new world of the twenty-first century."[1]

As his address proceeded, I soon recognized a predictable call-and-response pattern structuring the proceedings. When the left side of the assembly, populated by Democratic senators and representatives, rose to applaud the president's proposed policies and initiatives, the Republican senators and representatives on the right side remained seated and unsmiling. Rarely did they rise together to applaud the nation's forty-second president, my first in-person taste of the great divide of partisan politics in the US Congress.

I glimpsed Rosalyn in her gallery seat and our eyes met as we silently acknowledged the importance of this moment and our great honor in being present. The president concluded: "We don't have a moment to waste. . . . My fellow Americans, we have work to do. Let us seize the days and the century."[2]

Figure 3.2. State of the Union address, 1997. Courtesy of Architect of the Capitol

Clinton again shook hands with the Speaker and vice president, stepped off the rostrum, and was greeted by a scrum of supporters. We escorted him back through the crush in the House Chamber even more slowly than we had entered, then on to Livingood's office, where he was soon met by Hillary Clinton. We escorted the president and First Lady to their cortege and saw them safely off Capitol grounds.

It had been an honor to witness this powerful demonstration of our democratic process, but as a member of the Capitol Police Board, I was relieved to see this security risk to the core of our three branches of government reach a safe conclusion. During my tenure, I would see many Capitol building ceremonies that gathered key members of two or all three federal branches of government, ambassadors, heads of foreign governments, and other

dignitaries. The risks involved to the orderly continuation of government were significant, whether for a packed joint session of Congress, a presidential inaugural, or a Congressional Gold Medal ceremony in the rotunda. My nerves, and those of the sergeants at arms and officers of the US Capitol Police, were always alert to those risks and relieved when they were over and the dignitaries had safely departed.

It All Begins with Appropriations

The next week, I was introduced to the appropriations process, a journey into government bureaucracy that would affect day-to-day operations on the Hill and any initiative I hoped to accomplish during my ten-year term. Threaded through the core of our history is the ongoing odyssey of congressional decisions authorizing the Capitol's architects to design, build, redesign, rebuild, and repair the evolving US Capitol and its dome. When I took office, important structural issues, including serious leaks in the dome, had gone unresolved, delayed and delayed again, often for decades. At my first budget hearing before the House Appropriations Subcommittee, I focused on those needs by requesting a one-third increase in the architect's prior-year budget. It was detailed on a series of hastily prepared presentation boards, and I vowed that I would be better prepared at all future budget presentations.

The request was based on a list of priorities for our aging Capitol Hill buildings. I testified that many university complexes spend 1.7 percent of their replacement values on building upkeep. The Capitol complex of buildings was then worth more than $3 billion, which meant the Congress should have started appropriating a minimum of $50 million annually for decades to address the estimated billion-dollar backlog of deferred work. I also presented requests for the Botanic Garden Conservatory, which in 1990 had been slated for a $27 million restoration. Conditions had become so bad I would have to shut down the garden if $33.5 million was not quickly made available. Many other critical projects had been deferred due to appropriations caps, and as a result our national treasures were deteriorating. The committee heard my arguments, but I received a tutorial on the facts of Capitol Hill life: "Rep. James Walsh (R-NY), who chaired the House Appropriations Subcommittee, said he sympathized with 'Hantman's dilemma' but he noted that the House is still trying to cut costs for the Legislative Branch and may not be able to fund the full proposal."[3]

Hantman's Dilemma: Political Realities

I was in office only ten days. and already there was a name—"Hantman's dilemma"—for the physical condition of Capitol Hill's iconic buildings and the decades-long lack of will to adequately fund solutions for long-needed life-safety and security issues. This had all become my problem.

My job was to present Capitol Hill's critical needs to the Congress, prioritize their level of importance, and request funding to address them. Budget constraints meant a horizontal line would be drawn halfway down my list, and the projects below it would go unfunded, causing further deterioration in buildings already in poor condition. These then became *my* problems—not the problems of appropriators, not the problems of the Congress, but *my* problems. If something went wrong in the leaky dome, an unsafe conservatory, a nonexistent fire alarm system, or any unfunded project, that would also be my problem, my fault. My education had begun as life went on across Capitol Hill and I continued learning about many other agency responsibilities and issues.

A Heavy Lift: Moving the Women's Suffrage Portrait Monument

Three months into my tenure, a task I inherited from my predecessor suddenly became urgent—moving the fourteen-thousand-pound women's suffrage statue, known as the Portrait Monument, from the Capitol crypt up one level to the daylight of the rotunda. The monument, sculpted by Adelaide Johnson, was commissioned in 1893 by the National Women's Party to depict three suffrage movement leaders: Lucretia Mott, a Quaker minister, abolitionist, and peace advocate; Elizabeth Cady Stanton, architect and author of the suffrage movement's most important strategies and documents; and Susan B. Anthony, abolitionist, temperance advocate, and spokesperson.

The *New York Times*, in 1996, wrote that moving the Portrait Monument "will end a controversy that began in 1921, when Congress, then an all-male body, welcomed the monument at the rotunda with speeches and garlands, then quickly dispatched it to a downstairs storeroom, officially called the Crypt."[4]

Over the decades, multiple efforts to get Congress to agree to move the monument back had failed, but, according to Karen Staser, who conceived the National Women's History Museum in 1995, Senator Ted Stevens was the one who finally made it happen. "Stevens was an early supporter," Staser said, "and surprised us at a press conference by knowing the lyrics to the Suffrage songs! He explained that as a child he had attended suffrage rallies with his grandmother. He felt that our work was important enough for him to personally seek the support of his counterpart in the House, Speaker Newt Gingrich, because the project literally required an act of Congress."[5]

The Women's Suffrage Statue Campaign had raised eighty-two thousand dollars for the move, but before that could happen, we needed to create space for it in the rotunda. Congress agreed that the statue of Roger Williams, Rhode Island's founder, would be displaced, despite objections from Senator John H. Chafee of that state. Then a more sensitive issue was raised about the nineteenth century Black abolitionist Sojourner Truth. The *Washington Post* reported, "opposition by the National Political Congress of Black Women is so vigorous that it is beginning to divide women who are normally allies. In one example, Rep. Cynthia McKinney (D-GA), who is black and had previously endorsed the statue relocation, now plans to introduce legislation to block the move."[6]

The Portrait Monument was not to be moved until Sojourner Truth's image was carved into the rough chiseled stone mass that Johnson left behind the three figures, symbolically representing the women's movement's unfinished work. I initiated a detailed study and determined the stone was too fragile, with insufficient material left to carve another comparably sized bust. The move to the rotunda was cleared to go forward, while still leaving unresolved the issue of commissioning a statue of Sojourner Truth.

Figure 3.3. Portrait Monument to women's suffrage. Courtesy of Jeffrey Schwarz Photography

All of this was of little importance to Patricia Ghiglino and Reinaldo López of Professional Restoration, Inc., the firm hired to do the heavy lifting. They originally estimated eleven hours to relocate the monument from the crypt up to the rotunda. Moving such a massive weight proved to be a much more challenging logistical problem than anticipated as we maneuvered its bulk through tight passageways and onto the floor of an opened stairwell. After a long fifteen-hour day, we left the Capitol late Saturday evening, with the monument still on the crypt level, suspended from a three-story high chain-rigged scaffold.

A Swinging Proposal

On Sunday morning, May 11, Mother's Day, the moving crew of a dozen hoisted the Portrait Monument up a level to the top of the stairs and maneuvered it with just inches to spare between historic columns. By midnight the sculpture had successfully been moved across the rotunda, but now, after twenty-nine hours of intense effort, Mott, Stanton, and Anthony were still five long feet from their appointed place. All fourteen thousand pounds of the monument were still cradled by wide nylon shipyard straps suspended from the chain-hoist.

Several dozen members of the Women Suffrage Statue Campaign had been waiting since Friday with great anticipation and un-popped champagne bottles at the ready. Several generations were present, including Coline Jenkins-Sahlin, the great-great-granddaughter of Elizabeth Cady Stanton, and other members of the National Women's History Museum, including Karen Staser and Joan Meacham, who co-chaired the Women's Suffrage Statue Campaign, Connie Morella (R-MD), Anne E. W. Stone, and Joan Wages.

A tense and frustrated López suggested a new plan. He proposed swinging the statue across the last few feet of open space, and at the end of its trajectory, releasing the chain-fall to drop the Portrait Monument onto its new steel-framed base.

To the left of the monument's new base was the immense painting of the *Surrender of Lord Cornwallis at Yorktown* by John Trumbull (1820), and to the right was his painting *General George Washington Resigning His Commission* (1824). These priceless gilt-framed paintings are part of the original set of four commissioned from Trumbull. I could not imagine how López expected to release the chains of the hoist at the precise apex of the statue's northward swing and expect all fourteen thousand pounds to float down and gently come to rest, centered on its base.

I calmly told López that we would *not* be swinging the monument into oblivion, a disaster that would not only destroy national treasures, but would, secondarily, also bring my three-month tenure as Architect of the Capitol to an immediate conclusion. Finally, to my great relief, at 2:08 a.m. on Monday morning, after thirty-two hours of strategy and raw effort, the Portrait Monument was gently lowered onto the base in its place of honor—but not before representatives of the Women's Suffrage Statue Campaign, the Professional Restoration moving team, and members of my agency signed the bottom of the stone as it hung suspended above its base. In keeping with an old stone-mason tradition, we placed pennies beneath the statue for good luck. Champagne bottles popped amid great cheers and even greater relief.

The formal rededication ceremony took place on June 26, 1997. Speakers included Representative Connie Morella, who had proposed the successful concurrent resolution, House Speaker Newt Gingrich (R-GA), and Senator Olympia Snowe (R-ME) who said, "In many ways, the struggle to move the statue was emblematic of women's struggle for justice and equality throughout the history of the country."[7]

By legislation, after one year, a new bicameral commission was to determine a permanent site for the monument outside of the rotunda. Fortunately for my nerves, with ever-increasing numbers of women being elected to Congress, the political will to move it again has never materialized.

When I began my tenure during the 105th Congress, there were only 9 women in the Senate and 51 in the House of Representatives. As their numbers grew, women senators rightfully demanded dedicated gym facilities similar to those of their male colleagues. Senator Chris Dodd (D-CT), chair of the Senate Rules Committee, asked me to create a new women's gym at the site of the men's gym in the Russell Senate Office Building while concurrently improving the men's facilities. In the 118th Congress of 2023, the number of women in Congress grew to 25 Senate seats and 124 seats in the House of Representatives, a trend that will surely continue. A future Architect of the Capitol may well be tasked with downsizing men's gyms in the House and the Senate to accommodate growing space needs of congressional women in their march toward parity.

The architect's central offices, two levels beneath the Capitol Rotunda, is where we held many planning and coordination meetings with superintendents and staffs of all segments of our small city. The agency team supports inaugural ceremonies, state funerals, joint sessions of Congress, and other events and ceremonies held throughout the Capitol complex of thirty-nine buildings and hundreds of acres of historic landscape.

Daily operations include the mechanical, electrical, structural, and maintenance needs of Capitol buildings and grounds, as well as necessary improvements, planning, and design activities by architects, engineers, and construction managers. Our staff includes electricians, plumbers, upholsterers, carpenters and woodcrafters, painters and plasterers, masons, mechanics, roofers and sheet metal workers, grounds crew, horticulturalists, and other skilled

SOJOURNER TRUTH TAKES HER RIGHTFUL PLACE

Isabella Baumfree, better known as Sojourner Truth, was born into slavery in 1797 in Ulster County, New York, and she became a fierce advocate against slavery and for women's rights. Twelve years after the Portrait Monument was relocated to the rotunda, under the purview of my successor, Stephen Ayers, the 11th Architect, Sojourner Truth finally took her place of honor at another location in the US Capitol. A half million dollars had been raised to have Artis Lane sculpt the bust, which was cast in bronze, mounted on a pedestal, and is now displayed in Emancipation Hall.[8]

Figure 3.4. Bust of Sojourner Truth. Courtesy of Jeffrey Schwarz Photography

craftspeople who repair, maintain, and preserve the historic buildings, sculpture, artwork, and furnishings under our care. Facilities staff and administrators, custodial workers, and laborers complete more than one hundred thousand projects and work orders each year, providing building maintenance services throughout Capitol Hill.

Thousands of days, each one unique, flowed by within these walls. Extraordinary ones remain engraved in memory. After four months in office, June 5, 1997, was a truly notable day.

9:00 a.m.: Equal Employment Opportunity Program

Met with two Architect of the Capitol Agency officers, Ben Wimberly and Kathy Gause, to discuss the Equal Employment Opportunity Program, its statistics regarding case load, its projections, areas needing support and follow-up.

10:00 a.m.: Presidential Inaugurals and the Secret Service

Attended a Senate Inaugural Committee meeting to discuss changes to the physical configuration of the presidential stands and dignitary seating for future inaugurations. Safety considerations for presidential and crowd movements were presented, with modifications suggested by the Secret Service, the House and Senate sergeants at arms, and Grayson Winterling of the Senate Rules and Administration Committee. The architect is responsible for the overall inaugural design and construction process.

11:30 a.m.: Supreme Court and Justice Kennedy

Received a call from Supreme Court Associate Justice Anthony Kennedy requesting a meeting to discuss acoustical issues in the Court's Great Hall that he and Chief Justice William Rehnquist were concerned about. The justice also invited me to be his guest in the coming weeks to observe the workings of the court in session. I mentioned in passing that I'd be joining the House and Senate sergeants at arms in just a few hours to welcome Mother Teresa to the Capitol to accept the Congressional Gold Medal. Kennedy, half joking, asked that after she shook my hand, I not wash mine until we met, and I could shake his.

12:00 p.m.: Senate Budget Hearing Preparation

Worked on a statement to submit in advance of next Thursday's hearing on the 1998 Architect of the Capitol budget before the Senate Appropriations Subcommittee on the legislative branch, chaired by Senator Robert Bennett (R-UT). I knew that Senator Ted Stevens, chair of the full Senate Appropriations Committee, was likely to attend. This was to be my first opportunity to formally come before this committee in an open hearing.

2:00 p.m.: Newspaper Interview

Met with Robert Cohen, the Washington correspondent for the *Newark Star Ledger*, and his photographer for an interview about what it was like for me personally to serve as architect. His son had questioned Bob as he left his home for our interview, "But isn't the architect dead?"

3:20 p.m.: A Moment with Mother Teresa

Bill Livingood, Greg Casey, and I were honored to be among those welcoming Mother Teresa to the Capitol, where she was to receive the Congressional Gold Medal. We were instructed, "Don't reach out to shake her hand. Just put your hand out and let her take it in hers. She's just out of the hospital and very frail."[9] We stood in a receiving line on the East Plaza, south of the rotunda steps, as the cortege glided to a halt. A throng of sari-clad nuns and others in her entourage quickly surrounded the black armored limousine. An attendant opened the right rear door, and Mother Teresa was assisted into a wheelchair

Figure 3.5. Mother Teresa arriving at the Capitol. Courtesy of Architect of the Capitol

and slowly wheeled toward us at the carriageway entrance.

Greg Casey stood in front of me in the receiving line. His hand reached out as she turned to face him. After a few long moments Greg stepped back, and Mother Teresa was wheeled toward me. She was draped in her customary white sari, edged with the three blue stripes of the order of the Missionaries of Charity. I leaned toward her, offering my right hand to this woman whose life of sacrifice and devotion to millions of sick and needy was respected throughout the world.

She appeared incredibly small, her deeply lined face easily recognizable beneath her blue-striped headdress. Timeworn fingers of her left hand slipped beneath mine as she placed her right hand on top, embracing my hand between hers. She bowed her head toward me as a surge of energy coursed from her hands to mine. A long moment passed, she released my hand, and I stepped back as she moved on to the next person.

I stood there as she was escorted toward the carriageway entrance. I walked over to Greg and asked, "Did you feel that? That surge of energy?" He turned and focused on me, "You felt it too? That's amazing!" He paused and added incredulously, "But how could you have felt it? I'm Catholic, and you're Jewish!" We smiled, savoring this extraordinary moment in time.

4:00 p.m.: Congressional Gold Medal Ceremony

The rotunda was charged with anticipation as speaker after speaker lauded Mother Teresa's years of serving the needy. They spoke of how she expanded the work of the Missionaries of Charity to a hundred countries around the world and of how she had been awarded the Nobel Peace Prize in 1979 in recognition of her life of service.

With difficulty, she rose from her wheelchair, stepped haltingly to the microphone, and stood facing the thousand guests seated in the rotunda and the packed bank of TV cameras that brought her image and words to hundreds of millions around the world. Mother Teresa spoke slowly, thoughtfully. Somehow the voice of this frail woman resonated throughout the immense 180-foot-high rotunda. Astonishingly she found the strength to address us all in a powerful voice that rang with clarity, imbued with an aura of humility and grace. I was humbled to have been, ever so briefly, in the presence of this pure soul.

In September 1997, at age eighty-seven, just three months after her visit to the Capitol, Mother Teresa passed on. In 2016 she was canonized a saint.

June 17, 1997: Making the Case before Justice Anthony M. Kennedy

The next week, Bruce Arthur, my architecture department director, and I crossed First Street Northeast to the pristine neoclassical Supreme Court Building, where we were responsible for all preservation and facility management issues. We met with Associate Justice Kennedy in the Court's Great Hall, which is lined on both sides by monolithic Doric columns of cream-colored Alabama marble, as are all of the hall's wall surfaces. The rich red and blue art deco coffered ceiling partially scatters sound, but much like the marble wall surfaces, its hard plaster also reflects the sound back into the hall's volume where, like an echo chamber, it continues to reverberate.

When attorneys of the Supreme Court Bar come before the court, they cross a broad oval plaza, ascend the monumental stairs to the magnificent white Vermont marble portico, and enter through the imposing seventeen-foot-high bronze doors. The eight bronze door panels depict historic scenes in the development of the law, including the sixth-century Justinian Code, King John's Magna Carta of 1215, and King Edward I's Westminster Statute of 1275.[10]

Attorneys on a mission to plead their cases before the bench stride across the Alabama marble floor, unconcerned with the sound of their echoing footfalls in this wide processional corridor leading to

Figure 3.6. The Great Hall of the Supreme Court. Courtesy of Architect of the Capitol

the court chamber. The justices, however, had found that frequent banquets, lectures, and meetings of the Supreme Court Historical Society held in the Great Hall were negatively affected by poor acoustics. Justice Kennedy explained that speeches at these events are rendered virtually unintelligible, that incoherent sounds echoed from one stone surface to another, muddling voices and music, disturbing attendees, and embarrassing the chief justice and the court.

Kennedy proposed a solution. He had taught constitutional law at McGeorge School of Law of the University of the Pacific for more than two decades before President Reagan appointed him to the court in 1988. Since then, he taught at summer programs for McGeorge at the University of Salzburg Law Faculty Building in a renovated sixteenth-century Baroque-style palace in the center of the Austrian city. Kennedy recounted how thoroughly he enjoyed his summers at this stone palace, explaining that the rooms were quite comfortable. He believed the stone did not cause acoustical problems because old tapestries and draperies had been hung over them. Wouldn't this, he wondered, be a solution to the acoustic problem in the Court's Great Hall?[11]

I stood in that imposing space as Bruce Arthur and I discussed the problem with Justice Kennedy. Stewardship responsibilities demanded I preserve and protect the national treasures on Capitol Hill while finding workable solutions to problems. I told Justice Kennedy I was concerned that hanging volumes of fabric over the rich marble walls would compromise the strong architectural character of the hall. Bruce and I also doubted the justice's suggestion would solve the acoustical problem because the proportions of this long, lofty space are not conducive to the even distribution of sound. We suggested that instead a uniform system of speakers unobtrusively placed throughout the length of the Hall would be a more appropriate solution.

Kennedy considered this argument but was far from convinced. We suggested a test: the installation of a full-size drapery mockup in a single column bay of the hall to get a better sense of how this would look. Kennedy agreed, as long as it would not cost too much. The justices do not like going back to the Congress to request funding beyond the court's strict annual budgeting process. Over the next several weeks, my staff worked to plan and erect a realistic mockup utilizing old red velvet court draperies.

At our follow-up meeting, Kennedy greeted us and, with a hand on his chin, turned and moved about, thoughtfully studying the mockup from several angles, trying to visualize how it would look throughout the length of the Great Hall. To me, the draperies overpowered the space and compromised its architectural integrity. I calmly awaited the justice's judgment, prepared with new arguments to support my case. But to our relief, Justice Kennedy agreed that the effect of the draperies was unacceptable, thanked us, and said he would report this to the chief justice.

We soon installed a new sound distribution system with individual speakers alongside busts of former chief justices between each pair of columns. Attendees could now clearly hear lecturers in real time without sound bouncing unintelligibly from marble surface to surface. We had maintained the architectural integrity of the Great Hall and begun to establish a good relationship with the court. I had pled my first case before the US Supreme Court and won.

The *Statue of Freedom*: A Senator's Request

In May, when I had been architect for less than five months, Senator Daniel Akaka (D-HI) came to my office. Akaka, a civil and unassuming gentleman who embodied the aloha spirit of Hawai'i, had served for seven years as the first Native Hawaiian US senator and as a member of the House for thirteen years before that.

Akaka wanted to talk about the full-size plaster model of the *Statue of Freedom* that had languished in a remote warehouse for twenty-five years. In the 102nd *Congressional Record*, 1992, Akaka had eulogized a noted Hawaiian *kahuna lapa'au* (healer), Morrnah Nalamaku Simeona, noting that she had raised twenty-five thousand dollars to refurbish and restore the plaster model, including replacing missing fingers and stars. Akaka then led a successful effort to have the model installed in the high-domed basement rotunda of the Russell Senate Office Building, where its nineteen-foot height could be comfortably displayed. It had resided there, largely unappreciated, ever since.

The senator knew we were planning a Capitol Visitor Center and wanted me to include plans to display this monumental plaster model of *Freedom*. He was passionate about moving it from the basement of the Russell Senate Building so that it could be seen by the millions who would be welcomed to the visitor center. In a later interview with the Capitol Historical Society, Akaka expressed this hope: "for me that would mean *Freedom* returns to the

United States of America, and it'll be a place where people can go up to it—and there will be a second floor where they can look and see . . . the whole figure, and for me that's so important. . . . It'll be the shining light for my career here."[12]

I assured the senator I would consider his recommendation. In researching the statue and its design evolution, we found that Thomas Ustick Walter's 1855 drawing for the cast iron Capitol Dome portrayed a sixteen-foot-tall statue of a woman at its crest. As construction on the dome proceeded, Thomas Crawford, an American sculptor working from a studio in Rome, was commissioned to design the statue. Crawford designed an allegorical figure with her right hand resting on a sheathed sword and her left clutching a laurel wreath of victory and shield of the United States with thirteen stripes.[13]

Crawford created a full-size clay model, which he titled *Freedom Triumphant in War and Peace*, that was placed on an eighteen-foot-high pedestal. He cast it in plaster, then enlarged it from sixteen feet to nineteen and one-half feet tall. Secretary of War Jefferson Davis considered the liberty cap, a symbol of freedom and the French Revolution, to be inappropriate. Crawford eliminated it and instead replaced it with a helmet inspired by Native American culture topped with an eagle's head and feather arrangement.

The plaster cast was sent to America in six crates aboard a small ship that sprung multiple leaks and was unable to travel beyond Bermuda. The model was stored there until the crates could be shipped on another vessel, first to New York and then, in 1859, to Washington, DC, where it was first displayed in what is now National Statuary Hall.

A Foundry and an Enslaved Person

The bronze statue that now crowns the Capitol Dome was cast from this model by sculptor Clark Mills with help from his assistants, which included Philip Reid, an enslaved person brought to Washington when Mills moved there from Charleston. According to Mills, Reid was "smart in mind, and a good workman."[14] Reid successfully solved the problem of finding the joints and separating the plaster model into its five sections with a pulley system so that it could be transported from Statuary Hall to the foundry northeast of the Capitol.[15]

Reid had also been part of Clark Mills's twelve-person foundry when Mills won an earlier competition for a statue of Andrew Jackson on horseback at the Battle of New Orleans that is still in Lafayette Park, just north of the White House. According to William C. Allen, "A temporary foundry was erected south of the President's House and, through trial and error, Mills, Reid, and other workmen produced the first bronze statue cast in America. . . . The success of Mills's statue of Jackson . . . prompted the Secretary of War in 1860 to give him the commission for casting Thomas Crawford's *Statue of Freedom* for the top of the Capitol's new cast-iron dome."[16]

Reid was freed on April 16, 1862, when Abraham Lincoln signed the Compensated Emancipation Act, which freed enslaved people in the District of Columbia. On December 2, 1863, when the installation of the *Statue of Freedom* was completed, crowning the Capitol Dome, Reid had been a free man for more than a year. With the bronze casting safely atop the dome, the plaster model was reassembled and displayed in National Statuary Hall for a quarter of a century, then at the Smithsonian Institution's Arts and Industries Building, and most recently in the Russell Senate Building basement rotunda. Without Akaka's forethought, the plaster model might still be in the basement instead of being the very focal point of the Capitol Visitor Center, where it stands today.

Dome in Distress

Perfect in its geometry, the dome is more than the roof of the rotunda, more than a classic crown on a historic building. It serves as the physical embodiment of unity and cohesiveness, the focal point on Capitol Hill of the Congress and of our nation. In 1998, as the appropriators and their staffs continued to evaluate my budget requests, I was building a case to fund the dome's detailed inspection and full remediation. Guided by our Capitol building maintenance staff, I climbed into the space between the inner and outer domes to begin my stewardship efforts on behalf of the 4th Architect's creation. As they had reported, it was clearly in great need of attention.

This climb is physically challenging, with seemingly endless flights of stairs twisting and turning as they parallel the steeply arching curve of the dome's exterior skin. Climbers must duck beneath and between cast iron trusses where stairs narrow and continue rising sharply upward toward its apex beneath the base of the *Statue of Freedom*. As we climbed those steps on my first dome inspection it was easy to see that the dome was rusting. Old patched cracks had reopened, and cast iron decorative pieces were falling off, becoming embedded in roofs below. Bolted connections between pieces of cast iron railing had deteriorated so completely that only rust held the assembly together.

The sun was the major culprit, aided and abetted by Washington's significant freeze-thaw cycles. As the sun rises each morning, the eastern segment of the cast iron dome begins to heat up, causing the fish-scaled roofing plates to expand as they warm. As the sun arcs southward, new sections of the dome begin to expand, and the eastern sections, now out of the direct rays of the sun, begin to cool and shrink back to their original dimensions. This constant heating and cooling causes joints between adjacent cast iron pieces to open and close, rubbing against each other and making the creaking sound of metal-on-metal friction while opening pathways for water penetration.

A *New York Times* article in June 1997, with the headline "Leaks Aplenty in Capitol Dome," played on the double meaning of *leaks* to place the dome's immediate threat in a political context: "Yikes! The Dome of the United States Capitol has sprung a leak. Make that more than 200 leaks. And those are not the kind of leaks that Congress is famous for." I had requested funding to study the problem, but I ran "into a hitch that has nothing to do with bricks and mortar, and everything to do with politics."[17] Fiscally conservative House members were intent on freezing our budget. To convince them of these pressing needs, I initiated preliminary exploratory work on the dome to present at my next budget hearing.

Shutting Down the US Botanic Garden Conservatory

Later that summer, I confirmed that the dome wasn't the only structure in dire need of repair. The Botanic Garden Conservatory had been deteriorating for decades, and I had to advise the Congress that it was unsafe and could no longer remain open. This glass building's structural issues should have been addressed long before, but my predecessor, George White, cautioned me against shutting down this historic neoclassical revival landmark, assuming no funds would be allocated and it would be lost forever. George was certainly in a position to know, since he was forced to demolish the ninety-three-foot-tall Palm House in 1992 due to its extreme deterioration and Congress's denial of funding for essential repairs. Only a skeletal aluminum Stonehenge stood in bare testament to the stately Bennett, Parsons and Frost architectural gem that had graced the site.

In 1816 the Columbian Institute for the Promotion of Arts and Sciences first suggested the creation of a botanic garden.[18] At that time the United States was an agrarian society, and it was in the national interest to promote knowledge of useful seeds and plants from around the world. In 1827 Secretary of the Treasury Richard Rush sent a letter to representatives of foreign countries stating: "President John Quincy Adams was 'desirous of causing to be introduced into the United States all such trees and plants from other countries not heretofore known in the United States, as may give promise, under proper cultivation, of flourishing and becoming useful.'"[19]

Plants and seeds that were useful as food, shelter, textiles, and medicine were brought in from many countries, including China and Brazil. Even more important than this initiative was the six-ship, government-financed Wilkes Expedition of 1838–42 that circumnavigated the earth, explored the South Seas, and brought back "a large assortment of horticultural and botanical specimens" from around the world.[20] The Wilkes collection became the key impetus to reinstate the defunct Columbian Institute that had lobbied for greenhouses to exhibit this rare collection. The greenhouses were removed from the foot of Capitol Hill when the current Botanic Garden Conservatory was constructed in 1933, with the Architect of the Capitol now serving as acting director.

In 1997 I reported to Congress that I had no choice but to close the Botanic Garden Conservatory because dozens of greenhouse glazing panels rattled threateningly in their frames during high winds, electrical outlets had no ground fault protection and sparked when used, restrooms were not in compliance with Americans with Disabilities Act (ADA), and uneven paving stones were a tripping hazard. I knew if I closed the conservatory there was a real risk that George's prophecy would come true—that this architectural and botanic treasure would remain closed, but in fact the opposite occurred.

As the *Washington Post* reported in August 1997: "Repairs to Give Botanic Garden New Life. . . . At 5 p.m. Monday, the Conservatory's doors will close for three years of renovation. . . . The Palm House, the towering glass dome removed in 1992 for safety reasons, will be restored, and connecting houses will be added to the conservatory. . . . Earlier this year, Alan M. Hantman, newly appointed Architect of the Capitol, declared the Conservatory at Maryland Avenue and First Street SW unsound. Last spring, he informed three congressional committees that the building would have to be shut down for good if it did not undergo a complete overhaul soon."[21]

Faced with the choice of losing this national treasure or securing funding to correct its many problems, James T. Walsh, chair of the House Legislative Branch Appropriations Subcommittee, and Bob Bennett from the Senate Appropriations Subcommittee recognized the role the Botanic Garden Conservatory played in American history. They attached funding for the conservatory restoration project to an unrelated disaster relief bill, and the president signed it in June 1997.

We used copies of Lord and Burnham Company's original 1933 conservatory fabrication drawings to faithfully re-create the historic Palm House design.

Notes

1. Transcript of President William J. Clinton's State of the Union address, February 4, 1997.
2. Transcript.
3. Juliet Eilperin and Jennifer Bradley, "Leaky Dome Tops List of Projects for New Architect," *Roll Call*, February 13, 1997.
4. James Brooke, "Three Suffragists (in Marble) to Move Up in the Capitol," *New York Times*, September 27, 1996.
5. Karen Staser, "From the Crypt to the National Rotunda," National Women's History Museum, womenshistory.org.
6. Kevin Merida, "A Vote against Suffrage Statue," *Washington Post*, April 14, 1997.
7. Comments by Senator Snowe at Women's Suffrage Statue Rededication, *Congressional Record*, US Senate, June 26, 1997, S655–S656.
8. Neely Tucker, "Truth's Rightful Place on the Hill: Slavery's Towering Figure at Last Gets a Historic Bust in the Capitol," *Washington Post*, April 29, 2009.
9. Hantman, personal notes.
10. Building construction background facts are from an Office of the Curator of the Supreme Court information publication.
11. "Justices Kagan and Kennedy to Teach in Salzberg Summer Program," University of the Pacific, McGeorge School of Law, December 13, 2012.
12. US Capitol Historical Society, Senator Daniel Akaka Oral History Interview by Society President Ron Sarasin, March 16, 2007.
13. Statue of Freedom, Architect of the Capitol, S. Pub. 104-40.

14. Clark Mills, Petition to the Commissioners under the act of Congress approved the 16th of April, 1862, entitled "An act for the release of certain persons held in service or labor in the District of Columbia," June 20, 1862, National Archives, copy in "Casting Freedom" file, quoted in Allen, *History of Slave Laborers*, 15.

15. S. D. Wyeth, *The Rotunda and Dome of the US Capitol* (Washington, DC: Gibson Brothers, 1869), 194–95, quoted in Allen, *History of Slave Laborers*, 16.

16. Allen, *History of Slave Laborers*, 15.

17. Eric Schmitt, "Leaks Aplenty in Capitol Dome Repairs Fall Prey to Politics," *New York Times*, June 24, 1997.

18. *Science* 46 (July–December 1917): 508.

19. Fallen, *A Botanic Garden for the Nation*.

20. John Dickinson Sherman, "Botanic Garden Must Be Moved," *Haskell News*, March 31, 1932.

21. Janina De Guzman, "Repairs to Give Botanic Garden New Life," *Washington Post*, August 27, 1997.

FOUR

Of Christmas Trees and Capitol Domes

Newt Gingrich's "Holiday" Tree

In December, ten months into my term, Abe Lincoln's stone bust in the Capitol crypt, face burdened with his inner musings, took no notice of me and Rosalyn, offering no solace as we walked tentatively by. Lincoln's bust has lived in the Capitol since 1908, first in the rotunda and now in the crypt, pensively watching the sojourns of generations of the great and the mundane. Gutzon Borglum, of Mount Rushmore fame, sculpted the bust from Alabama marble of pure calcite, similar to the fine-grained white Carrara marble used by Michelangelo in sculpting his famous *David*. Borglum said this graining permitted him to achieve a look of kindness on Lincoln's face. This evening, however, Mr. Lincoln appeared withdrawn (fig. 4.1).

An hour earlier, on the West Front lawn, the podium settled unevenly into rain-soaked grass. The holiday tree, a stately sixty-three-foot-tall Black Hills spruce from South Dakota, rose majestically, directly in line with the imposing Capitol Dome. It was the thirty-fourth evergreen donated to Congress by the Forest Service from one of its 156 national forests across the country, journeying from a different state each year.

TV cameras and a thousand guests faced the tree. The US Marine Corps Band, the President's Own, sat twenty paces to the north, their metal folding chairs listing unsteadily on grounds saturated by the morning's heavy rains. On the opposite side of the tree was the Congressional Chorus, a volunteer group of Capitol Hill staffers that performed at tree lightings over the years.

A Politically Correct Tree

The first formal tree lighting ceremony was in 1964, and until 1994, they were called Christmas trees, not holiday trees. This was my first year as architect and host for the Capitol tree lighting ceremony, an honor conferred on each Architect of the Capitol since our agency had responsibility for selecting, transporting, erecting, and decorating the trees. I asked our senior landscape architect, Matthew Evans, who had traveled to South Dakota to select the tree, about this atypical naming practice. Matthew assured me that "holiday tree" was the correct term and had been for the past few years.

This practice led to multiple grievances from members of Congress, conservative lobbying groups, and my Capitol grounds crew, which petitioned me to restore the tree to its correct identity. It wasn't until years later, in a 2011 *Politico* article, that I learned how "holiday tree" became the accepted name instead of "Christmas tree." According to the article, "Newt Gingrich waged a quiet war on Christmas—or at least the Capitol Christmas Tree—shortly after becoming Speaker of the House in 1995. . . . In a time of heightened political correctness, Gingrich preferred 'Holiday Tree' over 'Christmas Tree,' according to sources familiar with the annual tree lighting ceremony at the foot of the Capitol. . . . People who worked in the [Architect of the Capitol]

Figure 4.1. Bust of President Lincoln in the Capitol crypt. Courtesy of Alan M. Hantman

office at the time recall the name-change mandate coming from Gingrich's office, the source said."[1]

The Republican Study Committee prodded Dennis Hastert, his successor as House Speaker, to direct me to change the name back, a change I welcomed since it had been difficult defending Gingrich's directive, which had always seemed surprising to me given his conservatism.

South Dakota's Gift to the Nation

The evening of December 10, 1997, was crisp and cold. The audience remained festive, even after sitting through speeches from officials of the Department of Agriculture and the National Park Service and several members of South Dakota's congressional delegation. Dozens of South Dakotans had accompanied their tree on its 1,800-mile journey from the Black Hills National Forest on a flatbed truck, making stops in Custer, Mount Rushmore, Rapid City, Sioux Falls, and other cities. Matthew had selected it because of its full symmetrical shape, its healthy color, its branching pattern, and its ability to graciously support ornaments. It traveled through Minnesota, Iowa, Illinois, and four other states to North Carolina, which would provide the following year's tree, before arriving finally in Washington.

Our grounds crew unwrapped the clear plastic covering used to protect the tree and keep it from drying out. Using a boom crane hung with multiple straps to distribute its load, our crew carefully lifted the tree from the truck bed and rolled it, swinging in its cradle, across the West Lawn to its ultimate destination.

Over the next several days the trunk was embedded four feet into the ground, secured with guywires, and a golden star fastened to the apex. The grounds crew then decorated the tree with thousands of colored lights and four thousand ornaments handmade by South Dakota's children. Many of those children now proudly awaited their moment of national celebrity when the formal lighting of the tree showcased their handiwork depicting pheasants, bison, Mount Rushmore, and other decorations symbolic of South Dakota. The Marine Corps Band finished playing "We Wish You a Merry Christmas," the last of its four holiday selections, as I invited the Speaker of the House to the podium.

Gingrich sloshed through the saturated lawn accompanied by young nieces and nephews. With good cheer, he addressed the audience and the TV cameras carrying his message live nationwide. He then invited the children; "At the count of three, let's press the button together." He opened the button's protective cover, and they all counted, "one, two, three!" and pressed.

Nothing happened!

The tree stayed dark and a profound silence enveloped the crowd, and Gingrich looked at me, then back to the children, again counting, "one, two, three!" They pressed the button again.

Again, nothing happened!

I turned to the band director sixty feet away, discretely calling out: "Play another song!" The band rustled through their music, and, after what seemed an eternity, they struck up another holiday song. They gamely played on and on as my electricians scrambled along the two-hundred-foot assemblage of yellow and gray extension cords, checking the route for disconnects or breaks.

Earlier that day, Matthew and I had discussed testing all electrical connections to be sure the tree would indeed light when the button was pressed. For the previous ten years, I had been part of the team responsible for New York's Rockefeller Center Christmas tree lightings. We always tested electrical connections the night before, and also an hour before the formal ceremony, when David Rockefeller would perform the honors on NBC. The Rockefeller Center trees had always been called "Christmas trees."

Matthew assured me the connections had been tested the night before, and they lit on cue, but I replied, "I am concerned because it rained this morning, and crowds of people have been walking all around the tree, stepping on the extension cords."

"Mr. Hantman," Matthew replied, "landscape architects before me have done it this way for more than thirty years, and we've never had a problem. I assure you that everything will be fine." With perfect hindsight, I knew of course I should have insisted on additional testing.

Gingrich and the children continued standing at the podium on national TV, while up the hill deep inside the underground electrical vault, a savvy electrician flipped an overriding switch, and the tree burst into glorious color, its handmade South Dakota decorations proudly announcing their state of origin. Rousing cheers rang out across the lawn, drowning out the strains of what was, at long last, the final song by the Marine Corps Band. Speaker Gingrich smiled as he calmly led the children up to admire the magnificent tree and South Dakota's handiwork with the entire audience enthusiastically joining them. The

Figure 4.2. Capitol Christmas tree from South Dakota, 1997, with grounds crew ready to start decorating.

Speaker's entourage soon walked up that hill to the Capitol for his private reception.

A *Tyrannosaurus Rex* Reception

Gingrich was escorted by his security detail up Frederick Law Olmsted's multitiered staircase, entering the Capitol through the same door used by presidents-elect walking to their swearing-in ceremonies, then continued up to the Speaker's second-floor office suite. Members of the local community soon drifted off, and South Dakota visitors left for their own celebration in the Rayburn House Office Building.

Our grounds crew mobilized, bustling across the lawn, loading crowd control stanchions, folding chairs, and the podium onto rolling carts. Despite all

Figure 4.3. Capitol crypt. Courtesy of Architect of the Capitol

this activity, it was unnaturally quiet at the foot of the tree. Rosalyn stood with me as Matthew struggled to regain his composure, uttering a few disconnected sentences, hoping his apology would penetrate my battered consciousness. I must have replied, but I have no recollection of what I said.

I turned to Rosalyn, her eyes apprehensive. We held hands crossing the soggy expanse of lawn toward the Capitol, climbing the same monumental stairways as the Speaker on the way to his holiday reception. The West Front Olmsted terraces build on themselves, flight upon flight, increasing in stateliness as they rise, providing a stable visual foundation for the Capitol building at the crest of Jenkins Hill.

That night those flights had become infinitely steeper, the stone beneath our feet unyielding, almost forbidding. We penetrated the dimness of the crypt, a dozen looming statues and the bust of Abe Lincoln silently observing our progress as we crossed the chamber. Twenty-two rings of paving stones surrounded the white compass rose at its center. Three concentric rings of Charles Bullfinch's 1820s Doric sandstone columns enclosed that multipoint stone marking the intersection of the four

quadrants of Washington, DC, as shown on Pierre L'Enfant's master plan.

A simple arched doorway beckoned us on to the Speaker's narrow spiral stone stairway leading to the second floor, each wedge-shaped tread deeply dished by footfalls of our nation's founders. The helical stairway had survived the great fire of August 24, 1814, set when invading British Expeditionary Forces took their torches to the Capitol in the War of 1812. This is one of the oldest surviving sections of the Capitol, and is lit by only three simple brass sconces, each sprouting a pair of unshielded bulbs. We could see the masons' original chisel marks on the underside of each tread above our heads as we climbed twenty-eight winding steps from the crypt to the rotunda level and the Speaker's suite. Crowds of staffers and holiday guests celebrated beneath four decorative chandeliers marching down the seemingly endless corridor leading to the Speaker's conference room, aptly referred to as the the Dinosaur Room by Republican House members. The malevolent stare of a huge *Tyrannosaurus rex* skull confronted us as we entered, its hollow eye sockets glowering, its dagger-like teeth bared.

Figure 4.4. Historic stone stairway. Courtesy of Jeffrey Schwarz Photography

That evening it seemed the Speaker had installed that fearsome skull to warn any who dared enter to abandon all hope. On loan from the Smithsonian National Museum of Natural History, Rex's plaster cast reminded me of the rampant stone lions flanking the gates of Mesopotamia's ancient capital of Nineveh to elicit fear and awe, symbolizing the immutable power of its ruthless and unforgiving ruler.

A dark carved wooden table stood at the center of the room, a single chandelier above with hundreds of crystals diffusing light to all corners of the space. The broad table could easily seat thirty souls locked in verbal combat around its generous perimeter, but now it overflowed with tray upon tray of holiday delicacies, a feast I would normally have dug into with appetite, but not tonight.

Do the Right Thing

People milled about in twos and threes, sampling, chatting, and laughing as Gingrich entered from his inner office, approached the table, and looked down to the far end of the room. He motioned me away from the crowd and over to the ornately draped window facing the brightly lit tree and the Mall beyond. We stood there together, my mind unable to frame any lucid thoughts. He looked directly into my eyes and said, "Mr. Architect, do the right thing."[2] Then, with a pat on my shoulder, he walked away, conversation ended.

I stood alone staring out the window, trying to absorb his words, trying to decipher the meaning surely hidden there. How did this relate to the crime committed earlier that evening, the unforgiveable crime of embarrassing the person second in line for the presidency before a national TV audience? I was numb, unable to focus.

I initially reasoned that perhaps the Christmas spirit and the beauty of the tree had fallen on my side of the scale of justice, outweighing whatever thoughts of retribution he may have harbored, or the Speaker may have simply been advising me not to screw up again. But in retrospect I realized that this was not the case.

Four months earlier, in August of 1997, Gingrich had traveled through several states on a political tour to sound out the possibility of a run for the Republican presidential nomination in 2000. While in Montana, he took a detour to meet with Dr. John Horner, a paleontologist and curator of the Museum of the Rockies. They publicly debated whether *Tyrannosaurus rex* was only a slow, short-armed scavenger, as Dr. Horner postulated, or the fearsome predator depicted in the movie *Jurassic Park*. Gingrich argued that *T. rex* was indeed a predator at the top of the food chain.

Given the Speaker's *T. rex* perspective, I believe that his admonition to "do the right thing" was a call for me to bite like a predator, eliminating whoever had direct responsibility for the embarrassing tree lighting debacle. I knew, of course, the ultimate responsibility resided with me, that despite my concerns about extension cords and rain, I hadn't directed that Matthew execute another lighting test before the ceremony. I would not turn him into a sacrificial lamb by firing him.

In a move designed to avoid cardiac arrest in future architects, I eliminated the thirty-year practice of using two hundred feet of plugged-together extension cords to light the Capitol Christmas tree. A waterproof underground conduit now runs from the electrical vault to the site where the annual tree is raised and decorated. Now, neither rain nor snow nor dark of night can short-circuit the button to be pressed by future Speakers of the House. At the conclusion of my ten-year term, I could claim to have batted nine out of ten for perfect, uninterrupted, Christmas tree lighting ceremonies.

Speaker Gingrich: Splitting the Capitol in Half

Over time I learned the difference between private and public sector decision-making. Once senior management at Rockefeller Center made a decision to move forward with a project, they stepped back and let the project team proceed, asking only that they be kept informed. Consistent leadership at the top of the corporation helped maintain project momentum. If changes or midcourse corrections were needed, quick decisions could usually be expected.

On Capitol Hill, congressional oversight was largely delegated to staff, who are typically generalists with little or no professional or facilities management experience. Early in my tenure, my agency's main line of communication with the Speaker's office ran through an inexperienced young person who had served in his front office for years. Her lack of architectural, engineering, facilities management, or any managerial experience at all appeared to be of little import. Her loyalty to Gingrich was her overriding credential for these important oversight responsibilities.

Each section added to the Capitol since its first wing was completed in 1800 was designed with an architectural sensitivity that respected and complemented earlier segments. The building as it exists today is perceived as a unified and cohesive whole, but the interests and actions of the House and Senate within are anything but unified, and communication between them is not what one might expect of Congress. An invisible yet fundamentally solid division runs down the central east–west axis of the dome and the rotunda, a division that cuts right across Capitol Hill.

The northern half of the Capitol is occupied by the Senate, the southern half by the House. Each body determines how its space is utilized and, in its oversight of the Architect of the Capitol's work, can choose different options as basic as how to clean and polish the floors. The Constitution clearly mandates the separation of power and responsibilities between the two congressional bodies, and this separation, this policy of turf protection, is powerfully illustrated by the Speaker's plan to split the physical operations and management of the Capitol building in half—directly along that east–west axis. This decision was not arrived at from any studied analysis but flowed from the inaccurate perception that the Office of the Architect was more responsive to the needs of the other legislative body. This concept, however, was not unique to America's legislative branch of government.

Visiting facilities management delegations of nations such as Canada, Australia, and the UK said that their bicameral legislatures made similar accusations, but they always performed their duties in an evenhanded way. Ireland's delegation, however, stated that the House of Lords has a less than equal status, since major decision-making and budgets are controlled by their House of Commons, making that chamber a bit more than equal.

The Capitol building jurisdiction has a staff of approximately 150. This is one of ten jurisdictions within the 2,300-person Architect of the Capitol Agency, each with a superintendent or director, dedicated staffs, and budgets. Jurisdictions include the Capitol building; Capitol grounds and arboretum; Capitol Police buildings, grounds, and security; Capitol Power Plant; House office buildings; library Buildings and grounds; Senate office buildings; Supreme Court buildings and grounds; US Botanic Garden; and the most recent addition, the Capitol Visitor Center.

Each superintendent is responsible for administering the budget of their jurisdiction, with some desiring greater independence and resisting the coordinating oversight of the Architect of the Capitol. Chief among these was the superintendent of the House office buildings, who had served for decades and believed he should report directly to the Office of the Speaker. He supported splitting Capitol operations in half, with little concern for how operations of the Senate side would be coordinated with those of the House.

After months of meetings and detailed safety, security, and operational reports, Gingrich was finally convinced that this division made no sense, simply because of the necessity of integrating life-safety and emergency egress, security, heating, ventilating, and air conditioning. It was essential that we coordinate the maintenance of the centrally located dome, rotunda, and crypt, including the erection and removal of inaugural stands and all special arrangements for security for other ceremonies and special events. This split would have created an untenable operations and life-safety nightmare.

Gingrich ultimately dropped his plan, leaving responsibility for the entire building within a unified Capitol building jurisdiction.

The Capitol's Three Domes

Central to the architect's design responsibilities and stewardship over the Capitol's history has been the evolution of the dome and the building it crowns.

Figure 4.5. Three domes. Courtesy of United States Capitol Historical Society

The juxtaposition of three different Capitol Dome designs in this powerful image parallels our nation's growth as it expanded from the original, tenuously bound thirteen colony-states to a nation ever more prominent in the world community as it grew across the width of North America.

The First Dome: William Thornton's Design

Dr. Thornton's winning 1793 Capitol building design was capped by a low, well-scaled dome, sensitively proportioned as an integral part of the planned Capitol building. Its construction was deferred while funding was provided for the design and construction first of the northern Senate wing, then of the southern wing for the House of Representatives.

Figure 4.6. Bulfinch's dome. Courtesy of Architect of the Capitol

The Second Dome: A President's Taste

Thornton's dome was never built, serving only decades later as Charles Bulfinch's conceptual starting point when he was directed by President James Monroe to redesign it to be seventy feet higher than originally conceived. This directive demonstrates that while each Architect of the Capitol needs champions to support important projects, such support can result in the unfortunate imposition of insensitive design preferences by those in authority.

The Third Dome: The Nation Expands

While Bulfinch's dome had been too large and ungainly for the Capitol's original four-hundred-foot-long base, three decades later, Architect Walter's House and Senate expansions yielded a 750-foot-long building that called for a dome of greater presence and proportionality.

Walter drew a beautifully rendered seven-foot-long elevation of the enlarged Capitol featuring an impressive cast iron fireproof dome. It is Walter's dome that has served as our greatest national icon for over 150 years.

The Dome and a Can of Rust

My investigation of this historic dome confirmed concerns that constant movement and water penetration had taken a significant toll on the dome's cast iron. My challenge was to decide how to present these realities to the Congress as I sought a significant funding increase for the next year's budget, which included funding to remove generations of dome paint to allow an in-depth inspection of cracks, fastenings, and other problem areas and the development of an overall remediation plan.

I've always used strong illustrations to emphasize key presentation points, and as I began my second year in office, I came to my budget hearings not only with renderings, charts, and lists but also with a two-phased plan of action complete with estimates

Figure 4.7. Walter's dome and Capitol expansion. Courtesy of Architect of the Capitol

Like many Americans, I believed President Abraham Lincoln had been determined to continue construction of the dome as a powerful symbol that, despite the enormous costs of the ongoing war, the Union would be preserved. This was compatible with my sense of patriotism and image of Lincoln as a far-sighted, thoughtful leader. But in 1861, at the start of the Civil War, the construction of the new cast iron dome had already reached a level above the thirty-six-column colonnade, almost completing the dome's visual base. At that time, the New York foundry of Janes, Fowler, Kirtland and Co. was contacted by the secretary of war, who "advis[ed] the firm not to expect payment for any further work on the Dome until the country's financial outlook improved. . . . Charles Fowler and his partners determined that there was no choice but to continue to hoist and bolt ironwork on the Dome. They had 1.3 million pounds of iron stockpiled on the site, and walking away from such valuable material would be irresponsible and costly. Instead the firm decided to continue building the Dome, trusting the government to pay when times were better."[3] This, in essence, was a unilateral business decision by the foundry, rather than one initiated by President Lincoln, who seized on this reality to create a powerful national rallying cry.

and powerful show-and-tell exhibits. At the hearings I also presented the members with "a piece of deteriorating metal and a coffee can full of rust gathered from the Capitol Dome."[4]

My heavy Maxwell House coffee can thudded onto the wooden witness table as I juggled several budget binders. Over the course of my ten-year term I testified at more than fifty hearings before a variety of House and Senate committees. My strategy at this hearing was to circulate the coffee can among the appropriators so they could personally lift and peer into it to find that two pounds of coffee had been replaced with ten pounds of much heavier rust, rust collected from the deteriorating cast iron dome. My message was, "Members of Congress, our dome is in your hands!"

I explained that no major repairs or renovations had been made to the dome since the 1960s and emphasized the importance of using environmentally safe methods to remove the lead-based paint on all of its surfaces. Multiple leaks onto the rotunda floor also demonstrated the critical need for these repairs.

> Representative José Serrano (D-NY) held the coffee can and asked, "That is a piece of the Dome, so to speak?"
>
> "That is a piece of the railing at the Dome," I answered. "We have bags of bolts that have rusted right out, and they were not holding anything in place."
>
> "This is rust?" he asked.
>
> "It is rust."
>
> "Looks like good coffee to me."[5]

The can of rust and chunks of cracked cast iron helped build a strong case for my budget request, but it still wasn't a done deal. Congress was under pressure not to appropriate funds above a set cap, so my $7.5 million first-phase dome budget was not approved. James T. Walsh wanted to be a good steward of our Capitol Hill treasures by supporting my request for the dome project, the US Botanic Garden Conservatory restoration, and necessary security

issues, but he was trapped by political pressure to avoid increases in that cap.

Creative Funding

Walsh accompanied me on an inspection tour of the dome and was convinced of the need when he personally saw multiple cracks and rusting all along our pathway, saying, "The Dome is a pretty important symbol to the country and the world, and we want to make sure we take care of it."[6] Senator Bob Bennett, the Senate's legislative branch chair, also supported funding for the dome's inspection and remediation, and was quoted in *Roll Call*: "I learned in business that one of the most expensive ways you can save money is to cut down on repairs in the short term."[7]

In a tight budget year, Walsh and Bennett saved the $7.5 million budget request for the dome, and the $33.5 million request for conservatory restoration and reconstruction; citing them as life-safety risks, they creatively attached them to the $8.6 billion disaster relief bill passed in response to massive flooding across many states. The relief bill was not part of the normal appropriations process and did not count against the rigid budget cap, an end-run around rigid conservative roadblocks.

We could now competitively bid contracts for both the Botanic Garden and for the removal of paint on the dome interior to permit its inspection. I awarded the paint removal work to the Aulson Company and called upon Hoffman Architects, a fine historic preservation and restoration firm out of New Haven, Connecticut, and LZA Technology, a nationally recognized structural engineering firm. I commissioned them to update and expand earlier studies they worked on with George White and prepare a comprehensive master plan for the next phase of dome restoration and repair.

Background of Dome Restoration

Many important architectural changes have been proposed and implemented at the Capitol over time, with the baton passed from architect to architect.

Figure 4.8. Dome repair of 1960 with lead-based paint primer. Courtesy of Architect of the Capitol

Partial efforts at restoring the Capitol Dome date to 1959, under the stewardship of J. George Stewart, the 8th Architect of the Capitol. Then, metal straps were fastened across cracks in the cast iron to hold them together, but they soon snapped with the pressure of constantly expanding and contracting iron plates. Joints were caulked, and a finish of dome white paint was applied over a new coating of red lead-based primer, which ended up creating an extensive environmental problem for his successors.

After a major 1990 storm created puddles on the rotunda floor and damaged Constantino Brumidi's frieze circling the top of the rotunda wall, George White investigated dome deficiencies and determined that the drainage problems and corrosion were due to cracked cast iron plates, joint leakage, and drains clogged by bird droppings. White initiated improvements to protect the gutters and maintain the dome and added catwalks to improve

worker safety. Ten years later, my emergency appropriation funded the first phase of a much more detailed dome restoration.

Two shifts of nine safety-suited workers were soon laboring twenty hours a day to remove eighty-eight tons of lead-based paint from the surfaces between the inner and outer domes. The Aulson team used air-powered blasters and needle guns on inner surfaces of the outer dome. We used less invasive vibration-free, citrus-based chemicals and hand-scraping on the inner canopy to avoid impacting Constantino Brumidi's masterful fresco, the *Apotheosis of Washington*, painted on the rotunda side of that surface.

Several of the twenty-one layers of paint removed from the dome were composed of as much as 30 percent lead, and we placed the area under negative air pressure with strong filtration systems to assure that lead was not released into the air. This work allowed us to inspect cast iron surfaces and document all existing problems, some of which dated back to the original construction of the dome. We blasted paint off each area of cast iron with needle guns and absorbent sponge particles impregnated with aluminum oxide. Surfaces were then thoroughly inspected for cracks and deteriorated connections, and a new base primer coat was immediately applied to prevent the bare cast iron from quickly rusting. We learned this lesson after areas that were cleared of old paint began turning rust-orange overnight. To resolve environmental disposal problems, I authorized shipment of the lead-based paint to Exide Battery Company in Indiana to be recycled for use in new car batteries.

Multilayered paint samples from the coffered dome of the rotunda were also gathered to determine original colors for future restoration and repainting. To protect members, staff, and visitors in the rotunda below, a donut-shaped protective netting was hung beneath the inner dome while still keeping the magnificent *Apotheosis of Washington* in view.

We discovered that major additional weather-related deterioration had occurred. Hoffman Architects documented the findings in a five-volume

Figure 4.9. Inner dome with rotunda ceiling protective netting. Courtesy of Architect of the Capitol

report, complete with drawings detailing the nature and location of 1,300 cracks, rusted connections, and other problem areas, and recommended methods of addressing them. The original cast iron trusses easily passed LZA's computer analysis, and we determined that the cast iron skin of the dome developed cracks due to expansion and contraction issues rather than from basic structural considerations.

Based on these reports, I requested funding for remediation of the cracked cast iron, removal of multiple layers of lead-based paint and primer from the dome's exterior, the recycling of additional tons of lead, and for the recasting of cast iron plates and decorations that were either missing or not reparable. This analysis ultimately became the blueprint for future remediation to be completed under the stewardship of my successor, Stephen Ayers, the 11th Architect.

Spanning the tenures of three architects, this multiphase, quarter-century-long project speaks to the importance of continuity, as each architect built on the efforts of his predecessor for the good of our nation's historic structures on Capitol Hill. It is extraordinary that with nine major phases of Capitol building growth, and many ongoing preservation efforts implemented over time, we can still celebrate a visually unified Capitol building that projects a spirit of architectural harmony, nobility and strength.

As a critical maintenance function we administered a triennial waxing to the *Statue of Freedom*, preventing ultra-violet rays from degrading the dome's crowning glory. The scaffolding erected for this three-year maintenance cycle also provided us an opportunity to concurrently replace lightning rods damaged over the years.

One of my joys as architect was climbing a narrow scaffold to the top of the statue for these inspections and looking out from the top of the Capitol Dome at the awe-inspiring sight of L'Enfant's dynamic pattern of city streets laid out below, just as he planned it.

Of Egos and Busts

Each US vice president also serves as president of the Senate and is entitled to a sculpted bust to be displayed in the corridors surrounding the Senate Chamber. On July 10, 1998, I led an expedition of Architect of the Capitol curators and Senate Rules Committee staff to see the current work of sculptor Frederick Hart to determine whether his recent stroke would prevent him from fulfilling a commission for a marble bust of J. Danforth "Dan" Quayle, forty-fourth vice president under President George H. W. Bush. The sculpture would join the busts of other vice presidents, a tradition going back to the 1885 bust commissioned for Henry Wilson, who served as vice president under Ulysses S. Grant.

Hart graciously welcomed our small delegation, escorting us on a mini tour through the new antebellum mansion he had built on his Virginia farm. He showed us to his weathered barn of a studio, where we saw larger-than-life plaster casts of President Jimmy Carter and Senator Richard B. Russell Jr. The senator's bronze casting had been dedicated in the rotunda of the Russell Senate Office Building two years earlier.

Rick's left arm hung limply, but he assured us that even though he could no longer use a hammer and chisel for heavy stonework, he could still work effectively in clay with his right hand and could still use rasps and files for fine finishing work. The heavy work would be accomplished by his longtime associate Vincent Palumbo, who worked under Hart's direction on the National Cathedral's statuary for many years. It was this earlier work on the Creation sculptures over the cathedral's main entrance and his *Three Servicemen* statue at the Vietnam Memorial that had recommended him to us.

Mortal Sculptors

Our visit confirmed that Hart could sculpt the Dan Quayle bust with Vincent Palumbo's assistance, but

DICK CHENEY UNVEILED

A bust of the forty-fifth vice president, Al Gore, was next in line chronologically, but William Frederick Behrends was commissioned first to sculpt the bust of the forty-sixth vice president, Dick Cheney, unveiled on December 3, 2015, in Emancipation Hall.

At the unveiling ceremony Cheney joked, according to the *New York Times*, about his bust preceding Al Gore's: "'Apparently there have been a few delays in the work on Al's likeness, it may be I'm easier to carve into stone.'"[8]

While Quayle's bust was placed in the quiet corridor to the east of the Senate Chamber, Cheney's bust, originally slated for the first floor, was prominently positioned near the famous 1815 Ohio Clock, where press conferences are frequently held, in a space not originally designated in the Senate curator's location plan for busts. Gore's bust, also by Behrends, was carved two years later and added to the Senate collection. Those of Joe Biden, the forty-seventh vice president, and Mike Pence, the forty-eighth vice president, have not yet been commissioned. They will either be placed in chronological order on the first floor or possibly in a more prestigious location, depending on the party holding the Senate majority at the time.

unfortunately, some thirteen months after he began, Hart died of lung cancer at age fifty-six. His assistant, Jeffery Hall, completed work on a clay model of the bust and turned it over to Palumbo for stone carving. Again, unfortunately, sixteen months after Hart's passing, Vincent Palumbo died of leukemia at age sixty-four. Both sculptors had died before the bust was completed. After complex negotiations with Hart's widow, Lindy, over how to best complete the commission, I selected sculptor Daniel Sinclair to finish the stone carving after Barbara Wolanin, our agency curator, and I met with him in his New York studio.

A fully detailed plaster cast was delivered to Sinclair, and within three months, after checking and rechecking hundreds of measurements from the life-sized clay model, he turned a block of Carrara marble into a faithful reproduction of Frederick Hart's original creation.

The bust was unveiled in the Capitol Rotunda on September 10, 2003, with former president George H. W. Bush, Vice President Dick Cheney, and the sculptor in attendance. Sinclair had successfully completed the bad-luck commission and lived to tell the tale. The bust was later moved to a corridor outside the Senate Chamber to join the forty-one other former presidents of the Senate, filling the last space designated for busts by the Senate curator outside the Senate Chamber on the second floor of the Capitol.

Notes

1. Jonathan Allen, "The Gingrich Who Stole Christmas?" *Politico*, December 8, 2011.
2. Hantman, personal notes, December 10, 1997.
3. Allen, *History of the United States Capitol*, 315.
4. Francesca Contigulia, "Senate Rules Panel Hears Concerns about Security," *Roll Call*, February 26, 1998.
5. "Part 2: Fiscal Year 1999 Legislative Branch Appropriation Requests—Hearing of Architect of the Capitol—Capitol Dome Project," House Hearing, February 4, 1998, 105th Congress.
6. Eric Shmitt, "Leaks Aplenty in Capitol Dome, Repairs Fall Prey to Politics," *New York Times*, June 24, 1997.
7. Jennifer Bradley, "Report," *Roll Call*, July 17, 1997.
8. Peter Blake, "Tribute and a Reunion for Cheney in Capitol," *New York Times*, December 4, 2015.

FIVE

Murders, Congress, and Security

The crypt lies one level beneath the rotunda's imposing volume, away from the brightness of the sun. Like the dome, it too measures ninety-six feet across, its vaulted stone ceiling springing from forty Doric sandstone columns set in three concentric rings. A stone multipoint compass rose marks the crypt's center, its white stone dished down by the shoes of millions who stood proudly at the point where the four quadrants of the District of Columbia come together, a spot where visitors often snap photos immortalizing their Capitol moment for friends and relatives back home.

Like the rotunda directly above, the crypt is shared territory, common to both the Senate and the House of Representatives. It therefore falls under the jurisdiction of the Joint Committee on the Library, with its chairmanship rotating each year from one body to the other. Statues or displays placed in these common spaces, as well as any proposed events, require the blessing of this committee.

The Gunman and the Cannibals

Two doorways lead from the crypt out to the Capitol's East Front, the Law Library door on the Senate side, and the Document Room door on the House side. Here, on Friday July 24, 1998, events occurred that shook the complacency of congressional lawmakers, reawakening slumbering, unaddressed security concerns.

"A gunman burst through a security checkpoint in the US Capitol yesterday afternoon," the *Washington Post* reported the next day, "and killed two Capitol Police officers in a terrifying exchange of fire that sent panicked bystanders diving for cover in the majestic marble building known around the world as a symbol of America and democracy."[1]

That Friday afternoon, Russell Eugene Weston Jr. stepped through the Document Room door with his father's old .38 caliber Smith and Wesson six-shot revolver in hand. He had come looking for "the ruby satellite" he believed was kept in a Senate safe. He later told a court appointed psychiatrist that "if he did not come to Washington DC, he would become infected with Black Heva . . . the deadliest disease known to mankind," and that the disease was spread by the rotting corpses of cannibals' victims.[2] The psychiatrist, Sally C. Johnson, wrote that Weston insisted that "the ruby satellite" was key to stopping cannibalism.

Officer J.J. Chestnut was on duty at his regular Document Room door post, manning the scanner and magnetometer. At 3:40 p.m., his attention was momentarily turned to visitors seeking directions when Weston walked through that door, set off the detector, and immediately pointed his gun at the back of Chestnut's head, firing before the officer could react. Chestnut fell mortally wounded.

Weston exchanged shots with Officer Douglas McMillan, who was returning to the door with a wheelchair for a tourist, then ran around a corner following a woman who was running for cover. They both burst through a door marked "Private Entrance" to Majority Whip Tom DeLay's suite. Behind that door, Detective John Gibson heard the

Figure 5.1. Capitol crypt compass rose. Courtesy of Alan M. Hantman

shots and yelled for DeLay and the office staff to take cover under desks. Gibson pushed the woman away to safety and confronted Weston, who shot him in the chest. Despite the wound, Gibson drew his gun and shot Weston in his legs. More shots were fired as other Capitol Police officers responded to the scene and arrested Weston.

DeLay and several of his staff hid in his private bathroom. Thanks to Detective Gibson's bravery, no one else in the suite of offices was injured. As DeLay's personal security detail, Gibson had become much like family. "I have no doubt that John saved the lives of many people today," DeLay said.[3]

Gibson later died during surgery at Washington Hospital Center. Chestnut was pronounced dead at George Washington University Medical Center, where Angela Dickerson, a tourist with minor bullet wounds to her shoulder and face, was treated and released. Weston, wounded in the torso, buttocks,

and legs, was aided on his way to DC General Hospital by a paramedic and Senator Bill Frist (R-TN), a heart surgeon.

Weston, who had a history of paranoid schizophrenia, recovered. Doctors said he opposed his attorney's plan to introduce an insanity defense because he saw a trial as his best chance to defeat the cannibals. Weston never stood trial.

The *Washington Post* reported: "Debates over how secure Capitol Hill really is have been raging for years, and yesterday's shootout is sure to give them a renewed sense of urgency. . . . Concerns about domestic terrorism in the 1990s have tilted the debate toward tighter restrictions . . . After Oklahoma City, the Secret Service shut down Pennsylvania Avenue to all traffic near the White House. And on Capitol Hill, traffic was eliminated or restricted on streets around three Senate office buildings."[4]

A serious option to help reconcile the mutually exclusive goals of accessibility and security was the plan to create a welcoming, yet secure visitor center. But Speaker Gingrich believed constituents should be able to climb the historic white stone steps of their Capitol to witness the workings of their Congress. He had been emphatic that he would not support a new visitor center, and he did not, until the afternoon of July 24, 1998.

Three days after the murders, the House voted to rename the East Front Document Room door as the Chestnut-Gibson Memorial Door. Gingrich thanked President Clinton for honoring his request to permit Detective Gibson to be interred at Arlington National Cemetery, even though he was not a veteran. On that same day, the Senate held a roll call vote on the resolution while standing in respect at their desks.[5]

Officer Jacob J. Chestnut and
Detective John M. Gibson

Officer Chestnut always greeted me with a smile as I walked through the Document Room door. He was a Vietnam veteran who had served in the Air Force for twenty years and in the Capitol Police for an-

ROLL CALL

THE NEWSPAPER OF CAPITOL HILL SINCE 1955

VOL. 44, NO. 7   MONDAY, JULY 27, 1998 $3.00

CAPITOL TRAGEDY

2 Officers Killed During Shootout With Gunman; Bedlam Erupts as Tourists, Staff Flee From Capitol

By Ed Henry

A gunman charged into the Capitol on Friday afternoon, killing two Capitol Police officers, seriously wounding a female tourist and plunging the building into chaos.

The gunman, Russell Weston, forced his way into the Capitol at 3:40 p.m. and fired at least 20 shots, according to eyewitnesses. Weston, who had previously made threats against President Clinton and was reportedly well-known to the Secret Service, was shot in the crossfire with the officers and was in stable condition Friday night at DC General Hospital.

Both of the Capitol Police officers, Jacob Chestnut and John Gibson, were married with three children each. Chestnut was an 18-year veteran of the force, while Gibson was an eight-year veteran.

The Capitol was closed for hours as hundreds of law enforcement officers, journalists, Members, staffers and tourists descended on the scene to deal with the first shooting in the Capitol since 1954, when Puerto Rican nationalists wounded five Members in the House chamber.

Sen. Bill Frist (R-Tenn), a heart surgeon who rushed to the scene,

AP Photo

One of the two slain Capitol Police officers is wheeled out of the building by emergency personnel on Friday afternoon. Both officers were married and each left behind three children.

Figure 5.2. Headline highlights murders. Courtesy of *Roll Call*

other eighteen. He carried himself with a respectful military bearing as he greeted members of Congress, staff, and hundreds of visitors each day. He was close to retirement and the father of five, grandfather of five, and husband to Mei Lei, a gracious and soft-spoken woman.

Detective Gibson served on the Capitol Police for eighteen years, recently assigned to protect House Republican Whip Tom DeLay. With his wife, Lynn, he was the father of three teenagers. A joint congressional resolution soon authorized the use of the Capitol Rotunda for a lying-in-honor ceremony for the two officers.

Flags flew at half-staff over the Capitol on July 28, 1998, as President Clinton presented wreaths and eulogized the fallen officers along with congressional

leaders of both parties. Officer Chestnut and Detective Gibson lay side by side on separate biers in the Capitol Rotunda with an honor guard of their fellow officers at attention in solemn respect. Police officers from across the United States and Canada circled their caskets in silent tribute, along with tens of thousands of visitors. Two hundred and sixty officers on motorcycles riding two abreast led the thousand-car funeral cortege past the Capitol on its way to Arlington Cemetery.

The cortege stretched fourteen miles, with thousands of respectful, flag-waving onlookers lining highways and roads along the way as it accompanied the fallen officers to their final resting places. Bagpipers from the Chicago and New York Police Departments joined the honor guard at the cemetery.

LYING IN HONOR AND LYING IN STATE

Lying-in-honor ceremonies are similar to lying-in-state ceremonies since they too are held in the rotunda, but with a police honor guard rather than a military honor guard, and most often without the Lincoln Catafalque. Lying-in-state ceremonies in the rotunda are authorized by concurrent action of the House and Senate to honor those who have rendered distinguished service to the nation, including presidents, senators, and members of the House. Generals John Pershing and Douglas MacArthur and unknown soldiers from major wars have also been so honored. Beginning with Henry Clay in 1852 and Abraham Lincoln in 1865, there have only been some three dozen such ceremonies in the nation's history, including for Presidents John F. Kennedy (November 24–25, 1963) and Dwight D. Eisenhower (March 30–31, 1969), and more recently Ronald Reagan (June 9–11, 2004) and Gerald Ford (December 30, 2006–January 2, 2007), Senators Daniel K. Inouye (December 20, 2012) and John McCain (August 31, 2018), President George H. W. Bush (December 3, 2018), Congressmen Elijah Cummings (October 24, 2019) and John Lewis (July 27–28, 2020), Supreme Court Associate Justice Ruth Bader Ginsburg (who lay in state in National Statuary Hall on September 25, 2020), and Senator Robert Dole (December 9, 2021). On January 12, 2022, Senator Harry Reid became the thirty-eighth person to have lain in state, while two months later, on March 29, 2022, Congressman Don Young became the thirty-ninth. Nine prominent citizens to date have lain in honor, four of whom were US Capitol Police officers.

I have never forgotten the sounds and images of shared mourning on that day.

We Remember the Bagpipes

We remember the mournful drone,
the pleated skirts of marching pipers,
soul-penetrating sounds stirring our emotions,
our melancholy.

We remember a dozen highway overpasses laden
    with fire trucks,
ladders fully extended forming towering archways,
house-sized American flags suspended beneath.

The long, silent cortege glided by police cars,
    ambulances,
pulsating lights insistent, unrelenting,
marking the loss of brothers in service.

We remember worship services,
caskets beside church altars,
heartfelt eulogies,
wives and children bowed in grief, dignified in loss.

We remember color guards,
a lone bugle crying out over Arlington's hallowed
    grounds,
rifle salvos saluting the fallen.

Two police officers murdered in Capitol halls,
Officer J.J. Chestnut and Detective John M. Gibson.

A deranged gunman invading the Capitol with
    unsettling ease,
shooting the lone officer stationed at the entry,
dodging through a random door to slay another
    defender.

These murders, this gross breach of Capitol
    inviolability,

MORE POLICE DEATHS: THE JANUARY 6, 2021, INSURRECTION

Twenty-two years later, on February 2, 2021, House Speaker Nancy Pelosi spoke at another rotunda ceremony: "It is my official and sad honor to welcome Officer Brian Sicknick and many who loved, respected and were protected by him, to the United States Capitol Rotunda for a recognition of his life."[6]

One month earlier, on January 6, 2021, the sanctity of the Capitol had been violated once again, this time by a rampaging mob of thousands of Donald Trump's supporters smashing their way into the Capitol, desecrating it in search of the House Chamber to stop the counting of the electoral votes formalizing Joseph Biden's presidential victory. They violated the same rotunda where presidents lie in state, where Mother Teresa, Martin Luther King, the Dalai Lama, and Ronald Reagan were awarded the Congressional Gold Medal, Congress's highest honor.

The rioters occupied the Senate Chamber just after Vice President Mike Pence and a number of senators were evacuated down a north stairway, grasp-ing the handsome 1859 bronze railing decorated with castings of cherubs, eagles, and deer as they hurried on. Rioters rappelled down from the mezzanine to rummage through senators' desks, posed for photos at the top of the vice president's dignified rostrum with *E pluribus unum* etched above, and left a note that they would be returning.

They pounded on the doors of the House Chamber as it was evacuated, and a rioter was shot and killed as she climbed through a smashed window at the Speaker's Lobby in pursuit of members. Members in the mezzanine held gas masks as they crouched, sheltering in place at the seats where the First Lady and her guests are honored at joint sessions of Congress.

Officer Brian Sicknick, who died while on duty during the events of January 6, 2021, became the fifth person to lay in honor in the rotunda, with an honor guard standing at the side of a black draped table holding his cremated remains and a folded American flag flown over the Capitol in his honor. President Joe Biden and First Lady Jill Biden paid their respects along with members of Congress and his fellow officers, but the Capitol building lockdown, due to both the insurrection and the COVID pandemic, prevented the general public from attending.

The 140 police officers injured in close-quarters fighting on January 6 suffered con-cussions, broken ribs, lost fingers, a lost eye, and lung injuries caused by bear spray, fire extinguishers, and bicycle racks and other thrown objects. Four other police officers, Howard Liebengood and Jeffrey Smith of the Capitol Police and Gunther Hashida and Kyle DeFreytag of the Metropolitan Police died by suicide in the following days. The Capitol Police chief and the House and Senate sergeants at arms were forced to resign in the wake of this insurrection. They had not prepared a strong security cordon to protect the Capitol in the face of threats they had been aware of and chose to downplay until the mob was at the Capitol. Four rioters also died.

President Donald J. Trump was impeached for a second time for his role in instigating the riot. Without a two-thirds vote in the Senate in favor of impeachment, his acquittal came quickly.

continues next page

continued from previous page

Senate Majority Leader Mitch McConnell, who had voted in favor of acquittal, rose afterward in the Senate chamber to state: "American citizens attacked their own government. . . . Fellow Americans beat and bloodied our own police. They stormed the Senate floor. . . . They did this because they had been fed wild falsehoods by the most powerful man on earth—because he was angry he'd lost an election. Former President Trump's actions preceding the riot were a disgraceful dereliction of duty."[7]

In the days following the insurrection, many in both parties agreed with McConnell in condemning the insurrection we had witnessed as it played out on our cell phones, computers, and televisions. In the coming weeks and months, however, many in Congress, fearing for their elective future, began echoing the falsehoods of a stolen election, further fracturing the illusion of *E pluribus unum*.

Weeks later, Officer William "Billy" Evans died of injuries sustained when an automobile purposefully slammed into him as he stood guard at the Capitol's north vehicular security gate. He was the fourth police officer to lie in honor in the Capitol Rotunda. Once again President Biden and congressional leaders came to pay their respects.

A year later, on February 8, 2022, Senate Minority Leader McConnell again pushed back, this time on the additional falsehoods and actions "that the Republican National Committee took on Friday, when it officially rebuked Ms. Cheney and Mr. Kinzinger for participating in the House Investigation of the Jan. 6 attack, accusing them of 'persecution of ordinary citizens engaged in legitimate political discourse.' Senator McConnell repudiated that description, saying of the events of Jan. 6, 2021: 'We saw it happen. It was a violent insurrection for the purpose of trying to prevent the peaceful transfer of power after a legitimately certified election, from one administration to the next. That's what it was.'"[8]

Almost two years after the insurrection, on December 6, 2022, a *Washington Post* headline read, "Congress awards gold medals to police who defended Capitol on Jan. 6."[9] The US Capitol Police and the DC Metropolitan Police and family members of those officers who died because of the insurrection were honored with Congressional Gold Medals in a Capitol Rotunda ceremony. House Speaker Pelosi thanked the officers for "putting their lives on the line to save the Capitol, the Congress and the Constitution." Senate Majority Leader Chuck Schumer addressed the officers in attendance, "history will forever note that democracy lived on because of you."[10] He also thanked the architect's staff for restoring the halls of the Capitol after the riot.

In stark counterpoint, "the Republican Party . . . officially declared the Jan. 6, 2021 attack on the Capitol and the events that led to it 'legitimate political discourse.'"[11] To date, this position is still supported by many even after leaders of the insurrectionists "were convicted of Seditious Conspiracy for plotting to keep President Donald Trump in power after his election defeat by leading a violent mob in attacking the Capitol on Jan. 6, 2021."[12]

In coming years, how many more rotunda ceremonies will be held to honor police officers attacked in full view of the Capitol Dome, dying in defense of our democracy?

revived old calls for strengthened security,
transcended political budget fratricide,
renewed enthusiasm for a Capitol expansion to
welcome all in safety.

George Washington never envisioned his Capitol,
designed for a country of four million,
one day welcoming millions each year,
never considered that this openness must be balanced against threats to Capitol sanctity.

Two officers murdered.
The mournful plaint of bagpipes awakened us to a
new reality,
our vulnerabilities exposed.

Congress's Response to the 1998 Murders of Chestnut and Gibson

The aftermath of Chestnut's and Gibson's murders led to much soul-searching at the Capitol as we worked to balance physical access to our democratic institutions and security concerns that clearly existed in real time. There was no perfect answer. Heated debates considered financial realities, politics, national ideals, and basic security implications of one decision versus another. The sense of loss, and of outrage that these murders could happen at the Capitol doors, drove members of Congress to cease procrastinating and address their fear of appropriating taxpayer funds for anything that could possibly be perceived as a perk of office, anything that could be interpreted as feathering their own political nests. Congress's position evolved over many months.

Going back decades, Congressman Vic Fazio (D-CA), chair of the House Appropriations Subcommittee on the Legislative Branch, had supported a visitor center since the November 1983 explosion in the Capitol's Senate wing by a group protesting US military involvement in Grenada and Lebanon. Fazio continued his support: "'Lawmakers such as Gingrich attacked the project as a congressional perk. . . . Newt was personally critical of this effort,'

Fazio recalled. 'It's only the demagoguery that we used to engage in every time we talk about spending a dime on the legislative branch that kept this from happening.'"[13] Still, James T. Walsh, the current chair, wondered if a visitor center could solve all threats, since a person with a gun could kill others no matter where confronted at the Capitol.

Congressman Walsh was partially correct, but a visitor center could decrease overall risk to the Congress and all who visit the Capitol. It could also provide services and educational opportunities never included in the building's design that would be needed as the annual visitor count continued increasing. The goals for the design would include visitor education and comfort and functional improvements while also preserving the Capitol and its treasured Frederick Law Olmsted landscape. Security, however, was the driving rationale members of Congress could unite behind to justify funding a visitor center.

Capitol Complex Master Plan

According to congressional records, George White was authorized to "prepare studies and develop a master plan for future developments within the United States Capitol Grounds . . . in order to provide within such areas for future expansion, growth, and requirements of the Legislative Branch and such parts of the Judiciary Branch as deemed appropriate."[14] White worked with the US Capitol Planning Group to assemble a team of consultants and a blue-ribbon National Advisory Group comprised of architects, educators, and social and political scientists as advisers to the design study team.

This master plan was based on both the original 1792 L'Enfant Master Plan for Washington and the 1902 McMillan Plan for the National Mall. It projected that the Capitol Grounds would expand to accommodate potential growth to the south and north of the Capitol, with the Capitol Hill Historic District to the east remaining a predominantly residential area.

Figure 5.3. Long visitor waiting lines. Courtesy of Architect of the Capitol

Another recommendation was to preserve and enhance the Mall area and other open spaces.

A Supermarket Parking Lot

The plan recognized the unsightly problem of row upon row of cars parked on the East Plaza of the Capitol and agreed that public transit should be encouraged, suggesting "the elimination of vehicles from the grounds immediately surrounding the Capitol, except for ceremonial occasions." It called for the "development of underground parking and support space beneath the paved area of the East Plaza . . . [to] allow it to be redesigned as a great pedestrian forecourt to the Capitol."[15]

The planners called for a three-level garage for five hundred cars, an auto and taxi drop-off, a truck dock area, as well as space for support services, offices, and storage, all connected to the Capitol by escalators, stairs, and elevators. These recom-

Figure 5.4. East Plaza parking lot. Courtesy of Architect of the Capitol

mendations were seriously considered before the 1993 truck bombing of the World Trade Center garage in New York highlighted major security risks created by parking beneath occupied buildings.

One of my first lessons on Capitol Hill seemed to be an eleventh commandment as important as the first ten—roughly rendered as, "Thou shalt not gore my parking spot!" At my own peril would I forget the importance of providing the Congress convenient and ample parking, including for senior staff who have the power to impact budgets and daily agency operations.

White wrote: "I had stated in 1971 that it was 'an incredible indignity' to the US Capitol, a worldwide symbol of freedom and democracy, to have a supermarket parking lot on the East Plaza. Of course, the 350 staff members and others who park there were not interested in this argument."[16] With foresight in 1962, a link into the Capitol for a possible future

underground garage had been built as part of the East Front extension. This turned out to be critical to the future location and design of the Capitol Visitor Center.

The Gingrich Compromise

Gingrich recognized that a visitor center was now politically palatable, but his aversion to expending funds led him to propose a compromise. Congress would appropriate $100 million for a new visitor center, but another $100 million in matching funds had to be privately raised.

Walsh was concerned that public funds might also be required to cover any shortfall left by private fundraising efforts, and this could be a political problem. But Gingrich expected support from his members, and Walsh complied. When I spoke with Walsh years after I completed my term, he told me he had only supported the visitor center and Gingrich's plan because the Speaker let him know that otherwise he could lose the chairmanship of his subcommittee.

The bill calling for $100 million in matching funds was a true compromise and was approved by a nearly unanimous Congress within four months of the July 1998 murders. The *New York Times* reported that Gingrich "called the Capitol the 'keystone of freedom. . . . No terrorist, no deranged person, no act of violence . . . will block us from preserving our freedom and from keeping this building open to people from all over the world.'"[17] These sentiments still need to be voiced in the congressional security debates that are ongoing in the wake of the 2021 Capitol insurrection.

With a dozen entry doors on all sides of the Capitol, the only thing preventing any armed terrorist from entering the Capitol in 1998 was the thin blue line of Capitol Police at each door, often just a single officer, occasionally assisted by an unarmed police aide with little training. Multiple studies by independent federal security agencies and consultants recommended a minimum of three officers at each post for effective backup. These same agencies also called for the politically unpalatable option of surrounding the Capitol building with fences, gates, and other systems similar to the hard perimeter installed around the White House.

Fortunately, Congress provided additional appropriations to enlarge and professionalize the Capitol Police force and design a perimeter vehicular security ring. Understandably, people reminisced about the days when they rode bikes up the monumental Capitol steps, drove their cars across the East Front Plaza, or enjoyed the sunset from the western terraces designed by Olmsted. In those days of innocence there were few security concerns. Access to entrances on all sides of the People's House had been virtually complete. The world of their Capitol memories had evolved into a more complicated place with notably greater risk levels. Our challenge was to balance conflicting needs for enhanced security with the imperative of permitting free and open

access to the Capitol. Visitors should still be able to view our democracy in action, witnessing free and open real-time debates in the House and Senate chambers.

In 1997 I prepared a perimeter security plan to replace the ring of deteriorating concrete flowerpots and concrete Jersey highway barriers with a perimeter comprised of specially fabricated steel bollards (similar to those at the White House), reinforced historic Olmsted stone walls, and retractable delta barriers to control vehicular entry. The Senate Rules and Administration Committee chaired by Senator Warner decided, according to a report in *Roll Call*, "to move forward unilaterally on parts of the perimeter security plan that the Architect of the Capitol unveiled [which] . . . requires joint House and Senate action . . . but House Oversight Chair Bill Thomas (R-CA) told Senator Warner he wanted more time to consider the plan . . . and how it would fit with the longstanding dream of a Capitol Visitor Center."[18]

Warner's frustration with the House's inaction convinced him to direct our agency to begin work he could unilaterally control on the Senate side of Capitol Hill. This included replacing Jersey traffic barriers with granite traffic circles that would also serve as attractive permanent planters on Delaware Avenue, C and D Streets Northeast. To keep potentially dangerous vehicles from getting too close to Senate buildings, access to Delaware and First Streets would now be restricted to senators and their staffs.

Meanwhile, the Capitol Visitor Center, a project that would also greatly enhance security, was beginning to move forward. *Roll Call* reported on September 28, 1998: "House and Senate Republican leaders have reached an agreement to move forward with plans for a Capitol Visitor Center and are preparing to include a $100 million fund for the project in an emergency spending bill that will come before Congress in the next few weeks."[19]

Although Gingrich assigned primary responsibility for perimeter security and visitor center construction to Representative Bill Thomas and his House Oversight Committee, this assignment did not become a functional reality because House in-fighting continued with House Transportation and Infrastructure Committee chair Representative Bud Shuster (R-PA). With no single force in charge, the center's schedule was placed in jeopardy. The $100 million emergency bill was passed to avoid having to count these funds against Congress's budget cap, with Gingrich directing that these funds be supple-mented by private sources for planning, engineer-ing, design, and construction of a Capitol Visitor Center.[20]

With the passage of this bill, it would be reason-able to assume we could proceed with in-depth proj-ect design, but political dickering continued. "I'm not going to be rushed into a decision" on a secu-rity plan, Thomas told *Roll Call*, "because someone writes an editorial or wants to turn a shovel full of dirt to create the impression of better security."[21]

He delayed the perimeter security project for a year and a half.

The passage of the $100 million bill, however, meant that my funding request for dome restoration was now denied. Congressional leadership was con-cerned that working on two major Capitol building projects at the same time would cause serious disrup-tion to daily congressional operations. They directed me to wait until the visitor center was fully con-structed before moving forward with dome repairs.

I spent many uneasy nights visualizing chunks of cast iron cascading down the dome's surface and causing a significant accident. It was no exaggeration to say that rust was the only thing holding the railing together at the top of the dome, and rust could yield to the force of gravity at any time. I also knew that if this happened, those in Congress who had denied my funding request would quickly point to me and blame me for poor stewardship and dereliction of duty. This was Hantman's dilemma.

An even greater risk than gravity was members' taking advantage of their special perk of scheduling personal dome tours for their constituents and do-nors, and I knew that pressure placed on the tholos-level railing by anyone leaning on it while enjoying the 360-degree panoramic view of the city could dislodge pieces and send them cascading down. To guard against this, we constructed a secure wooden railing inside the circle of the cracked cast iron railing to prevent anyone from leaning on the fragile metal. Despite the enormous life-safety risk, a dozen years passed as the House and Senate pushed off funding and the dome continued to deteriorate.

Moving Forward: The Botanic Garden

Around this same time, we were proceeding with a design for the Botanic Garden Conservatory. An accessible mezzanine walkway that would be twenty-four feet above the floor was added to the plans, providing an elevated view of the new tree canopy and jungle tableau of an abandoned plan-tation being reclaimed by nature. We put this res-toration project out for bids, awarded it to Centex Corporation, and held a formal ground-breaking ceremony on October 1, 1998, with key members of Congress voicing support.

James T. Walsh acknowledged, "the important educational role of the Conservatory, the promi-nence of the building, and the high level of public interest in the project." Senator Robert F. Bennett added the perspective of history when he mentioned that our founding fathers, in particular Washington, Jefferson, Madison, and Franklin, "were curious about the world, always looking to find the latest in-formation, inventions and discoveries."[22]

Our associate landscape architects, Rodney Robinson of Wilmington, Delaware, focused on cre-ating separate individually climate-controlled gal-leries where we could present collections of plants and flowers that tell stories of real-world ecologies. We included galleries for desert environments with cacti and succulents, a tropical rainforest for jungle climates, an orchid gallery, the Garden Court for plants used for economic and commercial products such as bananas and cocoa, and a Garden Primeval that displayed nonflowering plants dating to the age of dinosaurs in the Mesozoic era. Included in the Me-dicinal Plant Gallery is the Madagascar periwinkle

Figure 5.5.
Conservatory ground-
breaking. (*Left to right*)
Hantman, Bennett,
Livingston and Walsh.
Courtesy of Architect of
the Capitol

used to treat childhood leukemia and diabetes and the cannabis plant, the source of marijuana.

Walsh and Bennett, along with Representative Bob Livingston (R-LA), chair of the full House Appropriations Committee, joined me in breaking ground by "turning the first shovel" for the multiyear construction project.

When we finally received emergency funding for the project in mid-1997, the Botanic Garden's staff, under the leadership of Conservatory Manager Robert Pennington, began emptying it for the impending construction process. They were careful in determining which of the more than three thousand plant specimens to keep, prioritizing any that were rare, endangered, or of historical significance.[23]

Plants not kept were offered to twenty-two nonprofit or educational institutions including Smithsonian Horticultural Services, the National Zoological Park, the Capital Children's Museum, and the American Horticultural Council. Plant transfers were sometimes part of a reciprocal arrangement that called for those institutions to give plants from their collections back to the Botanic Garden upon completion of the project. Our historic specimens included several whose pedigrees could be traced back to the government-financed Wilkes Expedition. We could then begin the construction process.

From Speaker to Speaker to Speaker

In January 1997 Newt Gingrich was censured by the House and fined three hundred thousand dollars for ethics violations related to his practice of laundering money through charitable groups for pet political projects, such as televised classes. Challenges to Gingrich's leadership within his own party also grew from his passing most of his *Contract with America* legislation by assembling separate task forces to work directly from his office, thereby going around the entrenched House committee structure. In doing so he angered other powerful Republican leaders. I served under Speaker Gingrich until his party lost five seats in the 1998 midterm elections. He had mistakenly predicted that if his party continued pressuring Bill Clinton about the Monica Lewinsky affair that the president would be weakened, and the Republicans would win a minimum of six seats to as many as thirty.

Gingrich resigned under much criticism and pressure. "Mr. Gingrich stepped down tonight," wrote the *New York Times* on November 7, 1998, "facing a mutiny from fellow Republicans who insisted that his flaws could cost them the very majority he had created." His challenger for the Speakership, Representative Bob Livingston, told the *Times*, "Revolutionizing takes some talents, many talents. . . . My friend Newt Gingrich, brought those talents to bear, put the Republicans in the majority. Day-to-day governing takes others."[24]

Gingrich's tenure ended months after I helped convince him to abandon his attempt to carve Capitol building operations in half while also dropping his opposition to a new visitor center in the aftermath of the murders of Officers Chestnut and Gibson.

Adultery Leads to a Second-Choice Speaker

Livingston had served in the House since 1977 and was reelected eleven times. The Republicans' slim 1998 majority selected Livingston as Speaker-elect for the coming 106th Congress. Much changed over the next six weeks as the House prepared to impeach Clinton for perjury under oath in the civil suit regarding his affair with Paula Jones.

In December the *New York Times* reported: "Representative Robert L. Livingston, who confessed on Thursday night that he had had adulterous affairs, stunned the House this morning by saying in the impeachment debate that he would not serve as Speaker and would quit Congress in six months. . . . 'I must set an example that I hope President Clinton will follow,' Livingston announced to a shocked and silent chamber in an act that left the Republican Party in total chaos just hours before the vote to impeach President Clinton."[25]

On the other side of the Capitol, Senate Majority Leader Trent Lott did not have the sixty-seven votes needed in the Senate to find the president guilty, and Clinton, of course, did not resign.

Livingston founded the Livingston Group, a lobbying firm that represented Morocco in its free trade agreement with the United States and Libya in its settlement claims by families of those killed on Pan Am Flight 103, which was blown up by a terrorist bomb. He also unsuccessfully lobbied me as steward of congressional properties, representing a developer wanting to build an office building beside the Capitol Police Annex on South Capitol Street.

Another New Speaker: J. Dennis Hastert

Dennis Hastert (R-IL), one of Tom DeLay's whips, who had been reelected three times, was selected as a noncontroversial and respected alternative to replace Livingston. Hastert would remain Speaker until the Democrats regained the House majority in the 2006 midterm elections, and Nancy Pelosi (D-CA) succeeded him. He retired in 2007 and joined the Washington lobbying firm of Dickstein Shapiro. In 2016 he was sentenced to a fifteen-month term for bank fraud related to his sexually abusing boys when he had been a high school wrestling coach. *USA Today* reported that "Federal Judge Thomas Durkin called Hastert, 74, a 'serial child molester. . . . Nothing is more disturbing than having serial child molester and Speaker of the House in the same sentence.'"[26]

Flexing Political Muscle: Battle of the Logos

In March 1999 Representative Bill Thomas finally approved the House's half of the Perimeter Security design. The Capitol's perimeter had been compromised due to the House leadership's inability to control the whims of a key committee chair. An absurd reason was cited for the delay, a delay that placed the Capitol at risk of terrorist attacks similar to the Oklahoma City truck bomb mass murder for an additional year and a half. Thomas's spokesperson Jason Poblete told *Roll Call* that "at one point the Senate panels wanted to use the Senate logo on the bollards which would line their side of the Capitol. The House wanted a neutral logo on all of them . . . Then we finally agreed that we would have an eagle on all of them.'"[27]

Figure 5.6. Legislative branch bollard with eagle logo. Courtesy of Alan M. Hantman

Two Senate committees, one House committee, and the Speaker's office had approved the plan, but one committee chair delayed the project because of a logo design. We eventually obtained Thomas's approval, but only after significant pressure from the Speaker's office.

Our government's legislative process requires the review and approval by multiple committees of the House and Senate for any major Capitol Hill project, and this can uncover conflicting agendas. With no single oversight group to make informed and timely decisions, even on projects that involved significant life-safety risks, congressional gridlock can occur.

A Maze of Masters

Almost eight months after the murders of J.J. Chestnut and John Gibson, *Roll Call* published a story with the headline "Visitor Center Caught in a Maze of Masters." This "maze of masters" theme underscored the challenge of achieving consensus among multiple committees in both houses of Congress. Representative John Mica (R-FL), expressing his frustration, noted that nothing had happened in the ten years since George White began planning in earnest for a visitor center.

"The problem that you have right now is sort of the multi-jurisdiction of getting a project like this through," Mica told *Roll Call*. "You have the Appropriations [legislative branch] subcommittee, House Administration. You have the Transportation and Infrastructure Committee that has the building subcommittee. We have the Senate side and its counterparts and we have the Capitol Preservation Commission. There's a Capitol Commission overall, and on top of that you have the leadership to check off."[28]

Referring to a recent House hearing, the article noted that because of the multiple levels of oversight, "Hantman predicted he could break ground on the Visitor Center in 2003 and complete it in 2009."[29] At that hearing, I testified: "Each milestone of the project needs to be reviewed and approved, as we understand it, by some six different committees. A big part of any schedule that we have will be based on how long it takes to get approval at each step of the project. . . . What happens if committee 'A' and committee 'B' agree with the entire plan and approve it, but a third committee disagrees with component 'X,' and the fourth disagrees with component 'Y.' How do we get consensus among six committees to be able to move forward at all?"[30]

Chair Charles Taylor (R-NC) responded: "It has been my observation that government will mess up a one-car funeral and having to operate inside government on this important project is a necessary task, I suppose." He went on to say that "perhaps we can have joint meetings with the Senate and maybe put together leadership from both sides of the aisle to meet together rather than having you meet every time with six different committees." Finally, he proposed that they would "do what we can to speed that up as fast as is prudent."[31]

Mica and House Administration Chair Bill Thomas tried to resolve these concerns by introducing a resolution calling for three members of the House and three members of the Senate to form an oversight committee to make timely decisions, with Mica as the House Administration Committee representative overseeing the project.

John Mica was a steadfast supporter who never hesitated to speak out about the project's importance. When newspaper headlines trumpeted project bumps in the road, he was often the only one speaking in support, pointing to the many pitfalls beyond our control. Unfortunately, Mica's House Resolution 20 was never seriously considered, and the oversight debate led to the reactivation of the Capitol Preservation Commission (CPC) to serve as the single point of oversight. A bicameral body that had not met in the last half dozen years, the commis-sion consisted of nine members of the Senate, nine members of the House, and the Architect of the Capitol as ex officio member. Originally established in 1988, its purpose was to raise money for construction and improvements to the Capitol with its membership including majority and minority leaders of both houses and chairs of major committees.

Mica was now one of eighteen oversight members rather than one of six. The commission had no set meeting schedule nor staff of its own, with the legislation stating that the staffs of the secretary of the Senate and the clerk of the House were to serve as commission staff. Secretary of the Senate Gary Cisco optimistically told *Roll Call*, "the Commission will probably meet initially to consider the architect's recommendation and get together periodically from then on. . . . [It's] not anything that will require them to meet frequently." His hope was "that the

Commission will give Hantman the go-ahead before the October recess, and the architect's team can begin working while Congress is out of session."[32] This did not happen.

On the first anniversary of the police shootings a memorial service was held in Statuary Hall. A year had passed, but my agency had not yet been cleared to begin work on detailed plans. Senate Secretary Cisco recognized the difficult funding realities. "If past is prologue, the visitor center project is unlikely to move too quickly," he told *Roll Call.* "Even with oversight centralized under the Capitol Preservation Commission, appropriators are ever-present and will always have a look at the specific requests. . . . Appropriators said they've supported the project by spending $100 million on the cause in 1998—but that's not quite the whole story. The problem remains that the money must be released by the appropriators for Hantman to spend it. And each time Hantman wants to use some of the money, he needs to appeal to the appropriators to get it."[33]

The Choke Point: House Appropriations

Cisco was right. With my first funding request— $2.8 million to study the 1995 visitor center plan— the appropriators required an obligation plan so detailed it took months to complete before funds were finally released. It was clear the appropriators had more power than the Capitol Preservation Commission, compounding the difficulty of working with contractors and hampering our ability to make timely decisions. House appropriators would not allocate one lump sum, as is common in major construction projects, and insisted on carving the project budget into twenty-three separate, sacrosanct line items. This was zealously enforced by Representative David Obey (D-WI), a committed foe of the project, who referred to the Capitol Visitor Center as a giant "boondoggle."

We were required to prepare in-depth obligation plans throughout the life of the project and, before proceeding, wait for approvals from each body's appropriators. If funds remained unspent in one line item while another required additional funding, we were not permitted to move money within the project to resolve the problem without documented appropriator approval. Their insistence on line-item control and detailed obligation plans consumed tremendous management time and resources and seriously affected the project's progress and ability to quickly deal with construction problems as they arose.

Senate appropriators typically approved our requests immediately, while House approval took weeks or months longer, adversely impacting our ability to monitor and direct contractors, keep them on schedule, and pay them in a timely manner. It was a hardship that became part of an overall bureaucratic pattern seriously hamstringing the project and costing dearly in budget increases and missed project deadlines. Members of the CPC also delegated their oversight functions to staff, none of whom had architecture, engineering or construction experience. Despite Cisco's projection that the Capitol Preservation Commission "will probably meet initially to consider the architect's recommendation and get together periodically from then on," the CPC staff called my project management team to weekly oversight meetings asking them to report on project status and cross-examining and second-guessing them on design decisions.[34]

Rather than help resolve project issues, staffers seemed to see their primary function as protecting their individual senators or representatives and assuring that their member's fingerprints would not appear on any costly or controversial issue. Members of Congress never attended the meetings and voted by separate ballots on only a few occasions when major scope of work issues required approval. The commission staff never formally made any decisions throughout the life of the project. No minutes ever came out of these meetings; no attendance was taken; and no responsibility was accepted by the staff or their members, leaving the project team responsible for decisions our team did not make.

The Capitol Visitor Center design was inching slowly forward, but without established lines of congressional reporting or oversight.

Notes

1. Martin Weil, "Gunman Shoots His Way into Capitol, Two Officers Killed, Suspect Captured," *Washington Post*, July 25, 1998.
2. Bill Miller, "Capitol Shooter's Mind-Set Detailed," *Washington Post*, April 23, 1999.
3. Weil, "Gunman Shoots His Way into Capitol."
4. Michael Grunwald and Juliet Eilperin, "Protection vs. 'the People's House,'" *Washington Post*, July 25, 1998.
5. S.Con.Res. 113, To rename the Document Door of the Capitol as the Chestnut-Gibson Memorial Door, 105th Congress, 2nd Session, July 28, 1998.
6. Heard on a CNN telecast of the rotunda ceremony in honor of Officer Brian Sicknick, February 2, 2021.
7. "McConnell Speech after Trump's Impeachment Trial Acquittal," *US News and World Report*, February 14, 2021.
8. Jonathan Weisman and Annie Karni, "Party Censures Earn a Rebuke by McConnell, Leader Calls January 6th a 'Violent Insurrection,'" *New York Times*, February 9, 2022.
9. Eugene Scott, "Congress Awards Gold Medals to Police Who Defended Capitol on Jan. 6," *Washington Post*, December 6, 2022.
10. Hantman, notes from CNN coverage of Congressional Gold Medal ceremonies honoring police who defended the Capitol during insurrection of January 6, 2021.
11. Jonathan Weisman and Reid J. Epstein, "G.O.P. Declares Jan. 6 Attack 'Legitimate Political Discourse,'" *New York Times*, February 4, 2022.
12. Alan Feuer and Zach Montague, "Four Proud Boys Convicted of Seditious Conspiracy in Pivotal Jan. 6 Case," *New York Times*, May 5, 2023.
13. Juliet Eilperin, "Attack Stirs Interest in Visitor Center," *Washington Post*, July 26, 1998, A19.
14. Public Law 94-59, July 1975.
15. National Advisory Group, 1981 Master Plan, 1981.
16. White, *Under the Capitol Dome*.
17. Alison Mitchell, "Capitol Hill Slayings: Tightening Security, Congress's Goal: Guard House without Locking Out Public," *New York Times*, July 26, 1998.
18. Ed Henry and Jennifer Bradley, "Not Waiting for House, Senate Moves on Security Plan," *Roll Call*, November 3, 1997.
19. Joan Bresnahan and Ethan Wallison, "Visitor Center Moving Forward, Proposal Would Create $100 Million Fund for Project," *Roll Call*, September 28, 1998.
20. Omnibus Consolidated and Emergency Supplemental Appropriations Act, Public Law 105-277, October 21, 1998.
21. Ethan Wallison, "Warner Moves on Security, Thomas Won't Be Rushed," *Roll Call*, October 5, 1998.
22. Christine Flanagan, "Conservatory Renovation Groundbreaking," AOC Shoptalk Newsletter, November 1998.
23. Carla Pastore, "What Happened to all Those Plants?" AOC Shoptalk Newsletter, January 1998.
24. Alison Mitchell, "The Speaker Steps Down: The Career, The Fall of Gingrich, an Irony in an Odd Year," *New York Times*, November 7, 1998.
25. Katherie Q. Seelye, "Livingston Quits over Adultery Admission," *New York Times*, December 20, 1998.
26. Aamer Madhani and John Bacon, "Judge Sentences 'Serial Child Molester' Hastert to 15 Months," *USA Today*, April 27, 2016.
27. Stacey Zolt, "House Panel Approves Long-Awaited Perimeter Security Plan for the Capitol," *Roll Call*, March 1, 1999.
28. Stacey Zolt, "Visitor Center Caught in a Maze of Masters," *Roll Call*, March 11, 1999, 22.
29. Zolt, "Visitor Center."
30. Testimony of Alan M. Hantman, House Appropriations Legislative Branch Subcommittee Hearing, February 1, 1999.
31. Testimony of Alan M. Hantman.
32. "Planning for Capitol Visitors Center Inching Forward," *Roll Call*, July 22, 1999.
33. "Funding Foibles," *Roll Call*, July 22, 1999.
34. "Planning for Capitol Visitor Center Inching Forward."

SIX

Expanding the Capitol

Ever since George Washington's presidency, the US Capitol building has been built and rebuilt, extended and domed, re-domed and extended again. The need for further change, a Capitol Visitor Center, was clearly defined in George White's call for a master plan in the mid-1970s. A decade later, a bicameral, bipartisan leadership group, the Capitol Preservation Commission, authorized use of available security funds to develop a design.

To move forward with this long-delayed project, I requested funding to perform a congressionally required confirmation study of the recommended site and proposed design. When the funds were finally released five months later, I retained CRTKL, the design firm that had worked on the 1995 plan, to work with us based on their intimate knowledge of the program, alternative sites, and the specific physical building and foundation conditions on the East Front of the Capitol. We performed an in-depth analysis and update of the plans, recommendations and conclusions as a way of moving this forward. When I submitted the study to the Capitol Preservation Commission, my cover note stated: "I respectfully request approval by the Capitol Preservation Commission of this updated concept design as well as authority to request release by the Appropriations Committees of the House of Representatives and the Senate of funds required to complete the design development and the construction document phase of the project."[1]

Leonardo da Vinci offered this guidance to artists and architects as they conceived new initiatives: "Think well to the end, consider the end first."[2] With

that in mind, we asked ourselves what we wanted to accomplish with the visitor center. How did we want to relate to the Capitol building while respecting its integrity and the needs of the Congress and also addressing important security imperatives? Our answers were part of the 1999 revalidation report I submitted:

> The US Capitol Visitor Center has been conceived of as an extension to the Capitol, one that welcomes visitors to the seat of American government. It must do no less than embody the same principles that guided the foundation of this country: freedom, universal access, and a deep respect for representative democracy. . . . The open character and symbolic nature of the Capitol are perhaps its greatest attributes. Yet these very assets render the building and its occupants particularly susceptible to violence and terrorism. The tragic 1998 fatal shooting of two US Capitol Police officers underscores the degree to which security of the building and its occupants are at risk.
>
> The Visitor Center is a necessary means to reduce this risk. Such a facility will allow the screening of the vast majority of visitors to take place at a point remote from the Capitol itself. It will make feasible, but will not dictate, new policies for managing the flow of visitors for their own safety and security. . . .
>
> This, moreover, is not simply another improvement to the Capitol. The project is one of historic dimension. It constitutes the last

possibility to extend the Capitol within the historic framework of the grounds and the structure so recognizable to people throughout the world. As such, the Visitor Center must be designed in a manner worthy of that universal symbol of representative democracy. No building project at the Capitol of such significance has occurred for almost 150 years. Nevertheless, the project has been so designed that upon its completion the Capitol will be virtually unchanged from its appearance today.[3]

We confirmed the original project goals of security, visitor education and comfort, and the need for functional improvements at the Capitol and examined six potential sites with respect to security, accessibility, aesthetics and historic preservation. Our concerns echoed the historic 1850 design competition held to determine how best to expand William Thornton's original 1793 Capitol building design.

Design Competition—1850s Capitol Expansion

By 1850, with new states added to the Union, the Capitol building needed larger House and Senate chambers and additional offices and meeting rooms. William Allen described the process the Senate Committee on Public Buildings initiated in advertising a design competition to enlarge the Capitol by saying the possibilities were to add wings to the north and south of the current building or to build a new connected wing to the east. More than a dozen architects responded, with members of the House preferring an eastward expansion design prepared by Thomas U. Walter of Philadelphia, which would avoid the need to enlarge Capitol grounds beyond its existing perimeter.[4]

Allen continued, "The Senate Committee on Public Buildings asked Mills (Robert Mills of Washington) to study the entries and incorporate their best features into a new composite design. . . . The design was presented to the full Senate by Jefferson

Davis on February 8, 1851."[5] Northern and southern additions were shown attached directly to the Capitol, and the proposed additions were moved toward the east to avoid dealing with foundation problems on Capitol Hill's western slope. The Congress left the decision to President Millard Fillmore who, in an astute political compromise, chose a modified version of the Senate's north and south wing expansion scheme, while selecting Thomas U. Walter, the architect preferred by the House, to develop the detailed designs. Walter became the 4th Architect of the Capitol and went on to design not only the Capitol's northern and southern wings but also the iconic Capitol Dome we see today.

Early in our visitor center designs, we too analyzed multiple sites, a total of six: at the base of the Capitol's West Front, on a park northwest of the Capitol, north of the Dirksen Senate Office Building, south of the Cannon House Office Building, on park land north of the Capitol across Constitution Avenue, and on the East Front of the Capitol. The underground site on the East Front was the best option because it provided a direct, protected connection to the Capitol. All other sites would depend on the use of unsecured buses or trams to transport millions of visitors to the Capitol building proper, undermining the security measures that were a key goal of the center.

Design Criteria

Without question our revalidation report confirmed the appropriateness and viability of the preferred East Front site and provided major programmatic and design criteria:

Security

We confirmed the need for enhanced security, made possible with new screening technologies, risk assessment, and risk mitigation. This included screening visitors beyond a three-hundred-foot stand-off distance from the Capitol, creating separate visitor

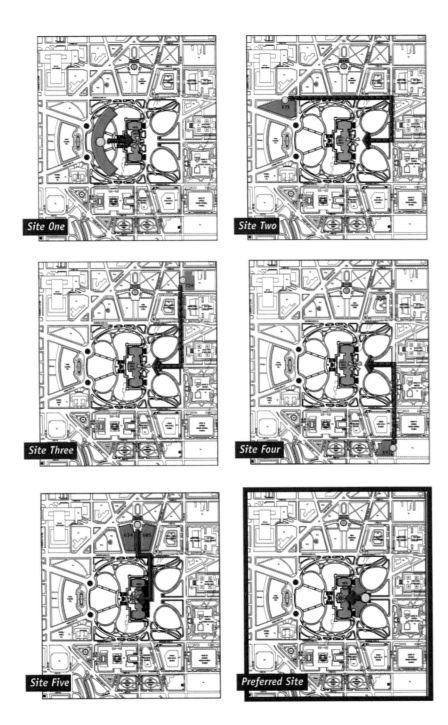

Figure 6.1. Six visitor center site options. Courtesy of CRTKL

flows for those returning to the CVC after Capitol tours, and integrating its design with the new perimeter security program to eliminate vehicular threat—all this while fostering an atmosphere of free and open access.

Visitor Education and Comfort

We confirmed the need to build a strong educational component by presenting a body of information and accessible resources on the workings and history of the Congress, the legislative process, and the mechanics of our representative democracy. Visitors were presented with the opportunity to access multimedia interactive stations, three-dimensional models illustrating the evolution of the Capitol building, and exhibits that introduce visitors to the Capitol as "Democracy's House," the place where the legislative branch of government votes on proposed legislation. We also provided visitors with amenities, comfort, and convenience appropriate to one of the world's most popular tourist destinations.

Capacity

We studied and then confirmed the optimal size of the visitor center to assure its capacity and amenities would be adequate to accommodate a growing tourist population and provide flexibility for future expansion. Based on this study, we determined the Capitol was already operating at or beyond its safe code-compliant occupancy during peak periods. The new visitor center could facilitate new ways of managing tour flow and access without compromising life-safety.

During peak visitation periods visitors typically waited outside for up to three hours, often under difficult weather conditions. The center is designed to screen 3,800 people per hour to eliminate those long waits. With all necessary visitor support facilities, up to 4,000 can be comfortably accommodated indoors, and 1,500 can be guided each hour from the visitor center into the Capitol on tours, with an additional 700 per hour on House and Senate gallery tours.

Design and Functional Improvements

The overriding principle guiding our design was the imperative of creating a facility that would stand beside one of the most historic and recognizable structures in the world. It was to complement the Capitol, never upstage it, with its materials reflecting permanence and durability. It was to embrace a simplicity, clarity, and vision with the flexibility

to accommodate future generations of visitors. In addition, the visitor center had to respond to the functional challenges of the Capitol as a working office building by providing adequate stairs, elevators, and circulation corridors; modern, efficient operations facilities for truck loading and deliveries; and constituent assembly rooms.[6]

We submitted our study, along with a model of George White's 1995 design, to a meeting of seven Capitol Preservation Commission members. Although the commission consisted of eighteen Senate and House members, this gathering was the largest leadership group assembled for any Capitol Visitor Center meeting during the project. When votes were required, multiple presentations were made to individuals or at most three or four members at a time. This had a significant impact on our schedule but was unavoidable since the commission consisted of the leadership of both parties in each chamber of Congress.

During this presentation, the members listened intently, asked detailed questions, and responded enthusiastically. I conducted additional presentations as other commission members became available one or two at a time. The Capitol Visitor Center would never have been funded if its primary function was perceived as serving the Congress. No senator or representative would place herself or himself at political risk by supporting the use of appropriated funds on a project that might be labeled a congressional perk. As George White said in his final design report: "The United States Capitol Building is a compendium of architectural contributions made by each generation over the past two centuries. Most of the additions to this most visible structure . . . have been made to accommodate members and staff. The proposed US CVC provides facilities to aid those who visit here rather than serve here."[7]

The only significant parts of the project directly related to member needs were the excavation and foundation work for future House and Senate expansion space, which at this point were to be built as empty structural shells with functional uses to be determined and built out at some later time.

Figure 6.2. Model presentation to Capitol Preservation Commission members (*left to right*): James Oberstar (D-MN), Dick Armey (R-TX), Trent Lott (R-MS), John Mica (R-FL), Tom Daschle (D-SD), Strom Thurmond (R-SC), Dennis Hastert (R-IL). Courtesy of Architect of the Capitol

Roll Call reported in October 1999 that "one of the project's largest obstacles was overcome late last month when President Clinton signed the legislative branch appropriations bill into law, which activated the Capitol Preservation Commission's (CPC) jurisdiction over the Visitor Center. . . . Now that the Architect's authorization is streamlined, Hastert believes things are on track."[8] It would have been remarkable if the review process had indeed been streamlined as Hastert said. But despite the CPC's intent, appropriator requirements for detailed line-item reporting took weeks and often months to process and approve.

Originally Projected Completion Date: 2009

At my February 1, 1999, House Appropriations hearing, I testified that the project completion date could be delayed to 2009 due to the multiple levels of congressional oversight and required approvals. I projected this completion date well before all the enormous changes in scope were brought about by 9/11, an anthrax attack, and other critical events in the following months and years, plus the consistent level of appropriations committee micromanagement. Unfortunately, this major project was politically locked into an artificially created schedule. My projected schedule was to be proven correct, with the Capitol Visitor Center ultimately dedicated in December 2008.

The Achilles Heel: An Immovable Presidential Schedule

Trent Lott, the Senate Republican leader, valued the two-century history of Capitol building expansions. He was proud to follow in the footsteps of Jefferson Davis, also from the state of Mississippi, who had been secretary of war from 1853 to 1857 and was serving his second term as senator when he left Washington to become president of the Confederate States.

As secretary of war, Davis fully supported the expansion of the Capitol building in the years before the Civil War and worked with the 4th Architect of the Capitol, Thomas Ustick Walter, and supervising engineer Corps of Engineers Captain Montgomery C. Meigs. Meigs had been championed by Secretary Davis to take charge of Capitol expansion projects including the new Senate northern wing, the House southern wing, and the monumental cast iron Capitol Dome Walter designed. Lott told me about his admiration for Davis and his commitment to expanding the building. I would find, much to my chagrin, that he intended to emulate his hero by bringing the Corps of Engineers to Washington to assume control of the Capitol Visitor Center project. More about that later.

Tom Daschle, the Senate majority leader, was also a strong advocate of the Capitol's preservation and restoration. He even offered his suite of offices as a testing laboratory for the restoration of cast iron window pockets and enframements that Walter had designed in the 1850s. Since the window pockets had been painted over many times, their raised floral patterns were unrecognizable blurs, and the windows themselves were inoperable. Daschle also recognized the Capitol had not been designed to accommodate millions of annual visitors and that something had to be done.

Daschle and Lott both saw the security imperative of a new Capitol Visitor Center and the responsibility to welcome visitors with respect, dignity, and educational opportunities. They favored completing the design and construction between the 2001 and 2005 presidential inaugurations, but President George W. Bush delayed the process for months by not signing off on this funding. In early 2001, almost eighteen months after we completed our report, Lott and Daschle went to the White House to press for an immediate release of funding with a promise that the

Capitol Visitor Center would be completed in time for the next inaugural, possibly Bush's second.

Jeri Thomson, the secretary of the Senate, soon informed me that Bush would release the funds but that I was expected to complete the project within the presidential schedule the senators had committed to. I expressed my concern that this was a tremendously difficult schedule and that with all the changes and delays that had already occurred, everything would have to go perfectly to meet that deadline. She essentially said this was my problem, and she would deny ever having imposed this political, and likely unachievable, scheduling demand. From this point on, this schedule fundamentally became the visitor center's Achilles heel.

But the senators' commitment to this presidential schedule had the impact they desired: President Bush signed-off on the appropriation, and shortly afterward, in February 2001, the House and Senate sergeants at arms and I welcomed the president to the Capitol for his address to a joint session of Congress. President Bush graciously apologized for his delayed release of the $100 million in funding. This was now a double-edged sword. While the funding was essential to move the project forward, the aggressive schedule that went along with it was already seriously behind.

Part of the delay was caused months earlier when senior staff noticed that areas allocated for the future House and Senate expansions were not exactly equal. The difference was approximately 1 percent of the total and was necessary to save the root systems of major trees close to the excavation. This disparity was unacceptable to senior Senate staff, and we were directed to reapportion and equalize the expansion spaces. This petty political requirement forced us to shift the two-story mechanical room toward the House side and redesign all piping and air handling ductwork located between the two expansion spaces.

We had to avoid any more design changes or scope increases. Everything had to go smoothly, but everything did not. Our Achilles heel haunted the

Figure 6.3. Footprint of Capitol Visitor Center. Courtesy of Architect of the Capitol and CRTKL

project, creating stress for the entire project team. It would later minimize the number of general contractors willing to risk committing to this extremely tight three-year schedule for such a high-profile and complex project.

With the appropriation sign-off by President Bush in hand, I requested release of project funds to move ahead with detailed design. Senate Appropriations approval was granted by the subcommittee chair, Senator Robert Bennett, and ranking member Senator Dianne Feinstein. Unfortunately, this was not a blanket approval, and in late 1999, I received this in response: "We are pleased to approve the following items: Item 1—Design Development, Item IV—additional studies, and Item V—Facility Administrative and Operating Plan." But the response also stated that "all approvals are conditioned on the design work being competitively bid."[9] This bidding was based on the so-called advertising statute, which involved a search for a new architectural design firm that could easily cause another year's delay.

Low Bidder versus
Best Value Design Architect

A decade earlier, when George White received an appropriation to design security enhancements for the Capitol Hill complex, he worked with a panel of professionals to select an architectural firm in a competitive process that evaluated experience, past performance, and other technical considerations. The panel chose CRTKL as associate architect, with a scope of work continuing through to completion of the 1995 visitor center design. I had worked with CRTKL during the first years of my term and was convinced this team could produce a fine design thoroughly compatible with the historic Capitol. There was little justification for investing a year in searching for a new firm and then initiating a new project learning curve to define design and security requirements.

I wrote to Bob Bennett and Dianne Feinstein that even though I recognized that statutory requirements for contract competition requires sealed bids and award to the low bidder, I reasoned that selecting the low bidder "would not be in the best interest of the government any more than a patient would be well advised to choose a surgeon for a major operation solely on the basis of price." I told them I intended to work with CRTKL because doing so would assure "the knowledge of various security measures currently in place and the upgraded security measures being contemplated, would be confined to one firm whose experience in security-sensitive work for the Government is exemplary."

I concluded my response: "Because . . . we have been operating . . . in conformity with the conditions set forth in your letter . . . I intend to enter into a contract with CRTKL for design development services in approximately thirty days unless I receive a prior direction from the Commission to the contrary."[10] Thirty days passed without a directive to stop work and initiate a new competitive selection process. We had dodged a bullet and could begin formal design in February 2000.

East Front Extension, 1959–60, and Proposed Garage

As our design proceeded, we studied the construction history of the thirty-two-foot East Front Capitol extension of 1959–60. William Allen writes that on July 4, 1959, President Dwight Eisenhower laid the cornerstone, spreading "cement on a foundation slab using the same trowel Washington wielded at the Capitol in 1793."[11] This ceremony followed years of heated debate in which many notable architects objected to the expansion plans that had been developed under the 8th Architect of the Capitol, J. George Stewart.

Allen explains, however, that Stewart was not the first to propose such an expansion. "The idea of building a new addition to the East Front had originated with Thomas U. Walter in 1863," he writes. It was "a means to correct the visual impression that the Dome was not adequately supported. Since then others had seen the project as a good

way to add more rooms to the Capitol, while covering the flaking sandstone wall with a new marble facade."[12]

To satisfy those who objected to the expansion, plans for an archaeological reproduction were drawn to exactly duplicate the elevation of the original deteriorating sandstone, but this time with a much harder and more weather-resistant stone, marble. The project was completed by the January 1961 inauguration of President John F. Kennedy. It not only created a new eastern front of special Georgia white marble but also included critical features that would, forty years later, help resolve the challenge of creating a smooth transition from the new underground visitor center into the Capitol building. The foundations for this expansion extended more than fifty feet beneath the East Plaza, with several rows of square concrete piers supporting the monumental stairs and majestic Corinthian columns of the portico above. Access to the Capitol from a future garage was to be between these tightly spaced piers, but since the garage was never built, this transition area presented us with a perfectly located connection to an underground visitor center.

George White's 1995 plan called for the spaces between those piers to be used for three sets of stairs, two escalators, and two elevators. Three sets of stairs were required because the narrow seven-foot spacing between the piers could not accommodate a single stairway wide enough for large numbers of visitors. Fortunately, the conference room at the symmetrical center of the Capitol, EF-100, was assigned to my agency to administer (since half of the room was on the Senate side of the Capitol and the other on the House side), and no one contested repurposing this area as the termination point for stairs and escalators. These existing physical characteristics made it possible to create a direct and respectful transition from the new underground Capitol Visitor Center into the Capitol building.

One of our great challenges in designing the visitor center was assuring compatibility with the building's historical neoclassical whole while also clearly relating it to our own time. A respectful design was

Figure 6.4. Excavation showing tightly spaced entry piers beneath central rotunda stairs. Courtesy of Architect of the Capitol

required, one that would build on the power and tradition of the Capitol building itself and relate to issues of compatibility of scale, materials, and color. But we would not be cloning the architectural vocabulary of the existing Capitol. Although senior Capitol Preservation Commission staff looked over our shoulders, wanting us to hew more closely to the historic Capitol's design, we instead focused on creating a unique addition, one that welcomes and invites visitors to experience the historic Capitol as their ultimate goal, not the addition itself.

Peer Review Panel and Architectural Design

Analyzing a design with a critical eye—turning it this way and that, throwing darts and reimagining solutions, playing with what-ifs—is important to the overall design process. This stage can be brutal, but it can also stimulate wonderfully creative solutions. Before a great deal of time and effort had been invested on an in-house analysis and refinement of the initial visitor center design, I believed it was critical to hold an objective peer review by convening a panel of distinguished architects and knowledgeable professionals from other government agencies to weigh in on the 1995 visitor center design.

In March 2000 I prepared to present our design challenges to the panel, together with CRTKL's chief executive officer, Harold Adams, and lead designer Rod Henderer, who was selected to replace his friend and associate, Goodluck Tembukiart, CRTKL's original visitor center designer, who had been tragically killed in a hit-and-run car crash.

Tembukiart was a dedicated designer with a great love of life. He had worked with George White over the course of nine years developing plans for perimeter security at the Capitol and the original 1995 Capitol Visitor Center plans. He was killed after working all weekend in preparation for a meeting with our team on Monday morning. He was deeply mourned by all who had the privilege of knowing him.

Janice Adams, also a principal with CRTKL, worked closely with Tembukiart and then with Henderer, providing project continuity. I referred to Adams's detailed journal notes to expand my narratives of the peer review discussions. She had a keen sense of history and was committed to creating a positive legacy for the work of our team, not only as we prepared for the peer review panel, but throughout the duration of the project.

How to Reimagine a Complex Building

On March 14, 2000, we presented the 1995 project design to the panel in our project conference room. Ten professionals from my agency were observers, along with additional design professionals from CRTKL and Ralph Appelbaum Associates, our exhibit designer. The discussion ranged freely across the design spectrum examining goals, intent, project parameters, and limitations.

The panel of experts listened attentively to the presentation while studying the white foam-core model of the 1995 design. Although it may be difficult for the reader to appreciate these experts' critiques in the absence of a three-dimensional model, the issues summarized below convey a sense of the wide range of freely expressed ideas and concerns.

Figure 6.5. Peer review presentation to (*left to right*) Ed Barnes, Harry Cobb, Hantman, Rod Henderer, Harold Adams, and Peter May (agency project manager). Courtesy of Architect of the Capitol

Sense of Procession and Visitor Flow: The panel questioned why the visitors followed a pathway from the center's entrance through long, circuitous Americans with Disabilities Act–compliant ramps to reach the orientation theaters on the floor below. Our follow-up studies solved the problem with a more direct solution by eliminating the ramps and providing large convenient elevators near the entrances and within the theaters, while placing theater entrances and stairway exits within visitors' direct pathways.

Symmetry: The panel questioned why visitor pathways are split in two and why there were two security screening areas, orientation theaters, information desks, and gift shops. We explained that the symmetrical allocation of space is critical to the design because of the absolute requirement that equal amounts of space be assigned to the Senate and House on their respective sides of the Capitol's east–west axis. What is done for one chamber must also be done for the other in equal measure.

Location of the Auditorium: The panel assumed that the auditorium was the visitor center's most important space, since it was the largest room in the 1995 plan. They thought it could be moved directly in front of the Capitol while moving visitor center spaces farther away. The auditorium, rather than serving visitors to the Capitol building, was originally included in George White's plans at the request of Librarian of Congress James Billington so he could present the library's extensive film collection to a larger audience. In the redesign process that followed, the Great Hall (later renamed Emancipation Hall) became the largest room and center of circulation and was located at the base of the rotunda steps to serve visitors most conveniently. The auditorium (which was to become the Congressional Auditorium) remained the element of the project farthest from the Capitol.

Orientation Theaters—Pulsing Visitor Flow into the Capitol: The panel questioned why two 250-seat orientation theaters were proposed rather than one large one or a series of smaller spaces, which could have flat rather than sloped floors. We explained that our studies had determined safe Capitol occupancy levels and then sized the two 250-seat orientation theaters to alternately pulse a controlled flow of guided tours into the Capitol every twenty minutes. This configuration was maintained in the final design and has worked well.

Addressing Underground Spaces: The panel debated whether the sense of the building being underground could be mitigated by creating major spaces, if the plaza above it needed to be made more interesting (possibly with low-profile skylights covered with water), and how to clearly identify the entrance within the Olmsted landscape. Even as these expert panelists disagreed on some of these issues, the creative flow of impressions, ideas, and critiques enriched the array of possibilities, leading us to question and reconsider basic 1995 concepts in meaningful ways.

Transformative Design Changes

The peer review inspired our new design team to return to the drawing boards. They shaped a visitor flow that seamlessly brought visitors down from grade level at East Capitol Street into an intuitive and expansive sequence of spaces at the heart of the visitor center. Our peer review, with its creative questioning and interactions, paved the way to the following major design changes, resulting in nothing less than a sun-filled, coherent, and welcoming sense of place:

Entrance: To create an easily identifiable open and inviting entrance to this underground complex, Alan Ward of Sasaki Associates, our landscape designers, proposed widening the ramps and adjacent landscape grading while framing them with curved and battered stone walls to echo the oval shape of Olmsted's landscaped "eggs."

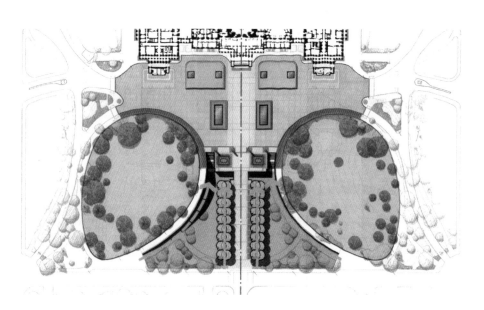

Figure 6.6. Entry pathways integrated into Olmsted Landscape (with arrows). Courtesy of Alan Ward, Sasaki Associates

Figure 6.7. Rendering, entry from the east. Courtesy of Michael McCann

Figure 6.8. Rendering, overlooking the Great Hall (Emancipation Hall) and skylight.
Courtesy of Michael McCann

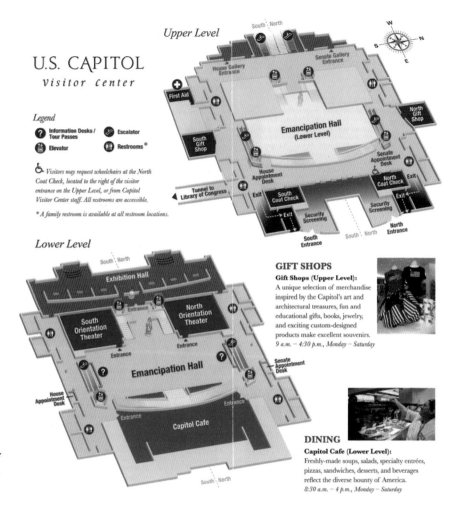

Figure 6.9. Visitor maps of the visitor center. Courtesy of Architect of the Capitol

This would give visitors a full view of the Capitol Dome as they descended the ADA-compliant ramps. The original Olmsted alee of tulip poplar trees, in line with East Capitol Street, was also re-created to frame the grand stairs as they too descend to the entry doors and security screening areas. This greatly strengthened the sense of entry and visitor procession.

Security Screening: Security screening areas could now flow more directly from the entry stairs and ramps into the visitor center, without a need for the 1995 intermediate skylights proposed for those locations.

Great Hall and Skylights: The procession of visitors from entry areas would lead to a dramatic mez-zanine level overlooking a gracious 30-foot high rectangular Great Hall that measured 80 by 200 feet. Two 50-foot-by-70-foot skylights punctuate the northern and southern ends of the Great Hall, sized and located to frame impressive views of the Capitol Dome from both the mezzanine and main floor levels of the Great Hall. All visitor center functions surround this new central space in an easily understandable and accessible pattern.

Grand Stairs: Symmetrical pairs of grand stairs and ADA-compliant elevators lead visitors down to the floor of the Great Hall with multiuse information and ticketing desks located at the northern and southern ends.

Orientation Theaters: This new Great Hall space was created by shifting both orientation theaters westward, closer to the Capitol. Access to the theaters is from the lower level, with rows of seating rising directly up to the main level of the Capitol tour marshaling areas, and internal elevators assuring total ADA accessibility. Large skylights here frame stunning views of the dome as visitors are marshaled for their tours and then escorted to the stairs and escalators leading up to the Capitol crypt level, where tours begin.

Exhibition Area: Ralph Appelbaum Associates consulted with us and CRTKL to configure a sixteen-thousand-square-foot exhibition area positioned to the rear of the orientation theaters and running the full length of the Great Hall. This consolidated the 1995 plan's scattered exhibit spaces into a single hall where the history of the Congress and its ongoing impact on our daily lives is presented.

Our revised preliminary designs were unanimously approved by the Capitol Preservation Commission, and only then could we proceed with final design and the development of detailed construction documents for public bidding. We refined these concepts and scheduled a second peer review work session, hosted by David Childs at his Skidmore, Owings and Merrill New York office. Our discussions reinforced our sense that important revisions had been made, particularly in the creation of the Great Hall with its large skylights and more direct and intuitive visitor flow. These and other changes were further refined as our design process continued.

The Congressional Auditorium: An Unfortunate Compromise

How can good architectural decisions be made in a timely way when the client is a commission composed of eighteen senators and representatives from both parties who represent the full spectrum of political philosophies and who must achieve consensus for us to move ahead? Senior staffers recognized that each vote could put members at political risk, and they protected them by avoiding votes and laying full responsibility for decisions large and small

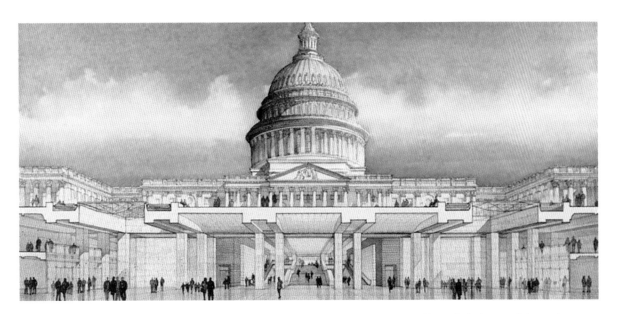

Figure 6.10. Cross-sectional view beneath the East Plaza showing the Great Hall, its skylights, and the earlier central stairway design leading directly up to the Capitol. Courtesy of Michael McCann

directly at my feet. A few votes could not be avoided, such as one on the basic issue of whether a major auditorium should be built.

George White's 1995 plan called for a large assembly space at the request of Librarian of Congress James H. Billington, who wanted a larger venue to showcase the library's extensive film collection. Billington also wanted a tunnel to connect the library's Jefferson Building to the visitor center, to tie it and the auditorium more closely into the library's complex of buildings. But once members of Congress recognized how useful an auditorium could be to them, they claimed it as a Congressional Auditorium, greatly diminishing the library's use. We developed several seating options for the full eighteen-member commission to review and vote on.

A 450-seat option, with 350 seats on a lower level and 100 on an upper gallery, would cost $20 million. This would barely hold all members of the House, with no room for staff, media, the public, or 100 senators for joint sessions of Congress. The largest option was for 750 seats, with 550 seats on the lower level and 200 on the upper that could accommodate all members of Congress, with room for staff, media, and the public. It would cost $33 million. I believed this was the best option since it could act as an alternative to the House Chamber for joint sessions of Congress. The House and Senate chambers sorely needed renovation and electromechanical upgrades to bring them up to modern life-safety standards. This would take some two years for each chamber, and alternative spaces convenient to the Capitol would have to be found during construction. The 750-seat option was designed with a center aisle to allow for seating divisions by political party. In traditional theater seating configurations, center aisles are typically avoided because they take up prime viewing area.

In February 2000 the design team presented these options to the commission along with relative benefits, drawbacks, and costs. Opinions ranged from those of fiscal conservatives, who did not want to build the auditorium at all, to those who proposed increasing its original design capacity from 450 to 750

seats to accommodate joint sessions of Congress. I lobbied for the 750-seat option but wasn't certain an auditorium of any size would be acceptable. A majority was cobbled together in a political compromise that reaffirmed the original $20 million budget and a 450-seat side-aisle version with wider seats for members, which could barely accommodate meetings of the full House. Eleven months later, in February 2001, we were directed to reconfigure the approved and now fully designed 450-seat auditorium to include a central aisle to clearly define political divisions.

Years later, as construction of the overall project was nearing completion, it was my pleasure to provide hardhat tours to senators and representatives. Pointing out the obvious, many asked why I had designed such a small auditorium, one that could not host a joint session of Congress. They assumed this was a mistake I had made and asked how the auditorium could be expanded. I had to inform them it could not because the reinforced concrete foundation walls were not movable.

A Home for the *Statue of Freedom*

One of the most significant design changes growing out of the peer review process was shifting the twin orientation theaters closer to the Capitol, permitting the consolidation of several smaller public spaces into the centrally located Great Hall. This monumental space became the access point for all visitor center functions that pinwheeled around it, including the orientation theaters, exhibition hall, Capitol Cafe, and House and Senate expansion spaces. Corridors on the east side of the Great Hall led to the Congressional Auditorium and the tunnel to the Library of Congress.

Our revised design proposed a monumental staircase between the orientation theaters that would lead to the mezzanine and then to a set of stairs and escalators up to the historic Capitol. It was this space, on the central east–west axis of the Capitol, that I envisioned as the perfect location for *Freedom*. Here, this impressive plaster model would be-

Figure 6.11. Rendering of niche created for *Statue of Freedom*. Courtesy of Michael McCann

Figure 6.12. *Freedom* as focal point of Emancipation Hall, with statues from the National Statuary Hall Collection. Courtesy of Alan M. Hantman

come the central focal point of the Great Hall and the entire visitor center.

To accommodate this, we split the broad monumental stairway into two symmetrical flights opposite one another against the walls of the orientation theaters. This created a space large enough for the statue and also formed the main entryway to the new exhibit hall behind it. We increased the floor's structural bearing capacity to carry the monument's fifteen-thousand-pound weight and vaulted the ceiling to comfortably clear the height of the nineteen-foot, six-inch *Freedom*.

With this revised design, visitors passing through the security screening area would enter the mezzanine overlooking the Great Hall and look out over this light-filled thirty-foot-high volume to focus on

Figure 6.13. CVC ceremonial ground-breaking. Courtesy of Jeff Trandahl, former clerk of the House

Freedom standing tall in her spacious alcove. The statue would lend both tradition and monumental scale to the hall, tying the visitor center to the historic Capitol. Twenty-four larger-than-life statues from the Capitol's National Statuary Hall Collection were also to be relocated here, further integrating the visual sense of the two buildings. I knew Senator Akaka would be pleased to see *Freedom* residing respectfully in her new home.

A Ceremonial Ground-Breaking

As the Capitol Visitor Center design progressed, it was essential to maintain support and a sense of physical momentum on Capitol Hill. Even though it could be years before excavation began on the site, the Capitol Preservation Commission decided to

hold a ceremonial ground-breaking on the Capitol's East Front to demonstrate leadership's commitment to move forward.

On June 20, 2000, a hot and sunny day in DC, all eighteen members of the bipartisan, bicameral commission, armed with ceremonial shovels, lined up on the future construction site with the Capitol building as an impressive backdrop. I was honored to serve as master of ceremonies and said:

> Honorable members of Congress, ladies and gentlemen: In the 1850s major extensions to the north and south sides of the Capitol were authorized with the great westward expansion of our nation and the resulting growth of Congress. . . . Back in the middle of the nineteenth century, no one could have anticipated the numbers of Americans and visitors from around the

world, who, each year, would visit our seat of government at the Capitol. . . .

Today's Congress understands that the people who come to their Capitol need and deserve a better opportunity to learn and more fully understand their Constitution, their Congress, and the history of their Capitol. . . . They require better amenities, better accessibility, and improved provisions for safety and security. Thanks to the leadership of Congress, the Capitol Visitor Center will give the people the improvements they need and deserve when they visit their Capitol. . . .

Standing with me today are the members of the Capitol Preservation Commission, whose support and commitment are making the Capitol Visitor Center a reality. And now it is my honor to introduce the Speaker of the United States House of Representatives, the Honorable Dennis Hastert.[13]

As Hastert spoke, Strom Thurmond, the Capitol Preservation Commission co-chair and Senate president pro tempore, sat in his wheelchair, suffering under the powerful summer sun. Matthew Evans, our landscape director, sensed the ninety-seven-year-old's discomfort and offered his straw hat to the senator. For decades the media had reported on the effects of the brutal summer sun Senator Thurmond experienced that day. In August 1997, *Roll Call* had reported "Tourists Are Dropping Like Flies: . . . Last month there were fifty cases of tourists experiencing fainting, dizziness or profuse sweating from the brutal Washington summer, according to the Office of the Attending Physician. . . . Some Congressional officials said the wilting tourists provide a strong case for why the institution should finally break ground on the long-anticipated Capitol Visitor Center, which would provide underground, air-conditioned waiting space for visitors."[14]

Anyone who witnessed the two-to three-hour long lines waiting to enter the Capitol understood the need to provide air-conditioned space. Press coverage, along with the critical security issues,

influenced Congress's decision to proceed with the Capitol Visitor Center. Hastert and Thurmond also unveiled a ceremonial cornerstone engraved with commission member names to mark this historic moment. (This ceremonial stone is now on display beneath the bridge between the security screening areas.) Members then enthusiastically wielded their shovels to dig into a trough of sand staged there for this symbolic ceremony.

This public demonstration of bipartisan congressional support was critical for design and planning to move forward. In the following months we conducted interviews to understand what each commission member thought important to convey in the exhibits and orientation film about the historic and current role of the Congress. Three months later, the CPC prepared to vote on approval of our plans. *Roll Call* reported:

> The Capitol Visitor Center moved one step closer to becoming reality last week. . . . Many members felt that the more modern looking original [1995] design, which called for using a lot of glass, did not blend with the classic and historic architecture of the Capitol. . . . "It looked like a mall," [John] Mica (R-FL) said of the original design proposal. "The new design is much more in concert with the existing structure and I think everyone likes it."[15]

How to Build the Visitor Center?

Looking at the historical record, in 1851 architect Thomas U. Walter recommended several construction alternatives for proposed Capitol extensions to President Millard Fillmore and Secretary of the Interior Alexander H. H. Stuart. "Walter recommended that the extension project be advertised for bids and placed under a single contract," William Allen writes in his history of the Capitol. "The second-best approach, in his opinion, would be to divide the contract into multiple parts to be sent out for bids. . . . Fillmore and Stuart agreed with Walter's

Figure 6.14. Ceremonial cornerstone displayed between security screening areas. Courtesy of Alan M. Hantman

second recommendation and instructed him to divide the work into as many parts as possible to enlarge competition to the greatest extent."[16]

In the present-day Capitol Hill, we consulted a Government Accountability Office (GAO) lessons-learned report that specifically warned against initiating such phased construction projects due to numerous reviews and approvals required at each phase, funding problems, complexity of design and quality of construction required on monumental buildings, and likelihood of numerous design changes.[17]

Tom Johnson, our GAO Assignment Manager, explained that these concerns were based on several major projects George White had built that were plagued by many congressional changes and tortuous review as well as approval and funding problems. Major construction issues had occurred during the design and construction of the Hart Sen-

ate Office Building (which had been transformed into a much larger project at triple the original cost estimate and taking twelve years to complete) and the Library of Congress's James Madison Memorial Building (which cost twice its original estimate and opened eight years later than originally planned).

For both projects, construction was split into multiple phases, yet members of Congress and the press criticized White even though these changes had taken place at Congress's direction.

Construction Review Panel

With GAO's construction lessons in mind, we explored alternative methods of constructing the center by assembling a Construction Peer Review Panel that included Bob Peck, director, General Services Administration (GSA) Building Division; Bob

Hixon, director, GSA Construction Excellence Division; GAO's Tom Johnson; a team from CRTKL, associate architects; and other construction experts. I was surprised when two Army Corps of Engineers officers showed up uninvited and unannounced to our initial meeting, but I thought their input could be helpful.

After our associate architecture firm, CRTKL, joined me in describing the project and its compressed schedule to those assembled, and solicited opinions on several potential contracting methodologies, we discussed the pros and cons of each construction method. The Army Corps of Engineers officers had not participated in the discussion, but they listened intently. When I asked for their thoughts, they simply stated, "We are taking over this project."

"Excuse me?" I asked.

The senior officer of the team responded: "I said we are going to be assuming control of this project."[18] The room went silent.

I had not been told about a takeover by anyone and was shocked by the matter-of-fact nature of this statement. I chose not to pursue the issue in the group's presence and continued the discussion around the table.

Two Mississippi Senators and the Army Corps of Engineers

Trent Lott knew the role Jefferson Davis played prior to the Civil War in the construction of the major Capitol building extensions for the Senate and House. As a loyal son of Mississippi, Lott spoke of a strong desire to follow in the construction footsteps of the man who became president of the Confederate States of America, and whose statue had been part of the National Statuary Hall Collection since 1931. With the Capitol Visitor Center becoming a reality, it appeared that Leader Lott saw a chance to play a critical role in the greatest expansion of the Capitol since Davis's tenure. It appeared that Senator Lott also saw an opportunity to emulate his hero as a supporter of the Army Corps of Engineers, one of the major job creators in southern Mississippi.

Newspaper Exposé: The Taj Ma-Vicksburg

It soon appeared that the fates were interceding on my behalf regarding this planned Army Corps of Engineers takeover. On Sunday, September 10, 2000, the *Washington Post* published the first of a five-part in-depth exposé of the Army Corps of Engineers, the corps' ambitious expansion plans, and the questionable multimillion-dollar projects proposed and built in areas that either did not appear to need them or for which there was little to no economic benefit. Many of these projects were considered harmful to the environment and Native American sites. In the second article, Representative Mark Sanford (R-SC) described the corps as "the ultimate candy store for politicians."

The article posed a question: "What does the Army Corps of Engineers do in Mississippi? Generally, whatever Senate majority leader Trent Lott and Senate Agriculture Chairman Thad Cochran want it to do. . . . Right now, the two Republicans have the Corps gearing up to build the world's largest water pump in the Mississippi Delta, a $181 million flood-stopper that Interior Secretary Bruce Babbit has called 'a cockamamie, godawful project.' . . . They moved the local Corps district to a sprawling campus that one agency memo called the 'TajMa Vicksburg,' and when the Clinton administration ordered the Corps to stop issuing permits for new casinos on the fragile gulf coast, Lott persuaded the agency to defy the order."[19]

The *Post* articles described how supporters of the corps in Congress rose to its defense when it was accused of producing biased studies, and they discussed the corp's Program Growth Initiative, which included plans to lobby Congress for even more work: "We intend to form a stronger partnership with congressmen and their staffs so that we become their agency of choice."[20]

The exposé pointed out that some within the congressional community hoped for corps reforms but could not secure sufficient support in the Congress. "Senate Minority Leader Thomas A. Daschle (D-SD), who has proposed moving the Corps to the Interior Department, states he 'can't think of a government agency in more dire need of reform than the Corps.' . . . The only problem, they say, is persuading colleagues to support their calls for change. . . . 'The Corps has some very powerful friends on Capitol Hill,' Daschle said. 'Even the people who agree with me tell me, "Look, I can't get into this, I've got a project in my state."'"[21]

Lott had asked our design team for a full-scale presentation in his office on Monday, September 11, 2000, the day the second article appeared. His request appeared to be a step toward the corps taking control, since we were asked to present our Capitol Visitor Center model, presentation boards, and samples for discussion. But once the exposé appeared, it became apparent that the corps was no longer anxious to march into the District of Columbia to take over this high-profile project, and Lott likely recognized that the timing was not right for this initiative. The presentation in Lott's office was canceled, and the corps never showed up to another project meeting.

Lott, however, continued to actively champion our Capitol Visitor Center project throughout the years of construction. After 9/11, Congress dictated major project changes and additions causing unavoidable budget and schedule issues. At that time Lott came to my office to talk about the challenges, pressure, and negative press generated as a result. He essentially suggested I fire the schedulers or project managers as a way of taking the heat off me.

I thanked him for his concern but said that under these extremely difficult circumstances, it was critical I maintain the project team's morale and would not want to sacrifice anyone, particularly those who had not caused these problems. From his rational political perspective, I am not sure he understood.

Notes

1. Letter from Alan M. Hantman to the Capitol Preservation Commission, in US Architect of the Capitol, "Revalidation Report."
2. da Vinci quoted in Dushkes, *The Architect Says*, 160.
3. Letter from Alan M. Hantman to the Capitol Preservation Commission.
4. Allen, *History of the United States Capitol*, 187–88.
5. Allen, 192.
6. Letter from Alan M. Hantman to the Capitol Preservation Commission.
7. White, "United States Capitol Visitor Center," 1.
8. Stacey Zolt, "Bipartisan Leadership Meets on Visitors Center Plans," *Roll Call*, Oct. 11, 1999.
9. Letter from the United States Senate Committee on Appropriations to Architect of the Capitol Alan M. Hantman, November 12, 1999.
10. Alan M. Hantman, letter to Senators Bennett and Feinstein, December 7, 1999.
11. Allen, *History of the United States Capitol*, 429.
12. Allen, 420.
13. Hantman, personal notes, June 20, 2000.
14. Ed Henry and Jennifer Bradley, "Tourists Are Dropping Like Flies in the Heat: Washington's Summer Takes Its Toll on Visitors Waiting to Tour Capitol," *Roll Call*, August 4, 1997.
15. Lauren Wittington, "Visitor Center Moves Ahead, CPC Members Voting on Final Design, Tunnel to LOC," *Roll Call*, September 21, 2000.
16. Allen, *History of the United States Capitol*, 202.
17. Comptroller General, "Conventional Design and Construction Methods."
18. Hantman, personal notes.
19. Michael Grunwald, "Working to Please Hill Commanders," *Washington Post*, September 11, 2000.
20. Grunwald.
21. Grunwald.

SEVEN

Design Approval and Obstructionist Removal

Design Approval Vote

The headline of the October 19, 2000, *Roll Call* editorial consisted of one word: "Superb." It went on to state: "Despite the partisanship that usually prevails around Congress, the final design for the Capitol Visitor Center has received unanimous bipartisan support from the eighteen-member Capitol Preservation Commission. And there's good reason why: The design is superb, grand enough to reflect the greatness of the institution of Congress *but* lacking the grandiosity of other Washington edifices."[1]

The commission vote was based on the study submitted one year earlier, along with my cover letter to the co-chairs, Speaker Dennis Hastert and Senate President Pro Tempore Strom Thurmond, in which I said, "This is not just another construction project. This is a project of momentous and historic importance. . . . Your decision to move forward will reflect confidence in our future ability to welcome visitors in a secure, educational, and convenient environment, yet will respect the past by preserving the Capitol and its historic setting."[2]

Our overriding aesthetic principle was to create a timeless design to complement the Capitol building, never to upstage it, and to embrace a classic simplicity and vision with flexibility to accommodate future generations of visitors. The visitor center was never meant to replace the historic Capitol as the ultimate visitor destination, but, as noted in our project description, to "enhance and celebrate the experience of visiting the Capitol, making it a richer and more meaningful experience for every visitor."[3] And to do

this while solving the functional challenges of the Capitol as a working office building, meeting center, and museum.

The commission's unanimous vote confirmed the preferred East Front site, basic project goals, and necessary functional improvements to the Capitol such as additional stairs, elevators, and secure truck docks. The murders of Officer J.J. Chestnut and Detective John Gibson more than two years earlier were the drivers that made enhanced security provisions necessary and gave Congress the courage and political cover to stop kicking the can down the road and finally commit appropriated funds.

Visitor Flow into the Historic Capitol

As we explained at our design peer review, we conducted a fire and life-safety study to determine how many people the Capitol building could accommodate. We determined the building could safely handle 1,500 visitors per hour on general tours, in addition to the normal congressional working occupancy. The separate House and Senate gallery tours could accommodate an additional 700 people per hour. This maximum number of hourly visitors became the basis for sizing all visitor center spaces and support facilities. To prepare the 1,500 visitors to tour the Capitol each hour, a pair of orientation theaters was designed to have three seatings each of 250 visitors per hour. At the end of the film, visitors would move up one level to the tour marshaling area and the escalators up to the Capitol. The separate

House and Senate gallery tours were served by two 25-passenger elevators to take visitors directly to the third-floor galleries.

The overall Capitol Visitor Center was sized to comfortably accommodate four thousand visitors at any time as they viewed the orientation film, marshaled for a Capitol tour, visited the exhibition hall, explored the House and Senate gift shops, or enjoyed breakfast or lunch in the Capitol Cafe. Our plans included excavating well beyond the visitor center's footprint to allow for future, yet undetermined, needs of the Congress. The maximum size of this area was limited by the Capitol building to the west and Olmsted's historic landscape on the remaining three sides. A total of 170,000 square feet of future congressional space was to be built on three levels, divided between the House and Senate sides of the building. Visitor Center plans called for building only the structural shell and foundation walls for these future needs. No one could anticipate how quickly the future would come.

A Tunnel to the Library of Congress? Kingston Says *No!*

Several major congressional decisions remained, the first being the Librarian of Congress's request for a tunnel from the visitor center to the library's Jefferson Building. James H. Billington often introduced me by saying, "I'm the 13th Librarian of Congress, but Mr. Hantman is the 10th Architect of the Capitol."[4] He and his staff worked closely with me and my agency as we requested funding for and managed the library's capital projects, providing design services and construction oversight.

Billington was proud of the library's collections and told me he wanted to "let the champagne out of the bottle" by increasing library visitation, which he hoped the tunnel would do. The Library of Congress's grand Beaux-Arts Thomas Jefferson Building is a wonderful blend of art, architecture, and a heavy classical, almost theatrical, level of ornamentation. It was designed by John L. Smithmeyer and Paul J.

Figure 7.1. Great Hall in Library of Congress's Jefferson Building. Courtesy of Architect of the Capitol

Pelz with Edward Pearce Casey supervising the building's public interiors, among the most richly decorated structures in the United States.

The Jefferson Building featured the most cutting edge improvements available at the turn of the twentieth century, including the first use of electric lighting for a building in Washington. Its light bulbs were left unadorned as a wonderful design element celebrating this emerging technology. Opened in 1897, it was renamed the Thomas Jefferson Building in June 1980 to honor the former president's role in establishing the library by selling his collection of 6,487 books to the Congress after its original collection was destroyed in the fire set by the British in the War of 1812.

Billington had appealed to key members of Congress for his tunnel, as well as for a controlling role in planning activities and exhibits in the Capitol Visitor Center, which would turn it into a virtual extension of his library operations. He ultimately achieved the first of these goals, the tunnel, but not the second.

I was authorized to spend private Capitol Preservation Commission donations to study the tunnel's feasibility, and we determined that the connection could be made if it were dug low enough beneath First Street Southeast to clear the Amtrak tunnel in its path.

Strong objections from Representative Jack Kingston (R-GA), chair of the Appropriations Legislative Branch Subcommittee, delayed detailed design for many months, until Speaker Hastert and the commission intervened to determine the tunnel's future. In opposition, Kingston frequently repeated his offer to provide an umbrella to any member of Congress concerned about getting wet while crossing First Street Southeast from the visitor center to the Jefferson Building.

Billington and I were in a sensitive position since we both reported to Kingston's appropriations subcommittee. The chair directed me to keep costs from rising, to refuse to make project changes called for by Congress, and to report back with a list of at least ten ways to cut out major costs. The analogy he used was: "If I am planning an addition to my house and the projected costs come in high, I will cut out things such as a bathroom to stay on budget."[5] Kingston expected me to eliminate restrooms and the cafeteria he considered unnecessary, downgrade the quality of finishes, and cut out Billington's tunnel.

I told the chair we could not eliminate restrooms because building codes specified the number of fixtures required based on occupancy, and that current dining facilities were inadequate to accommodate three million annual visitors. I also was strongly against cuts that would prevent the smooth functioning of the center or degrade the finishes on a project that was to last for generations. The decision about the $10 million funding for the tunnel to the library was to be voted on by Congress.

Many in Congress disagreed with Kingston's approach to reducing the quality of finishes to cut costs. At my 1997 confirmation hearing, Senator Kaye Bailey Hutchison had clearly voiced concern, warning me to not replicate on the visitor center what had been done on the Capitol courtyard infill project years earlier. There, inexpensive wallboard and other finishes had been used, making the project look, in her words, "like a Howard Johnson's."

While I was obligated to prepare a list of potential project cuts for Chairman Kingston, I certainly did not support their implementation. At his direction the elimination of the Library of Congress's $10 million tunnel topped the list. Despite his protests, however, Congress appropriated funding for the tunnel. It would appear that Jack Kingston had taken on the wrong dignitary in Billington, who was then at the height of his power.

A Tunnel to the House Wing of the Capitol? Kingston Says *No!*

Kingston also set his sights on another proposed tunnel, this one beneath the House carriageway, directly accessing the visitor center. But again he ran into many influential House members, including Hastert. Kingston, as one of thirteen appropriations

Figure 7.2. Construction of library tunnel sloping down to pass beneath First Street Southeast. Courtesy of Architect of the Capitol

subcommittee Cardinals, delayed the decision on this tunnel for several months before the Speaker finally stepped in to overrule him.

While Kingston lost this battle, his opposition had taken the tunnel out of its proper construction sequence. Concrete foundation work had already been completed near the House carriageway. We remobilized and cut into a completed section of the foundation wall to create the new connection. Doing it this way significantly raised the costs and delayed overall work in that project area. Politics, again, had an impact on budget and schedule.

Kingston continued his drive to cut costs, with Hastert recognizing that these obstructions were causing significant problems. The Speaker finally took the unprecedented step of dissolving Kingston's appropriations subcommittee, removing him from the Capitol Visitor Center appropriations approval chain. The Capitol Visitor Center project was now to report to the full House Appropriations Committee under Chair Jerry Lewis (R-CA). Our budget was now reviewed and monitored by this full committee, whose mission was to oversee the entire national budget including multibillion-dollar execu-

tive branch agencies such as the Departments of Defense, Education, Homeland Security, Agriculture, Energy, and Commerce.

This change was to be a double-edged sword. Congressman David Obey, ranking minority member of the full House Appropriations Committee, became our project's most enduring obstructionist, negatively affecting our schedule and budget to a far greater extent than Kingston had. Obey, of Wisconsin's seventh congressional district, ultimately served in the House from 1969 to 2011, making him that chamber's third-longest-serving member. He had been against the Capitol Visitor Center project from its inception, throwing roadblocks into appropriations reporting and approval requirements, hindering progress and costing millions more in delays and contractor change order claims. This meant that the Architect of the Capitol and the Capitol Visitor Center project had fallen from the frying pan into the fire.

Essential approval and authorization requests began to encounter additional congressional roadblocks as the project developed, from the same members who had voted for it initially. The Capitol Visitor Center would face roadblocks similar to those that mid-nineteenth-century projects had experienced. History was coming full circle.

History Repeats Itself

President Millard Fillmore's selection of Thomas U. Walter to design northern and southern extensions to the Capitol in the competition of 1850–51 began a design and construction odyssey that spanned the Civil War and tripled the size of the Capitol.

Almost two years had passed since Walter began work when Franklin Pierce became president and Jefferson Davis of Mississippi became his secretary of war. Davis was committed to the expansion project and had been active in the design and architect selection process as a member of the Senate Committee on Public Buildings. According to William Allen, he now convinced Pierce to move the extension project from the Department of the Interior to the War Department, under his control. He then appointed Captain Montgomery C. Meigs of the Army Corps of Engineers to manage day-to-day affairs.[6]

This appointment effectively meant that Walter was put under military rule for the next nine years. Meigs and Walter had strong ideas regarding design and construction issues, as they fought for influence with Pierce and key members of Congress. Meigs, with Davis's support, prevailed and tried to take credit for many of the architect's design initiatives.

Naysayers Stop the Project

Also during that time, the project collected several enemies who tried to stop it from moving ahead. The pressures of budgets, schedules, and the application of political power was similar to what we experienced with the visitor center project.

Naysayers, as discussed by William Allen, included Representative John McNair of Pennsylvania, who opposed the project based on incorrect information received regarding the integrity of the foundations. Representative David K. Carter of Ohio

opposed the project since he and others wanted the Capitol moved out of the District of Columbia to western states at the physical center of the country. And Senator Solon Borland of Arkansas: "questioned the cost of the project, rejecting the architect's estimate as deceivingly low and warning against greedy workmen who wanted the government to operate 'a great national almshouse' for their benefit. He painted a dramatic and exaggerated picture of doom and destruction if construction were allowed to proceed." Borland also proposed stopping the project and abandoning the foundations that cost $100,000 to date.[7]

The Senate Committee on Public Buildings investigated the foundations with the assistance of the Army Corps of Engineers and determined the materials and workmanship to be excellent. "Senator Borland was unmoved. Facts could not change his mind about the architect or his belief that the Capitol extension was a waste of money. . . . At every opportunity, Borland and his lieutenants threw obstacles in the path of the appropriation."[8] Ultimately the House and Senate agreed to a resolution appropriating $500,000 for the extensions and workmen returned to work in April 1852. When the Civil War broke out, Davis left Washington to serve as president of the Confederate States of America from 1862 to May 5, 1865, when it was dissolved.

Twenty-First-Century Naysayers

Fast-forward 150 years to find twenty-first-century naysayers inexorably opposed to the Capitol Visitor Center project. They created appropriations roadblocks causing significant delays and cost penalties throughout the life of the project. With Republicans in the House majority, the ranking Democrat on the House Appropriations Committee from 1995 to 2007 was Congressman Obey, who seemed to relish speaking negatively about the project.

Obey, as mentioned earlier, imposed onerously detailed reporting criteria on the Capitol Visitor Center project and successfully delayed reviews of invoices and payment submissions. Requests for budget increases to fund changes imposed by the Congress and oversight agencies following the 9/11 and anthrax attacks ran the gauntlet of prolonged adversarial hearings and extended approval processes.

Congressman Obey became our twenty-first-century Solon Borland.

Olmsted Landscape and Restorations

Planning for the Capitol Visitor Center was always framed by the imperative of respecting the integrity of two historic landmarks, the Capitol building and the Capitol grounds. The size of the Capitol and the nature of its grounds had changed tremendously since George Washington first laid the cornerstone in 1793.

Since the early 1850s, legislation to enlarge the Capitol grounds had been proposed to enhance the view of the Capitol building and its sense of importance, with, according to William Allen, the Senate in support of this concept and the House opposed. By 1867 the new Capitol extensions and dome were almost complete, but the building could still not be seen to advantage on the cramped Capitol grounds with saloons and restaurants right across the street. Legislation to enlarge the land surrounding the Capitol had been debated since the early 1850s. In 1872 Senator Justin Morrill of Vermont introduced legislation that called for purchasing the full squares of private property across A Streets North and South and adding it to the Capitol grounds. The bill quickly passed the Senate, and after much debate, a modified version passed in the House and was signed by President Ulysses S. Grant.[9]

With the Capitol grounds growing to a total of fifty-eight acres, Morrill understood that a quality landscape master plan was needed, and he reached out to Frederick Law Olmsted, the country's preeminent landscape architect. Morrill chose him based on Olmsted's achievements, including Central Park in Manhattan, Prospect Park in Brooklyn, South Park in Chicago, and the Buffalo New York Park System, carried out through a partnership with architect and landscape designer Calvert Vaux. In *Frederick Law Olmsted: Designing the American Landscape*, Charles Beveridge and Paul Rocheleau quote Olmsted's belief that "the Capitol and its grounds must help 'to form and train the tastes of the Nation.' . . . In his parks Olmsted subordinated architecture to the landscape, but in planning the grounds for a great structure like the Capitol, the landscape design was subordinated to the building."[10]

For the east side of Capitol grounds, Olmsted used an open neoclassical style for hardscape elements defining the eastern edge of the expansive open area for strolling, parking carriages, and large inaugural crowds. He planned a naturalistic approach with extensive lawns and trees for the remainder of the site but encountered difficult circulation problems. "Olmsted noted that twenty-one streets touched the Capitol Grounds," Beveridge and Rocheleau wrote, "while footpaths and carriage drives entered at forty-six different points."[11]

His plan resolved these issues brilliantly on the east side by curving walkways and drives to create open egg-shaped greens on the north and south, fringed by groupings of shade trees. Olmsted highlighted the strength of the Capitol building's design and its magnificent dome by creating view corridors through openings in these tree groupings. Paintings of that period depict women with parasols, horse-drawn carriages, riders in top hats, and clusters of people enjoying the ambiance of the Capitol building forecourt.

In the years since Olmsted's time, the East Front was paved as a blacktop thoroughfare from north to south and as a parking lot for some 350 cars. This sea of cracked and patched paving was demeaning to the visual image and importance of the Capitol building. We wanted to create a welcoming forecourt, on what would be the roof of the Capitol Visitor Center. At the center of the East Plaza, breaking up the large expanse of undefined opened space, are the large Great Hall skylights, surrounded by fountains and low black granite seat walls, inviting visitors to sit, meet friends and family, and enjoy close-up views of the Capitol building. To achieve a human scale for

Figure 7.3. Olmsted's 1874 General Plan for Capitol Square. Courtesy of Architect of the Capitol

the full expanse of the plaza, we created a twenty-five-foot square pattern of granite paving blocks that incorporates the skylight seating areas, welcomes visitors to traverse it, and creates an appropriate and respectful forecourt for the Capitol.

Olmsted's rich East Front landscape had also been compromised over the years, and many large trees were in decline, among them the tulip poplars lining East Capitol Street Drive. A number of memorial trees were also in trouble.

Several hundred-year-old tulip poplar trees had died and been removed, leaving an irregular gap-toothed pattern framing the entry road. During our preconstruction period, we had hundreds of trees evaluated to determine which were still viable, which could be relocated outside the center's planned perimeter, and which had to come down. This survey helped establish the location of the visitor center's eastern wall as we tried to preserve as many trees as possible. Of 346 trees on the east side,

99 were memorial trees, and of these, we were able to relocate 8, but 5 were in decline. Still 62 others had to be removed and replaced. Our plans called for removing any trees obstructing view corridors and planting more than those removed, resulting in a Capitol landscape that more accurately conformed to Olmsted's vision.

A critical design challenge was to integrate this major expansion into the historic Capitol grounds and graciously transition visitors from street level at East Capitol Street down eighteen feet to the center entrance, while avoiding any sensation of descending into a basement. To achieve this, we looked to Olmsted's 1874 plan and tilted his pathways from East Capitol Street down to create gracious entry ramps for universal access while echoing the curves of his open egg-shaped lawns. To excavate in this area and build the ramps and stairs, we first had to relocate the Maryland Liberty Tree.

The Liberty Tree

The Maryland Liberty Tree, planted in 1978, was one of four seedlings grown from the Liberty Tree at Saint John's College in Annapolis, under which colonists had gathered to plan a rebellion against the British Crown. Liberty Trees were at the sites of many notable political events leading up to the Revolutionary War, the most famous of which was Boston's Liberty Tree, an old elm tree where angry colonists began meeting in 1765 to protest actions of the English Crown. It was torn down by loyalists and British soldiers in 1775, as were others throughout the colonies, with the Maryland Liberty Tree now said to be the oldest one surviving.

The seedling of this tulip tree (*Liriodendron tulipifera*) had grown to sixty feet and was expected to continue growing, potentially to ninety feet. This is one of the largest species in the mid-Atlantic region, one reason Olmsted chose the same species for the alee of trees framing the eastern entry to the Capitol grounds. This tree had to be saved, but it was the most difficult one to be moved. A three foot-deep, twenty-four-foot-diameter ball of roots, earth, and clay was dug beneath the tree in preparation for its move out of the visitor center footprint some fifty feet closer to First Street Northeast. Steel pipe-rollers were driven beneath the root-ball, which was rolled onto tracks and jacked up, and then the hundred-ton package was hoisted onto a truck for its short ride to its new location.

We assured that the leaves of the Liberty Tree and all trees in the work area were kept clear of construction dust so they could breathe, and we protected them from construction equipment by fencing them off. We could now replant Olmsted's alee of tulip poplars along a series of steps gently descending to the visitor center entrances to frame the inspiring view of the Capitol and dome for visitors as they descend to the visitor center entrance.

Exhibit Design Pressure Points of Power

Visitor education about congressional history, the legislative process, and the mechanics of our representative democracy was a key rationale for the visitor center project. A twelve-minute orientation film and an exhibition hall featuring rotating exhibits were designed as primary venues for this information. This educational project was distinct, yet interwoven with the physical stone and concrete visitor center construction project.

Considering the diverse political, cultural, and religious perspectives represented in the US Congress, this other project was destined to flex and shift with ever-changing pressure points of power. This project faced the challenge of reaching an impossible consensus on what version of history would be presented to millions of visitors to the people's house each year. One year into my tenure, *Roll Call* wrote that during testimony at a hearing, "Hantman said that the construction of the building is not the difficult task, but rather deciding which parts and whose perspective of congressional history will be highlighted inside the visitors center." They also quoted Wendell Ford as saying the "center is 'a must' and that 'how to depict history' is the hard part."[12]

Figure 7.4. Rendering of ramp and stair leading to visitor center main entry keeping dome in view as ultimate destination. Courtesy of Michael McCann

As architectural design proceeded, we retained Ralph Appelbaum Associates to lead our exhibit design efforts. This firm's portfolio included many of the world's most recognizable public learning institutions in more than fifty countries, among them the National Museum of African American History and Culture and the US Holocaust Memorial Museum. Appelbaum Associates had worked well with powerful and diverse groups to achieve consensus and create meaningful visitor experiences.

Forming the foundation of the exhibit design process, our research included interviews with congressional leadership and members of the Capitol Preservation Commission compiling their thoughts about potential exhibit documents, objects, events, and historic figures. At many of these interviews I was struck by members' depth of input, their personal reflections, and commitment to our constitutional system of government. Their responses were uniformly serious and positive, welcoming new exhibits as important opportunities to provide information about Congress to Capitol visitors, particularly children.

We knew that political controversy had to be avoided to the greatest extent possible while telling the story of the Congress and its impact on the lives of US citizens over the course of our nation's history. There had been recent controversy over a proposed *Enola Gay* exhibit to be mounted at the Smithsonian Air and Space Museum. This was the B-29 plane that dropped the atomic bomb on Hiroshima in 1945, helping bring World War II to an end. The exhibit was ultimately canceled because of the reaction to curators who criticized established political consensus and influenced powerful members of Congress to argue against it. We knew that, for our exhibits, a wide diversity of opinions would be voiced no matter what the exhibits presented and, conversely, did not present.

To avoid historical inaccuracies and public criticism in our presentation of the story of Congress, we created a Content Working Group of historians, convened by the new exhibition project director, Martha Sewell. This group included representatives of the Congressional Research Service of the Library of Congress, the Smithsonian Institution, the National Archives, the National Museum of American History, the Architect of the Capitol, members of Congress and senior staff, and historians and curators representing the House and the

Senate. Together they provided expertise, scholarship, and a broad overview of potential exhibit elements. The group's task was to draft vision and mission statements, a set of interpretive goals, and an over-all thematic structure for Visitor Center exhibits.

The "Preliminary Interpretive Principles and Themes" report stated that the mission of the exhibits "is to foster in the visiting public a deeper appreciation for our unique system of American representative democracy by strengthening the connection of visitors with Congress and the US Capitol through a broader understanding of their functions, their structures, and their histories."[13]

The Content Working Group organized its work into three major themes:

National Aspirations and the Legislative Process: an exploration of significant acts of legislation that have moved the nation closer to its ideals.

History of Congress and the Capitol: a look at how the history of Congress and of the complex that houses it have grown and evolved as the country has grown and evolved.

The People and the Process: a presentation of the unique responsibilities, traditions and cultures of the House and the Senate, and of the dynamic process through which representative democracy happens.

The group also defined four major interpretive principles as the framework for the exhibit's design:

Access: The visitor center is designed to accommodate visitation of up to eighteen thousand people a day in a safe, welcoming, and comfortable environment while guaranteeing a meaningful and enjoyable experience.

Authenticity: Original documents will be used to illustrate themes and stories presented. Rare documents from the Library of Congress, the Na-

Figure 7.5. Exhibition Hall Interpretive computers and Wall of National Aspirations: Freedom, Unity, Knowledge, Common Defense, General Welfare, and Exploration. The hall was redesigned in 2022. Courtesy of Ralph Appelbaum Associates

tional Archives, the Smithsonian Institution, and the Congress's own collections will be changed as exhibits are rotated out.

Relevance: Connections between the legislative work of the Congress and its links to the daily lives of visitors in their home states will be stressed. The many ways visitors can engage in our representative democracy will be emphasized.

Connectedness: The visitor experience will be designed as an integral part of a continuum between the visitor center and the Capitol through use of traditional artwork to tell stories, statues from the National Statuary Hall collection, gallery exhibits, the orientation film, and the quality of the finishes themselves.

With congressional support for these principles and themes, our exhibit designer began working closely with our architectural design team to prepare floor plans and themed design concepts for the first museum dedicated specifically to the history and role of the Congress.

Unfortunately, the direct involvement of congressional leadership and the many Content Working Group experts were not sufficient to insulate the project's exhibits and films from the objections of religious historians who found bias and religious omissions in the carefully crafted exhibits and who wanted to impose their versions of our nation's history and founding principles as the exhibit design was developed over several years.

Meanwhile, events of great consequence continued to influence life in the Capitol, including in the House Chamber, where the formal counting of electoral votes of the contentious November 2000 presidential election played out.

Counting Electoral Votes

I was seated in my customary place in the cluster of chairs to the left of the House rostrum reserved, during joint sessions of Congress, for the sergeants at arms of the House and Senate, the secretary of the Senate, and the Architect of the Capitol. The visitor gallery was half empty as Rosalyn took her seat beside the press cameras. This constitutionally mandated session was held to formalize selection of the next president and vice president: either Republicans George W. Bush and Dick Cheney, or Democrats Al Gore and Joe Lieberman. This was the culmination of the political rancor that had divided the nation since the inconclusive election two months earlier.

The outcome had been preordained by the US Supreme Court in favor of Bush and Cheney when it effectively foreclosed hand-counting of the incompletely punched ballots in four Florida counties, the "hanging chads," ending Gore's efforts to win that state's popular vote and the presidency. In his concession speech the day after the Supreme Court ruling, Gore stated:

> Now the US Supreme Court has spoken. Let there be no doubt, while I strongly disagree with the Court's decision, I accept it. I accept the finality of this outcome, which will be ratified next Monday in the Electoral College. And tonight, for the sake of our unity of the people and the strength of our democracy, I offer my concession. I will also accept my responsibility, which I will discharge unconditionally, to honor the new president-elect and do everything possible to help him bring Americans together in fulfillment of the great vision that our Declaration of Independence defines and that our Constitution affirms and defends.[14]

Bush held a razor-thin Florida plurality of 537 votes statewide, giving him all 25 electoral votes, for a total of 271 and the presidential victory. Democratic members of the House were expected to object to the acceptance of Florida's contested electoral certification. I transcribed the following direct quotes from a CNN real-time video.[15]

With three sharp raps of the gavel, Speaker Hastert declared, "The House will be in order. Members will please take their seats. Sergeant at Arms!"

"Mr. Speaker," declared Bill Livingood, the thirty-fifth sergeant at arms of the US House of Representatives, "the Vice President and the United States Senate." Two pairs of House pages led the procession, each carrying an impressive leather-wrapped chest holding electoral certifications. The vice president and senators inched their way toward the rostrum, greeting members along the way. We shook hands as Gore mounted to the uppermost tier and was welcomed by the Speaker. The two leaders stood before a sparsely filled chamber with more than two hundred vacant seats, the room virtually devoid of Democrats.

Gore gaveled the session to order: "Open the certificates in alphabetical order and pass to the Tellers the certificates showing the results of the electors in each state, and the Tellers will then read, count, and announce the result in each state." The certificate from Alabama was removed from the chest and read. There were no objections, so the count proceeded on to Alaska, Arizona, Arkansas, Delaware, the District of Columbia, and then to Florida. Chaka Fattah (D-PA), one of four tellers, announced, "This is the one we've been waiting for." He read through the legal language and concluded: "Mr. President, the certificate of the electoral vote of the state of Florida seems to be regular in form and authentic, and appears, therefore and therefrom, that George W. Bush of the state of Texas received 25 votes for president, and Dick Cheney of the state of Wyoming received 25 votes for vice president."

Gore asked, "Is there objection?" This opened the floodgates, with Congressman Alcee Hastings of Florida the first to rise: "I must object because of the overwhelming evidence of official misconduct, deliberate fraud, and an attempt to suppress voter turnout," he said. Gore gaveled him down, and since Hasting's point of order had not been co-signed by a senator, Gore ruled, "The point of order may not be received."

Other representatives went through the same gavel-rapping process, accompanied by intermittent sighs of frustration from the chair. Illinois Representative Jesse Jackson Jr. rose to speak, "Mr. President, I am objecting to the idea that votes in Florida were not counted." His voice rose as he shouted, "It is a sad day in America, Mr. President, when we can't find a senator to sign these objections."

The gavel rang out repeatedly, but Jackson continued speaking over Gore's objections. "The gentleman will suspend!" Gore, with arms spread wide, and a frustrated half smile, said, "The president thanks the gentleman from Illinois, but . . ." he paused, looking at the passionate representative, appearing to be unable to find an appropriate response to address this outburst. Instead, Gore smiled and said in a questioning tone, "Hey . . . ?!"

He appeared to be saying, in effect, "I can't do anything, I'm sorry!" The Republicans in the chamber laughed and applauded at this. Gore had let his guard down with this one demonstration of emotion. Thirteen Democratic congresspeople rose with points of order. With the advice of the parliamentarian, Charles W. Johnson III, all were rejected, yet they still pressed to have their objections noted. Gore sacrificed his personal goals and political and social agenda acting on what he believed best for the unity of our nation by assuring no senator would co-sign a point of order.

Vice President Al Gore confirmed his own defeat. I believe many in the chamber that day, of both parties, regarded this man with respect for his bearing and integrity. I certainly did. He concluded with, "May God bless our new president and our new vice president and may God bless the United States of America." With a final rap of the gavel, Gore declared the joint session of Congress dissolved. In apparently good humor, he signed autographs for the tellers, for me, and for others as he left the rostrum.

Figure 7.6. "Hey!" VP Gore Counting the Electoral Votes, 2001. Courtesy of *Washington Post*

Like Al Gore, Supreme Court Justice Stephen Breyer (who retired from the court in 2022) disagreed with the court's ruling in *Bush v. Gore*, saying: "I didn't think *Bush v. Gore* was right. I was in dissent. But I heard Harry Reid [Senate Democratic leader] who I also think did not think it was right, I heard him say the following when he was at the Court at dinner. He said, 'You know, the most remarkable thing about that case is a matter hardly ever remarked, and that is this. Although half the country thought it was just terrible and really disagreed with it, there was no violence in the streets. People didn't kill each other.' And that, he said, 'was a good thing.' And that is what I think. I think it was a good thing."[16]

Rosalyn joined me in my office after Gore concluded the joint session with his words of national unity: "May God bless our new president and new vice president and may God bless the United States of America." We were drained by the passion we had witnessed, the love of country, and commitment to the democratic process Gore exhibited in defeat. We too were glad there was no violence in the street.

The Counting of Abraham Lincoln's Electoral Votes

The 2001 counting of the electoral votes was an important moment in our nation's history, but it was not the first time this constitutional formality had been contested or even imperiled in the sacred halls of the Capitol, nor would it be the last. On February 13, 1861, a joint session of Congress convened to formally count the electoral votes of the November 1860 presidential election, won by Abraham Lincoln. After decades of debate and violence surrounding the issue of slavery, members of Congress came to the House floor armed with pistols and Bowie knives for their own protection. Newspapers such as the *Baltimore Sun* were filled with concerns that "the counting of the electoral votes would never be peacefully accomplished."[17] The possibility of taking over the Capitol, or even the city, by sending in Virginia's militia or other means, was openly discussed.

The army security cordon surrounding the Capitol was commanded by Lieutenant General Winfield Scott, who, despite being a Virginian, was loyal to the Union and was not about to allow any disruption to the constitutionally mandated counting process. A *New York Times* article "The Capitol Takeover That Wasn't" states, "When a secessionist senator from Texas, Louis Wigfall, asked Scott if he would dare to arrest a senator for treason, Scott exploded, 'No! I will blow him to hell!'"[18]

In 1861 John C. Breckinridge of Kentucky was vice president serving with President James Buchanan, and he honored his oath of office by faithfully presiding over the counting. Breckinridge later joined the Confederacy and in 1865 became its fifth secretary of war. Lincoln might have been denied the presidency without the honorable actions of two Southerners remaining true to their oaths in support of the peaceful transfer of power.

Enemies Foreign and Domestic

During my term as architect, my colleagues and I were dedicated to honoring and upholding the oath of office we had taken to "support and defend the Constitution of the United States against all enemies, foreign and domestic." In 2021, as a private citizen, I was shaken to my core as members of both the Congress and the executive branch violated that oath in the pursuit of a political agenda that attempted to overturn a demonstrably fair and open election and undermine the basic principles on which our country was founded. In recounting here my personal experiences as an officer of Congress at the 2001 counting of electoral votes, I am compelled to contrast those experiences with the events of 2021, when insurrectionists violated and degraded the same chambers, corridors, and halls of the Capitol I committed to maintain and protect.

Like Breckinridge in 1861, and Gore in 2001, Vice President Mike Pence stood at the House dais in 2021 following a divisive and heavily contested election. Lawsuits attempting to invalidate Joseph R. Biden's electoral wins in six battleground states had been rejected by courts at all levels, infuriating Donald Trump, who still claimed the election was stolen.

Trump instructed Pence to overturn the electoral college results in those states won by Biden. Pence issued a formal statement before the session was convened confirming that the Constitution did not empower the vice president to determine which electoral votes to count, or do anything other than tally the duly certified ballots and announce the victors. At Trump's Save America rally on the morning of the ballot-counting session, Trump told tens of thousands of supporters that he was disappointed in Pence and that the only way to "take back our country" was for his supporters to go to the Capitol and "fight like hell" or they wouldn't "have a country left."

When Arizona's electoral votes were called in favor of Biden, Representative Paul Gosar (R-AZ) objected. Unlike in 2001, when no senator signed on to the objections of several Democratic representatives, this time Senator Ted Cruz (R-TX) signed onto Gosar's objection, triggering the requirement that both chambers deliberate on the objection for two hours and then vote. The world watched Pence preside over the Senate Chamber's deliberations as a mob of thousands responded to Trump's directions to "Fight like hell" and swarmed down Pennsylvania and Constitution Avenues to the Capitol, attacking Capitol and Metropolitan Police who were protecting the Congress and the Capitol building.

They succeeded in interrupting the counting process as the vice president, members of the Senate and House, and their staffs went into hiding. It took hours for reinforcements to arrive to clear the chambers, halls, and corridors of insurrectionists desecrating our Capitol.

There were two major differences between the insurrection of January 6, 2021, and the insurrection averted on February 13, 1861. The sitting president in 1861, James Buchanan, did not deny the results of the election and send a mob to stop the electoral vote counting, and importantly, security at the Capitol was entrusted to an honorable, well-prepared officer, Lieutenant General Winfield Scott, who had the unilateral authority to stand firm with his troops against the treason of his fellow Southerners.

At the opposite end of the spectrum, the sitting president in 2021 did not accept the electoral results and sent his supporters to stop the counting and reverse the vote, and as the Capitol was under assault, additional forces needed to support the Capitol Police were delayed for hours by their chain of command. What should have been a quadrennial formality, the ceremonial counting of electoral votes, was transformed into an existential threat to the core of our democracy. Fortunately, Pence followed in the footsteps of all of his vice presidential predecessors and honored his oath of office.

Presidential Inaugurations

The Capitol building is a multiuse stage supporting Congress's ongoing operations, where citizens can observe their government in action and mourn presidents and other individuals of note, and where figures of national and international significance can be celebrated. Every four years, the West Front of the Capitol is where we enact a core part of our democracy: the peaceful transfer of power from one president to the next as the chief justice of the Supreme Court administers the oath of office.

I was retained as a consultant to the Inaugural Committee to assist in planning and constructing President Bill Clinton's inaugural stands a month before I was sworn into office. As architect I continued working on the organization, execution, and evaluation of Clinton's second inaugural, which took place on January 20, 1997. This was solid preparation for George W. Bush's first inaugural four years later, in January 2001, where we provided the inaugural stands; seating for 30,000 guests; coordination with US Capitol Police and Secret Service; fencing, installation of flags, buntings and decorations; installation of sound systems and scaffolded media towers; and carpentry, electrical, mechanical, and plumbing services.

Washington's weather in January is difficult to predict, and on the night of January 19, 2001, a snowstorm passed through Washington. My team, with the assistance of the National Guard, managed to clear the snow from thirty thousand chairs in time for the next day's events. Taken before the snow was cleared, the wonderful aerial view in figure 7.7 highlights the seating pattern and breadth of inaugural preparations.

Existing plans for the inaugural stands had been in use for years, but there were significant design flaws caused largely by the requirement that we provide as much seating as possible within the multilevel geometry of the Olmsted terraces. Poor view angles resulted for many seats, and a serious bottleneck and life-safety risk was caused since guests seated on the main level had to enter and leave through the same door used by the president and his entourage. A smaller number of guests on the upper terrace level were able to enter from several other access points.

We wanted to solve the seating problem before the next inaugural, and Jim Crapp, a member of our construction division, designed an amphitheater-like configuration which gave all guests easy access to both levels of the stands with multiple paths for safe egress while also maximizing the number of seats and improving view angles. Jim built a model of his comprehensive design, which was fully endorsed by the full Joint Congressional Committee for use at the next inauguration. Our construction division and carpentry, electrical, mechanical, and plumbing shops, and grounds crew implemented this new design for George W. Bush's second inaugural in 2005, surpassing all expectations.

Members of the carpentry shop (Peter Meneghini, Jeffrey Walters, and Jeffrey Hagan) used wood from the platform's decking to shape a set of gavels as a gift to the new president to commemorate his inauguration. The number of gavels is traditionally based on the new president's number in the presidential sequence. George W. Bush received forty-three gavels and I had the honor of presenting this token of respect to President Bush in the Oval Office.

Figure 7.7. Snow the night before George W. Bush's first inauguration, January 2001. This wonderful aerial view, taken before the snow-clearing effort, highlights the seating pattern and the breadth of inaugural preparations. Courtesy of Architect of the Capitol

Figure 7.8. Overview of inaugural stands, January 20, 2005. Courtesy of Architect of the Capitol

He later gave them to members of his Cabinet and his top advisers.

New York's Junior Senator Takes Her Seat

On the evening of February 27, 2001, before President Bush's address to a joint session of Congress, the secretary of the Senate hosted a generous buffet dinner in the Senate Reception Room, one of the most elaborately decorated spaces built during the Capitol extension project of the 1850s. Ornate scagliola plasterwork overlays the wall and ceiling surfaces simulating carved marble moldings and door surrounds, adding to the opulence throughout. Portraits of Henry Clay, Daniel Webster, John Calhoun, and other Senate notables, framed by gold-leafed decorative moldings, occupy places of honor about the room, with empty framed spaces awaiting future senatorial portraits.

A mix of round and rectangular tables were placed about the room, and chairs were filling with members of the most exclusive club in the world and their companions, dining, talking, laughing. A scattering of senators and spouses gathered at the buffet and bar in the adjacent LBJ Room, connected by a pair of ornately paneled wooden doors. The walls of the LBJ Room were lined with rectangular buffet tables, a bar positioned diagonally at one corner, and at its center was a large circular flower and food-laden table beneath a historic crystal chandelier.

Rosalyn and I stood in line at the buffet as a new senator arrived. With a final aside over her shoulder, she entered, walked across the richly colored Minton tiles, head erect, face framed by golden hair, her staffers lingering in the corridor beyond.

The LBJ Room had a notable history. First intended as a library, Thomas U. Walter's design morphed into a room dedicated for the Senate Committee on the District of Columbia. The 1902 McMillan Plan was formulated here, serving as a model for the City Beautiful movement across the nation and profoundly shaping Washington's development in harmony with Pierre L'Enfant's original vision. Gracing its walls were portraits of John Adams and Thomas Jefferson, hand-colored engravings of 1830s Washington, and Norman Rockwell's 1964 composition of President Johnson, designed to grace the cover of *Look* magazine. Constantino Brumidi's lunette representing history looked down from above with Father Time holding an hourglass and scythe.

This room was known to be Johnson's favorite, first when he was Senate majority leader and later as vice president under John F. Kennedy until the 1963 assassination catapulted him into the presidency. Now called the LBJ Room, it was valued in its rich reality as an integral part of Senate life in the Capitol, fully accepted, unlike the senator now standing alone at its center. She was standing beneath the imposing crystal chandelier originally hung in Ulysses S. Grant's White House, which was then brought to the room by the 6th Architect of the Capitol, Elliott Woods, who purchased it at President Theodore Roosevelt's sale of White House furnishings during its 1902 renovation.

Hillary Rodham Clinton, the junior senator from New York, quietly contemplated her surroundings. Some considered her a carpetbagger, invited to the state by local political powers seeking a high-profile candidate. She moved to New York in September 1999 while still a polarizing First Lady, seeking the seat of the retiring senator Daniel Patrick Moynihan (D-NY).

It's possible that some of the more established senators resented this foray into their exclusive club by the wife of the outgoing president. Whatever the reason, she stood alone that February evening. None of those standing at the buffet, getting drinks at the bar, or talking in groups around the perimeter of the LBJ Room welcomed her to her first Senate dinner. Intentionally or not, they appeared oblivious to the new senator's presence. Rosalyn and I sensed her discomfort.

I approached Senator Clinton and reintroduced myself from past meetings, and asked if everything was going well with her new suite in the Russell Senate Office Building. I introduced her to Rosalyn, we spoke for a while, and I escorted her to the buffet. Shortly after Rosalyn and I took our seats, Clinton

Figure 7.9. Senate reception room with portraits of John Calhoun and Henry Clay. Courtesy of Jeffrey Schwarz Photography

entered the LBJ Room, scanned the scene, selected her seat among Senate peers, and joined in the conversation. John Calhoun and Henry Clay appeared to look out upon the assembled crowd with reserved amusement.

A Fundraising Astronaut: Senator John Glenn

Early in 2000 the CPC approved the creation of a not-for-profit 501(c)(3) to oversee the new visitor center private fundraising effort for the $100 million needed to match the funds appropriated by Congress. The board of the fund was made up of a distinguished group of dignitaries and former Republican and Democrat congressional leaders to both direct and lend gravitas to the fundraising process.

Representatives of the fund contacted wealthy individuals and corporations with limited success. The effort had virtually stalled, primarily because naming rights could not be granted in return for donor generosity. Conversations with comedian Bob Hope's estate fell apart when a $5 million donation would not secure naming rights for a Bob Hope Auditorium. Others demurred because they wanted

more public recognition than an inscription in a book of donors. A soft drink company that was denied exclusive rights to sell their products in all Capitol Hill buildings also walked away without donating. Despite this constraint, donations totaling more than $35 million had been raised.

The fund reinvigorated its efforts by having its blue-ribbon members publicly stress the importance of the project with their strong personal support, but an additional incentive was needed. In a letter to the Pew Charitable Trusts' Rebecca Rimel, the interim board chair of the fund, congressional leaders (Senate President Pro Tempore Strom Thurmond, Speaker of the House Dennis Hastert, Senate Majority Leader Trent Lott, Senate Democratic Leader Thomas A. Daschle, and House Democratic Leader Richard A. Gephardt) reiterated their support for the board's efforts and offered an incentive: "In an effort to show our appreciation for your hard work and for the early and consistent commitment of the Pew Charitable Trusts, and to appropriately recognize donors to the fund for the Capitol Visitor Center for their generosity, we reiterate our commitment to join you at a reception/dinner to be held on a mutually agreed upon date this fall."[19]

The hope was that such a meeting with congressional leadership, and a push for public awareness, would encourage big-ticket donors to support this important education and security-based project.

The funds raised to date had come from donors including the Pew Charitable Trusts, the Bill and Melinda Gates Foundation, and the Annenberg Foundation. Senator and astronaut John Glenn served as the fund's national spokesperson, and former vice presidents Walter Mondale and Dan Quayle were recruited to the honorary board of directors to enhance its national profile and help raise the additional $65 million.

In August 2001 *Roll Call* noted that, "under federal law Congress must have all the money needed for the project in the bank before crews can begin digging." The piece quoted Glenn, who said, "That's what puts the heat on it right now. We just hope that it all comes through, and we can get this thing started and get it done on time. There's nothing magic about the next inauguration, but it would be a nice thing to have it open at that time."[20] Glenn's remark about the next inauguration was a reminder that a promise had already been made to the president that the project would be completed by then—the project's Achilles heel.

We planned a kick-off media event for a strengthened initiative, the unveiling of a detailed scale model of the Capitol Visitor Center, and a photo session to take place in the Capitol crypt, one level beneath the Capitol Rotunda.

The Media Briefing That Never Was

The briefing was to take place at noon on September 11, 2001, followed by the annual meeting of the board of directors of the Campaign for Democracy's

The Board of Directors of the Fund for the Capitol Visitor Center

cordially requests your presence at

A Preview Reception and Dinner

for the

Capitol Visitor Center

with honorary hosts

The Honorable Tom Daschle
Majority Leader, United States Senate

The Honorable J. Dennis Hastert
Speaker of the U.S. House of Representatives

The Honorable Trent Lott
Minority Leader, United States Senate

The Honorable Richard A. Gephardt
Minority Leader of the U.S. House of Representatives

and

The Honorable John Glenn
Former United States Senator
and
Project Spokesman

Tuesday, September 11, 2001
Washington Court Hotel
525 New Jersey Avenue, NW
Washington, DC

6:00 p.m. Reception
7:00 p.m. Dinner
Business Attire

To R.S.V.P. or for further information please contact:
Rachel Hirschberg
phone (202) 347-9177   fax (202) 347-9190

Figure 7.10. Invitation to September 11, 2001, media briefing, reception, and dinner hosted by the Campaign for Democracy's Front Door. Courtesy of Alan M. Hantman

Front Door. I was to address the directors and share a brief history of the Capitol Visitor Center and its critical importance to the Capitol. The board of directors was also scheduled to hold a reception and dinner for the visitor center later that evening at the Washington Court Hotel for major donors with all congressional leaders in attendance, for a meet and greet with project spokesman Senator John Glenn.

That noon press conference never took place. Nor did the annual meeting, or reception and dinner scheduled for later that same evening, as promised six months before.

Notes

1. "Superb," *Roll Call*, October 19, 2000.
2. US Architect of the Capitol, "Revalidation Report."
3. "Capitol Visitor Center: The Nation's Front Door to Democracy," US Architect of the Capitol, Washington, DC, 1998.
4. Hantman, personal notes.
5. Hantman, personal notes.
6. Allen, *History of the United States Capitol*, 215.
7. Allen, 203.
8. Allen, 203.
9. Allen, 343.
10. Beveridge and Rocheleau, *Frederick Law Olmsted*, 188.
11. Beveridge and Rocheleau, 188.
12. Frances Contigulia, "Senate Rules Panel Hears Concerns about Security," *Roll Call*, February 26, 1998.
13. Ralph Appelbaum Associates, "Preliminary Interpretive Principles and Themes."
14. CNN, December 13, 2000.
15. All direct quotes of the joint session proceedings were transcribed by Alan M. Hantman directly from a CNN video made in real time on January 6, 2001.
16. Adeel Hassan, "'Law Requires Both a Head and a Heart': Breyer in His Own Words," *New York Times*, January 27, 2022.
17. Historical Highlights, House Office of the Historian, Joint Session to Count 1860 Electoral College Votes, quoting the *Baltimore Sun*.
18. Ted Widmer, "The Capitol Takeover That Wasn't," *New York Times*, January 8, 2021.
19. Letter from House and Senate Leadership (Senate President Pro Tempore Strom Thurmond, Speaker of the House J. Dennis Hastert, Senate Majority Leader Trent Lott, Senate Democratic Leader Thomas A. Daschle, and House Democratic Leader Richard A. Gephardt) to Rebecca Rimel, Pew Charitable Trust Interim Board Chair of the Fund for the Capitol Visitor Center, March 20, 2001.
20. Lauren W. Wittington, "Visitor Center Fund Begins Final Push," *Roll Call*, August 9, 2001.

The World Changed

September 11, 2001

My commute on that crystal clear morning passed historic Rock Creek Cemetery, the United States Soldiers' and Airmen's Home, and Prospect Hill Cemetery. A last turn onto North Capitol Street brought the Capitol Dome into view, its silhouette etched into the distant sky. Framed at first by rows of single-family homes, then by a wall of mid-rise office buildings, the dome grew larger with each traffic light, its classical details and its crowning glory, the *Statue of Freedom*, coming more sharply into focus.

That morning, Rosalyn and I hugged each other much like we had on a thousand Washington workdays since my term began four years earlier. But after this September day our complacency would be shaken to the core, and we no longer took our daily patterns for granted.

My assistant, Kaye Burke, excitedly called me into her office to see a news flash: a plane had crashed into a New York City tower. The image on her small TV was fuzzy, the reporters' voices uncertain, nothing substantive to report. This had to be a reprise of the 1945 incident when a B-25 Mitchell Bomber lost its way in a dense fog over New York City and crashed into the seventy-eighth and seventy-ninth floors of the Empire State Building. Fourteen people had been killed that Saturday morning, but the building was back in operation two days later. That accidental loss of life was a tragedy, but nothing that changed the course of history. But half an hour later, Kaye shouted, "Another plane crashed!"

Two burning towers, scenes of falling debris, rising plumes of smoke and flames. Our senses were overwhelmed with images filling the screen, of people running in panic, of horrified voices describing the scene. We soon heard about the attack on the Pentagon, just outside Washington in Virginia. This was clearly a coordinated attack on our country. What cataclysmic act would come next?

Capitol Police radios warned that another plane was heading toward Washington. Officers rushed from office to office, ordering people to evacuate immediately. Chaos ensued as members and their staffs scrambled down stairways toward the western door, through the same corridors presidents-elect pass on their way to inaugural ceremonies. They ran alone, in pairs, in small groups, out to the National Mall. A few carried purses, briefcases, or armloads of papers—all appeared stunned, scared. Some ran out of their shoes without stopping to reclaim them, the only sounds that of rushing footfalls. Many knew the World Trade Center towers in New York had been attacked and that a plane was approaching Washington from the north. Some didn't know a third plane had crashed into the Pentagon . . . until they saw black clouds wafting across the Mall.

I checked our area of the building to be sure everyone was out and I was among the last to leave. I exited the western door into the late summer sunlight, blindingly bright as it reflected off Frederick Law Olmsted's monumental white stone stairway. A Capitol Police officer directed everyone away from the building. I sprinted to Capitol Police Headquarters, passing many members of Congress standing just a few hundred feet from the Capitol, appearing stunned, still on the lawns and sidewalks of Capitol Square, still in harm's way, along with groups of curious onlookers. Phone service was intermittent, crashing from the overload. No way to communicate.

Unprepared

The Senate and House sergeants at arms and I conferred with Capitol Police leadership at their command center and monitored incoming feeds from government and network television sources. Dozens of senators and representatives soon found their way to headquarters, occupying conference rooms and available offices while awaiting updates that in reality contained little new information other than what could readily be seen on television broadcasts.

The White House evacuation had begun only at 9:20 a.m., after the attacks at the World Trade Center and just before the plane crashed into the Pentagon at 9:27 a.m. Even after this third attack, the Capitol evacuation was not initiated until 9:48 a.m., and only after the Federal Aviation Authority warned of another hijacked plane headed from the north toward Washington, DC.

First Lady Laura Bush was on Capitol Hill that morning, preparing to testify at a Senate Education Committee hearing in the Russell Senate Office Building. When the hearing was abruptly canceled, Mrs. Bush paused to join Senators Edward Kennedy (D-MA) and Judd Greg (R-NH) for a press photo-op before she was finally evacuated, after 10:00 a.m.

Speaker Dennis Hastert, second in line for the presidency, was on the floor of the House of Representatives when the evacuation began. His security detail took him to a secure location by helicopter after he stopped to cancel a joint session of Congress with the prime minister of Australia. According to his oral history, recorded in 2012 for the Flight 93 National Memorial, the joint session was to be attended by "Vice President Cheney . . . the President's Cabinet, the President's Joint Chiefs of Staff, the Supreme Court and members of the Diplomatic Corps, all in

one room. And I'm thinking: this is probably not a good idea and if this is a thing that could happen in New York, it could happen here. . . . And my gosh, here we are a sitting duck up on this hill, and it's a clean shot right down the Mall, and I think we need, we better get everybody out of here."[1]

That morning, Nellie Neumann, a Capitol tour guide, was giving a special tour to nine members of the British Parliament when a Capitol Police officer came to the door of the Old Senate Chamber and ordered the delegation to evacuate immediately. They exited the east side of the Capitol, and in Neumann's oral history, recorded in 2012, she recalled another police officer shouting,

> "Run as far and as fast as you can!" And I stopped for just a moment. . . . I just had to have one more look at the United States Capitol, and I have to admit, I fully expected it was the last look I'd ever have. For all I knew, it was the last look I'd have of anything before I was buried beneath the rubble of the Capitol, because there was a plane coming towards us. . . . But as I glanced around . . . representatives were pouring down the front steps. The same was happening on the Senate side. But I think what struck me at that moment was how so many of them were frantically dialing cell phones that didn't work. . . . And I thought to myself: here they are, the power brokers, really, of America, and yet their faces really reflected utter terror and, I mean, a helplessness, like, "Somebody, please help me," because no one knew what to do.[2]

House Sergeant at Arms Bill Livingood's recorded testimony described going to the Speaker's office, looking out the window and seeing the smoke from the Pentagon curling across the Mall:

> And the Speaker said, "Let's evacuate." And I said, "We need to evacuate everything, not just the Capitol." . . . So we evacuated the entire campus at that time. . . . I went to one of our last exits

that was open. I said to the two police officers there . . . "Okay. You all shut the door. Get out of the building. You can stand off and watch the door from a distance." And the two said, "Sir, we're going to disobey because we're concerned if a plane hits this building, if there's someone that we missed, we might hear them yell, and that's why we want to stay here." That's the unsung heroes that I . . . always talk about.[3]

In its long history, the Capitol had never been evacuated, and no viable evacuation plan was in place in the event of fire or threats of any kind. No fire annunciator system or workable public address system was in place to provide clear instructions, and there had been no significant rehearsals to prepare building occupants to safely exit in the event of an emergency. I believe many felt they were too busy to be bothered. Complicating everything, communications among multiple federal security agencies were poorly coordinated.

The Fourth Plane: United Airlines Flight 93

I often think about those who had hugged their loved ones that morning and traveled by car, bus, or train to their offices in the World Trade Center or the Pentagon—or those who boarded planes in Boston or New York on business trips, vacations, school commutes, or visits to those they loved—just another routine day, until terrorists took their lives and forever fractured the lives of those left behind. As horrific as the losses were from the first three planes, if the fourth one had reached its target, the Congress could have been decapitated. "I think of those people on that 9/11 flight, Flight 93," Dennis Hastert said in his oral testimony, "if they hadn't acted as quickly as they could, we would have had thousands of people in the Capitol when that plane would have come through the front door of the Capitol of the United States. . . . And so, it was the bravery of these spirits, of these people that knew that they were doomed one way or another, and

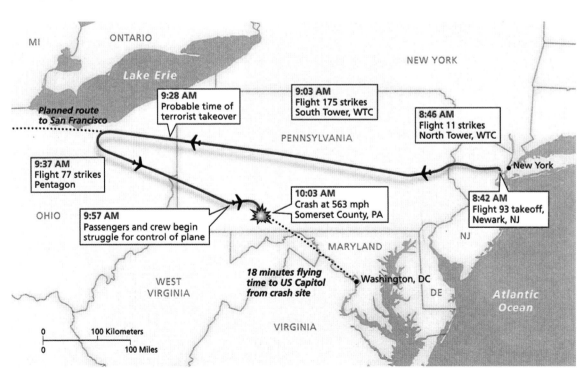

Figure 8.1. Route of United Airlines Flight 93. Courtesy of National Park Service, Flight 93 National Memorial

they took it upon themselves to . . . take the control of that plane."[4]

United Flight 93 left Newark, New Jersey, twenty-five minutes late due to heavy air traffic. It was a Boeing 757 bound nonstop to San Francisco with thirty-three passengers and a crew of seven. Approximately forty-five minutes out, at 9:28 a.m., while flying over Pennsylvania, the plane was hijacked by four terrorists and turned onto a new flight path, southeast toward Washington, DC.

The passengers and crew frantically phoned loved ones once they understood they were being hijacked, only then learning that two other planes had been hijacked and crashed into the World Trade Center towers and another had destroyed an entire section of the Pentagon. These heroic passengers then voted to retake control of the aircraft—the ultimate democratic act in a moment of crisis. Their plan to regain the cockpit did not succeed when the terrorists flying the plane crashed it to prevent the passengers from assuming control.

No one survived the fiery impact as the plane plowed into a remote field in Shanksville, Pennsylvania, and seven thousand gallons of fuel exploded, incinerating all. Flight 93's thirty-three passengers and seven crew sacrificed their lives preventing an even greater disaster since it is strongly believed that the intended target was the Capitol building. I think about all of us on Capitol Hill who also could have been lost, about the possible destruction of the Capitol building itself impacting the image and standing of our nation on the world stage.

Rosalyn and I and several friends traveled to Shanksville to pay our respects to those who are memorialized there in their final resting places. We stood at a low wall at the field's edge, a hundred yards from the crater dug by the doomed plane as it plowed into the earth. I placed a small replica of the *Statue of Freedom*, one that stood in my Capitol building office on that horrific day, into a small wall niche. We lit memorial candles and offered our silent prayers.

At the 2015 dedication of the new Flight 93 Memorial Visitor Center, designed by Paul Murdoch

Figure 8.2. Wall niche at Flight 93 Memorial. Courtesy of Alan M. Hantman

Architects, the National Park Service invited me to speak about my 9/11 experiences at the Capitol to let the families know their loved ones' bravery saved so many lives and the Capitol building itself.

The Families

Rosalyn and I were honored to meet Flight 93 families at a luncheon following the dedication ceremonies that day. The mother of flight attendant CeeCee Ross Lyles shared photos of the bronze monument created in Lyles's memory and passionately described the memorial ceremony and the visits of schoolchildren to their hometown of Fort Pierce, Florida. Lyles's mother had chosen to honor her daughter at the crash site to be in the presence of the other families.

The voicemail Lyles left for her husband, Lorne, relives the tense moments of the counterattack being planned by the passengers and crew members. She and another flight attendant boiled water to scald the hijackers. The recording of her voice, clear and

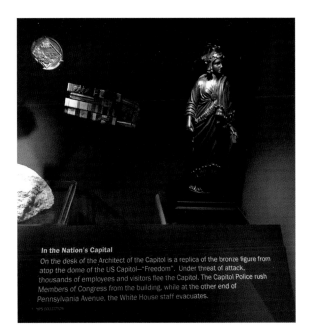

In the Nation's Capital
On the desk of the Architect of the Capitol is a replica of the bronze figure from atop the dome of the US Capitol—"Freedom". Under threat of attack, thousands of employees and visitors flee the Capitol. The Capitol Police rush Members of Congress from the building, while at the other end of Pennsylvania Avenue, the White House staff evacuates.
NPS COLLECTION

Figure 8.3. *Statue of Freedom* displayed at Flight 93 Visitor Center. Courtesy of Alan M. Hantman

strong, can be heard at the Flight 93 Visitor Center: "I hope to be able to see your face again, baby. I love you. Goodbye."[5]

At a remembrance ceremony later that evening, Deborah Borza spoke of the loss of her daughter, Deora Frances Bodley, a twenty-five-year-old college student returning to school in California after visiting friends in New Jersey. Borza was told about her daughter's death while in church and recounted how the strength she derived from the three hundred loving members of her congregation had sustained her.

A procession began at Memorial Plaza just before dusk. A family member or representative of each lost hero carried an illuminated lantern in their honor, walking in slow, silent procession, each separated by three paces, punctuating each person's painful loss. A seemingly endless row of 2,937 candles lit the processional pathway, one for each of the innocents killed at the World Trade Center, at the Pentagon, and in Shanksville. This runway of glowing candles was protected by translucent containers shielding them from night breezes as the solemn procession

approached the memorial wall. The bearers placed their lanterns at the foot of eight-foot-high stone slabs inscribed with the name of each hero. The clear, cool night enveloped us all. Candles flickered in honor and memory of the souls lost on 9/11 in this Pennsylvania countryside. No words were spoken. None were needed. Each September 11, Rosalyn and I return to Shanksville on 9/11 to pay our respects.

God Bless America

On the evening of September 11, 2001, two hundred members of Congress gathered for a hastily called press conference on the Capitol's East Front Rotunda stairway. Instead of attending a Capitol Visitor Center media event and fundraising dinner originally scheduled for that evening, I stood at the East Front Capitol steps as a bipartisan group of senators and representatives gathered before the world in a rare sense of unity, proclaiming that the United States of America could not be intimidated, that we would stand up to murderous terrorism.

House Speaker Dennis Hastert emphatically stated: "When America suffers, and people perpetrate acts against this country, we as a Congress and a government stand together to fight this evil threat. Those who brought forth this evil deed will pay the price."

We observed a long moment of silence. I teared up as I joined with members of Congress singing "God Bless America," and was keenly aware of the privilege of returning home that day, of safely driving back up North Capitol Street only because of those who had sacrificed their lives and come to rest in Shanksville, Pennsylvania.

In the days following 9/11, the DC Army National Guard was mobilized around the Capitol building and the city of Washington. According to their newsletter, "Task Force Capital Guardian, consisting of 100 soldiers, was called on by the US Congress to provide perimeter security on the Capitol grounds. Their mission was to help police secure the restricted area around the Capitol. It was the first time since the 1968 Washington riots, following the Dr. Martin Luther King Jr. assassination, that the DC National Guard was called to protect the Capitol Grounds."[6]

The streets of Washington were deserted. Soldiers with assault rifles were stationed at virtually every Capitol street intersection, and we established new vehicle inspection checkpoints on the sections of Constitution and Independence Avenues that cut across Capitol Hill. Few tourists traveled to Washington or visited the Capitol due to the heightened security, and this seriously affected business at hotels and restaurants. Eleanor Holmes Norton, the DC delegate, urged me and the other members of the Capitol Police Board to provide greater public access to Capitol Hill buildings while still providing complete security. This was impossible in the aftermath of 9/11 without first fully reevaluating security provisions.

Congressional staffers were anxious and expressed concerns about their personal safety, questioning whether they should continue working in Capitol Hill buildings that were targets of terrorism. Over time, Congress appropriated funds for a variety of new security installations, including steel bollards to create a vehicular stand-off perimeter, the reinforcement of historic walls, and new vehicle access barriers. We closed sections of streets bordering the House and Senate office buildings to public use and constructed new granite traffic islands to channel vehicular flow.

Freedom Without Fortresses

Long before 9/11, the nation debated how architecture, engineering, and urban design decisions should respond to potential terrorism. In the decades since, there has been substantial agreement on basic physical security elements, including improvement of structural systems, methods of public communication and egress, detection, alarm and suppression systems, filtration systems, and the use of laminated safety glass. Many building codes have

been revised and others will continue to be examined and upgraded. With persistent occurrences of worldwide terrorism and security threats raised to new levels with the appalling specter of domestic mob terrorism threatening our very democracy, it is obvious that consensus on security measures will become more difficult to achieve.

Two months after the 9/11 attacks, in November 2001, these security issues were debated at a symposium entitled Freedom Without Fortresses, held at the National Building Museum in Washington, DC. Daniel Patrick Moynihan, who had recently retired after serving in the Senate for twenty-four years, was the keynote speaker.

Moynihan made significant contributions over the course of forty years toward the transformation of Pennsylvania Avenue into a grand connection between the White House and Capitol Hill. In 1962 Moynihan wrote a proposal for President John F. Kennedy for the redesign of Pennsylvania Avenue. He also prepared guidelines on federal architecture that became the General Services Administration's Design Excellence Program for its national portfolio of federal buildings, a program that has significantly improved the quality of federal buildings nationwide.

The symposium proceedings quoted Moynihan: "architecture is inescapably a political art, and it reports faithfully for ages to come what the political values of a particular age were. Surely ours must be openness and fearlessness in the face of those who hide in the darkness. A precaution, yes, sequester, no."[7]

Other senators wanted to close off the Capitol Hill campus to all exterior vehicular traffic and implement some version of the 1987 Whips Plan to fence in the Capitol. At the symposium, security concerns were also voiced about the Senate gallery regarding the installation of glass barriers to prevent visitors from physical contact with senators below. I noted Moynihan's statement favoring precautions but not sequester.

Security concerns also forced the cancelation of countless events, among them a nascent program

Rosalyn initiated that Delegate Eleanor Holmes Norton supported. Administrators of Anacostia High School and Cesar Chavez Charter School had worked out an agreement with the US Capitol Historical Society, with the support of the clerk of the House and the secretary of the Senate on behalf of their respective chambers, for students to be involved in a pilot program that would prepare them to assist tour guides in the Capitol. Rosalyn recalled that Anacostia High School's administrator declared "the Anacostia River separating our students in southeast Washington from the Capitol might as well be an ocean," since her students, living in the shadow of the Capitol Dome, seldom crossed that river and had little connection to the federal government so close to their homes.[8]

Impact on Visitor Center: New Legislation

The September 11 attacks rekindled security concerns raised more than three years earlier in the aftermath of the 1998 murders of Officer J.J. Chestnut and Detective John Gibson. Memories of those tragedies were fading, and support for a new security-based visitor center had waned, but 9/11 decreased the political risk of using appropriated funds for the design and construction of the center. Speaker Gingrich knew the project would be significantly delayed if funds had to be raised through private sources, so the Campaign for Democracy's Front Door, spearheaded by Senator John Glenn, was shut down.

Chair James Walsh was no longer concerned about potential political criticism if his House Appropriations Subcommittee supported funding for the Capitol Visitor Center. Virtually unanimous bipartisan, bicameral support was now assured.

Congress now worked to create a form of terrorism insurance to protect airlines from liability lawsuits if they were hijacked and for construction contractors if terrorists once again struck buildings. The Department of Homeland Security was created under the Homeland Security Act of 2002 to oversee and coordinate more than twenty separate offices and agencies related to homeland security issues, including the Coast Guard, Secret Service, and immigration agencies.

HOMELAND SECURITY SHORTCOMINGS

Ninety senators voted for the Homeland Security Act, including former Senator Barbara Boxer of California. According to her official website, Boxer "has made improving homeland security one of her top priorities. Senator Boxer wrote the law to allow pilots to carry guns in the cockpit . . . [and] authored the provision of the 2001 Aviation Security Law to require that air marshals fly on high risk flights."[9] But in the wake of the death of George Floyd in police custody in May 2020 and the actions Homeland Security forces used to put down ensuing largely peaceful First Amendment protests in Washington, DC's Farragut Square and in Portland, Oregon, Boxer now regrets her Homeland Security Act vote: "There was no protection built into this bill to stop a power hungry president from misusing a powerful federal police force, hidden in disparate agencies, controlled by one agency head. . . . No federal agency should be roaming the streets of America in unmarked vehicles and unmarked uniforms, arresting people exercising their constitutional right to free speech. That's called kidnapping, and it's what dictatorships do. . . . I never thought that the Department of Homeland Security would be used against our own people."[10]

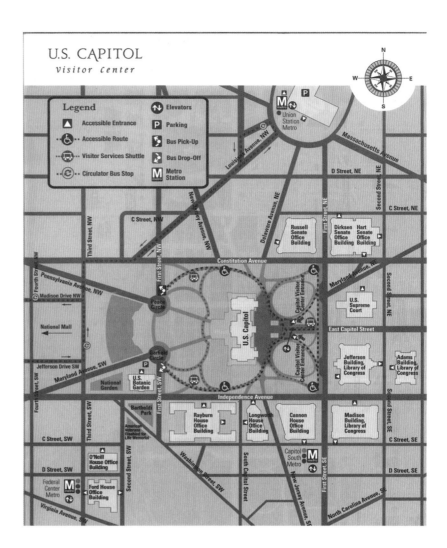

Figure 8.4. Capitol Hill area. Courtesy of Architect of the Capitol

Interface with the City of Washington

Cooperation between the City of Washington, DC, and Capitol Hill is critical to both entities. The National Mall is defined by the district's two major east–west avenues, Constitution Avenue on the north and Independence Avenue on the south. Both avenues run through the Capitol Precinct, where they are under the operating control of the US Capitol Police. They are closed off during high-security events such as presidential inaugurals and State of the Union addresses. After 9/11, there was much discussion about closing these streets permanently for all but limited access, even though this would have

a serious impact on traffic flow throughout the city proper.

It was decided instead to permanently close several secondary streets in front of House and Senate office buildings and the Capitol while allowing critical traffic to flow through the Capitol Precinct under Capitol Police monitoring.

We designed a new security perimeter around the Capitol complex to protect against car and truck bombs since some 80 percent of terrorist actions worldwide occur that way. We eliminated unsightly and ineffective sewer pipes and concrete highway barriers around Capitol Hill buildings and replaced them with a coordinated system of bollards, traffic roundabouts, new walls, and reinforced historic walls, all supported by an enhanced Capitol Police presence. This perimeter minimizes negative visual and physical obstructions on Capitol Hill while creating a more pedestrian-friendly and accessible area. The public could still walk on Capitol grounds, celebrate presidential inaugurals, attend tree lightings, enjoy a sandwich in the gardens at Bartholdi Park, tour the Capitol, visit a member of Congress, or mark the passing of a president in the Capitol Rotunda.

The visitor center's design was based on balancing security imperatives with a sense of openness and accessibility required of a democratic society. I cannot imagine any major building project having a site in a more security-sensitive location than one right next to the fully operational Capitol building. Security requirements for all construction workers included background checks and time-consuming daily security screenings. Each construction vehicle entering the site—and there were more than sixty thousand—was screened remotely for the duration of our project.

Another Attack—This Time Bioterrorism

The 9/11 trauma hung heavily over Capitol Hill. Buildings were closed to the public, and staffers spoke of the risks of working on the Hill. Few tourists visited. Just weeks later, on October 15, 2001, Grant Leslie, an intern for Senator Tom Daschle in the Hart Senate Office Building, opened an envelope from the senator's daily pile of letters and found a handwritten note along with a fine white powder that spilled onto her desk and clothing. It was soon determined to be a virulent dose of anthrax spores. The note read:

09-11-01
YOU CAN NOT STOP US.
WE HAVE THIS ANTHRAX
YOU DIE NOW
ARE YOU AFRAID?

DEATH TO AMERICA
DEATH TO ISRAEL
ALLAH IS GREAT.

The return address on the envelope mailed to Senator Daschle was "4th Grade, Greendale School, Franklin Park, NJ 08852."[11]

Capitol attending physician Rear Admiral John Eisold and his attending staff quarantined the Hart Senate Office Building and immediately tested members and staff with nasal swabs and provided sixty-day prescriptions of the antibiotic Cipro. A second letter was mailed to Senator Patrick Leahy of Vermont, chair of the Senate Judiciary Committee, but it was safely transferred unopened to a research lab for investigation.

This attack followed a series of anthrax letters received a month earlier by the *New York Post* and NBC News. American Media in Florida, publishers of the *National Enquirer*, also received letters laced with anthrax, and Bob Stevens, a photo editor with American Media, died of anthrax inhalation on October 5, 2001, the first recorded anthrax death in a quarter century.

Investigators retraced the mail delivery carts from Daschle's office back to the freight elevator, to the Dirksen Senate Office Building mailroom, to other mailrooms in the Ford House Office Building, and the Washington, DC, Brentwood Post Office, where two postal workers later died. Thirty-six other post offices that received mail from Brentwood for local Washington, DC, distribution were tested, and more than ten thousand postal employees received precautionary antibiotics.

On Capitol Hill, eleven suites in Hart ultimately showed traces of anthrax, as did mailrooms in the Dirksen Senate Office Building and several House office buildings.

The Capitol Police Board: A Three-Legged Stool

Members of the Capitol Police Board were not always of the same mind. The board oversees the 2,200-member US Capitol Police Department, which is responsible for the security of Congress, staff, visitors, and the general public on the Capitol Hill campus. The Police Board chairmanship rotates each year between the House and Senate. Bill Livingood, the House sergeant at arms, was a thirty-three-year veteran of the US Secret Service, and his perspective was shaped by his career as a security professional. Greg Casey was serving as Senate sergeant at arms when I was first appointed architect. He was a creative problem-solver and a political appointee of Senate Majority Leader Trent Lott. Each Sergeant owed his primary loyalty to his respective chamber.

The Architect of the Capitol, as an officer of the Congress, is the only member of the Capitol Police Board who serves both bodies of the Congress and is the third leg of the board, committed to balancing security and openness and maintaining an overall sense of accessibility and welcome.

Daschle had risen to Senate majority leader several months before the anthrax attack when Senator Jim Jeffords of Vermont left the Republican Party and became an Independent who caucused with the Democrats, giving them the majority. Daschle selected a new Senate sergeant at arms, retired US Army major general Alfonso E. Lenhardt. This occurred one week before 9/11, with the anthrax attack coming just weeks later, an unenviable welcome for General Lenhardt as he assumed his new responsibilities on Capitol Hill.

As the new chair of the board, Lenhardt quickly appointed an independent incident commander and called for immediate support from the Environmental Protection Agency (EPA), the federal agency responsible for the removal of hazardous substances. Under the EPA's Superfund program, other federal agencies including the Center for Disease Control and Prevention (CDC), the Federal Emergency Management Agency, the Federal Bureau of Investigation, and elements of the US Coast Guard were activated to assist. The EPA fund supported each organization as well as contractors and expert consultants. All quickly descended on Capitol Hill, joining the Capitol Police in our investigation and remediation efforts.

Within forty-eight hours, we evacuated fifty senators with offices in the Hart Building, while the other fifty senators remained in the Dirksen and Russell Senate Office Buildings. In the Capitol, Hastert had also received a letter laced with anthrax, but fortunately it had remained unopened.

Senators and their staffs moved into cramped quarters and hideaways in the Capitol and to office spaces shared with the General Accounting Office, a congressional agency with offices a short distance from Capitol Hill.

Modular office buildings located directly across from the Capitol Police Headquarters now became the Incident Command Center, overflowing with staff from more than a dozen federal agencies and supporting contractors. Tents were also erected on Massachusetts Avenue and D Street Northeast to provide more space and establish an orderly chain of command. We could not, however, use space in any occupied building that had received mail since it would therefore be at risk.

A Glass Palace as Incident Command Center

When the attack occurred, my agency had just completed a three-year gut renovation, restoration, and expansion of the US Botanic Garden Conservatory, a historic neoclassical revival national treasure built in 1933 at the southwest corner of Capitol Hill. This was the only Capitol Hill building that had not received mail because its plant collection was still being reinstalled and the building was not yet open to the public.

I recommended using the conservatory as the Incident Command Center to supplement the temporary modules and tents. We borrowed office furniture by the truckload from unoccupied government office space in nearby Crystal City, Virginia, and amid Royal Palm trees and flourishing exotic plantings, the conservatory became a sylvan, ecologically correct center for our bioterrorism experts. Another problem arose, however, as all of these efforts had become so time-consuming, they negatively affected the operations of the Senate, and to a lesser degree the House of Representatives. The Capitol Police Board, the Environmental Protection Agency, and its team of federal agencies and consultants accelerated our efforts, working around the clock to investigate, analyze, and solve problems while working to control expenditures. But experience should have taught us that, when politics is involved, no positive initiative goes unpunished.

On March 6, 2002, the Senate Committee on Finance put out a press release:

> Sen. Chuck Grassley (R-IA), ranking member of the Committee on Finance, has learned the cost of cleaning the anthrax from the Hart Senate Office Building and other Capitol Hill Buildings is already at more than $23 million, and the tab is still running, according to the Environmental Protection Agency (EPA). "That's a lot of money," Grassley said. "Unfortunately, the EPA's response is so lacking in context and answers to all my questions that it's difficult for the taxpayers to judge whether their money was used properly. The EPA's work to make the Hart building safe is important, but so is a full accounting of how the agency handled the cost. I plan to learn more about the details of the project."

Grassley directed GAO auditors to investigate the EPA, including details on "how each contractor was paid, whether by the hour, per task, or per contract, and details about food, housing and transportation costs."[12]

The GAO's 2003 report stated that the EPA alone had committed 150 staff to the cleanup as well as fifty "on scene coordinators" pulled from nine regional offices who oversaw "the contractors during shifts that ran twenty-four hours a day, seven days a week, for about three months." The report also said the "EPA used ten of its existing competitively awarded supply and security contracts for additional support." The minor sole-source contracts had been authorized because "the emergency situation created the urgent and compelling need to obtain services and supplies without going through the generally more time-consuming competitive bidding process."[13]

The EPA's ability to quickly address evolving needs during this still-developing emergency was critical to its safe and successful resolution. Responding to Grassley's requests took several more months, but unfortunately, it appeared that quickly resolving unique life-threatening emergencies takes a back seat to more standard bureaucratic accounting and operating procedures. Grassley noted that because it was Lenhardt who had called in the EPA, the major general must also be the one to justify the rising costs of the remediation project and his role in overseeing it.

Had our remediation team followed normal procurement and approval processes, the crisis would have affected the Senate for far longer than the three months it did. Capitol Police spokesman Lieutenant Dan Nichols properly assessed the situation when he said that our bottom line was to insure public safety, and that it cost what it cost.

Grassley has served in the Congress since 1975, three terms in the House, and in 2022 was elected to serve an eighth term in the Senate. When I see power residing in the same individual for such a great number of years, I believe Newt Gingrich had it right in his 1994 *Contract with America* when he committed to term limits, after which House Republicans brought a constitutional amendment for a floor vote to limit members of the House to six two-year terms and Senate members to two six-year terms. The bill did not receive a two-thirds majority then, and there currently does not appear to be any real interest in the term-limit concept in the House or the Senate. In 1811 Thomas Jefferson wrote, "there is a fullness of time when men should go, and not occupy too long the ground to which others have a right to advance."[14]

Earlier, on October 20, 2001, Daschle reported on the status of the investigation on the Senate floor: "It has been ten days now since the letter containing anthrax was opened in my office in the Hart Building. We now have the final results on all the nasal swabs collected by the attending physician's office. Of the more than 6,000 swabs, 28 were positive for exposure."[15]

Attending physician Eisold and his team of navy doctors proactively administered a sixty-day course of Cipro to more than four hundred people. "As for the buildings," Daschle continued, "the Capitol itself has been open all week for official business. After virtually around the clock environmental testing, a number of other buildings in the Capitol complex have begun reopening.... We are looking at the most appropriate way with which to remediate the Hart Building."[16]

The Hart Senate Office Building, designed by John Carl Warnecke, was constructed under my predecessor, George White, and first occupied in 1982. Its modern, hard-edged design was faced in three-inch-thick white Vermont marble and built abutting the neoclassical Dirksen Senate Office Building. Even though the two buildings' floor levels do not align, they are connected by corridors, ramps, and stairways, permitting staffers to walk between them. Together these joined buildings fill the entire long block just south of Constitution Avenue, with the single exception of the historic Sewall-Belmont building that houses the National Women's Party and its Museum of the Women's Suffrage Movement. Fortunately, Sewall-Belmont remained free of anthrax contamination.

The continuing fallout from 9/11 and the expanding anthrax investigation and remediation process under way put enormous pressure on Daschle and Lenhardt to resolve the crisis and permit senators to resume normal operations in their offices.

Lenhardt was impatient. He wanted Architect of the Capitol employees to seal off the connections between the buildings immediately so Dirksen could be occupied while Hart underwent major remediation work. Our employees had already used remote radio communications to guide Centers for Disease Control workers clad in high-level personal protective equipment to locate a safe with keys to Hart Building offices locked by evacuating occupants. CDC workers bagged and removed thousands of samples for off-site remediation procedures. This included important Senate papers and personal items from Senate offices that were potentially contaminated. All of these items were safely returned at the conclusion of the operation.

Eisold, Lenhardt, and I met in a conservatory office to discuss sealing off the Hart Building. The sergeant at arms pressed to immediately seal it off so it could be safely fumigated. This was a reasonable request since Architect of the Capitol personnel in our construction division had high levels of safety training and could suit up in rated personal protective equipment (PPE). Because of the high risk, though, I asked Dr. Eisold to administer Cipro to our employees just as hundreds of Senate staffers had already been protected. As we discussed my concerns, Lenhardt demanded, "After two weeks, we know everything we are going to know about the anthrax contamination and where it is. The experts told us that it can't be aerosolized and spread to the locations your people have to work in. You need to get them in there now! This is a failure in leadership!" He then stormed out of the office.

Lenhardt's demand for immediate action was based on preliminary assumptions that would have jeopardized my staff's safety. Experts soon determined the attack used a highly processed form of anthrax that had indeed been aerosolized. More than two trillion spores had been released, and to their surprise, it was far more dangerous and widespread than initially assumed. In 2005 the National Academy of Sciences Board on Life Sciences issued a report entitled "Reopening Public Facilities after a Biological Attack." Its key message was: "After the 2001 anthrax attacks, decision makers sometimes relied on assumptions that later proved unfounded; their subsequent actions resulted in significant

Figure 8.5. Hart Building open atrium with Alexander Calder's sculpture *Mountains and Clouds*. Courtesy of Architect of the Capitol

problems with communicating the degree of risk involved to the stakeholders."[17]

Fortunately, Eisold agreed to provide the Cipro. My agency's construction staff, suited up in personal protective equipment, entered the vacated buildings with their tools and materials, including sheets of plywood, rolls of plastic, and two-by-four studs, and successfully sealed off the Hart Building, preparing it for fumigation by the CDC. If they had not received that precautionary drug, they would have been at serious risk from the aerosolized anthrax.

How Best to Fumigate Hart

The US Botanic Garden Conservatory was at the heart of the process, with one side gallery functioning as a conference room where most major decisions were made. Anthrax trails were also found in House office buildings, including the Rayburn,

Longworth, Cannon, and Ford buildings. Four offices in the Longworth Building tested positive for traces of anthrax, and spaces in the Ford Building had to undergo a series of air sampling and decontamination cycles due to movement of people in the trail of the anthrax letters.

Thousands of samples were brought to off-site laboratories to determine the most appropriate method of remediation. We soon understood that this form of aerosolized anthrax could not be neutralized by normal cleanup methods such as HEPA vacuuming or disinfecting foam. The problem was far more complicated and required a solution that had never been used on a building-wide scale. After thorough testing, chlorine dioxide in its gaseous form was determined to be the best alternative. Sabre Technical Services, an EPA consultant, was to pump this gas into the Hart Building after determining the right concentration, contact time, temperature, and relative humidity. The Hart Building was to become a beta test case.

Sabre had to first determine how to inject the gas safely into a nine-story, ten-million-cubic-foot building. The gas had to be safely pumped in sufficient concentrations to reach all potentially contaminated surfaces while making sure this poisonous gas didn't leak out of the building and into the surrounding neighborhood. The EPA's fumigation contractors would not begin work without indemnification against potential liability. As assurance the gas would not escape from the Hart Building, we erected a meteorological tower to actively monitor ambient air for chlorine dioxide. Possible methods of gas injection were studied, with the decision ultimately made to construct barriers inside the ductwork to isolate contaminated areas before fumigation could begin. The goal was to remediate 99.99 percent of the contaminate.

Once fumigation was completed, extensive sampling of offices and the heating, ventilating, and air conditioning systems was performed, demonstrating that the process had been highly effective. The Environmental Clearance Committee was assembled to review findings and had to vote unani-

mously before the Hart Building could be cleared for habitation.

Carpeting and furniture had been damaged, and Daschle's entire suite of offices was gutted and stripped of all furniture and furnishings, down to bare walls and floors. Three months after the anthrax letter was opened, the Hart Senate Office Building was reopened, and the US Botanic Garden was returned to the architect's office to prepare for the conservatory's grand public opening. On January 23, 2002, the *Baltimore Sun* reported,

> The Hart Senate Office Building, which had been sealed for months as an anthrax hot zone, reopened yesterday like a time capsule. . . . Bagged lunches awaited their owners, moldy in office refrigerators. Long lost jackets and dress shoes sat at desks. Calendars were frozen on October 17, the last day that workers had occupied their offices. . . . "Look what I found," said Carrie Markey, an asst. to Sen. Harry Reid, a Nevada Democrat. In her hand was a note: "Make X-Mas list."[18]

Christmas had come and gone on Capitol Hill, and Congress had managed to work through a period of great risk and inconvenience. Most importantly, no one on the Hill, no one connected to the Congress or Capitol Police, no one on the investigation and remediation teams, and no one in the surrounding neighborhood was injured during the process. Fortunately, everyone who swabbed positive for anthrax at the beginning of the process received Cipro, and none were infected.

Opening the Botanic Garden Conservatory

The anthrax attack delayed the opening of the restored Botanic Garden Conservatory for almost two months. A team mobilized from several sections of our agency then reinstalled the stored exotic trees and plants throughout the greenhouse structures. The conservatory now provides code-compliant life-safety conditions and a state-of-the-art auto-

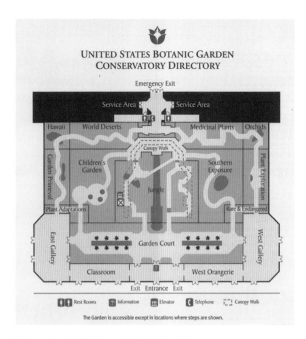

Figure 8.6. US Botanic Garden Conservatory directory. Courtesy of Architect of the Capitol

mated environmental control system that creates ideal conditions for four thousand plants by monitoring the weather, controlling a misting system that adjusts humidity, and operating retractable shades that help manage temperature and light.

The *New York Times* described the conservatory as "DC's Other, Calmer Hothouse" and reported that "an atmosphere of hope and renewal surrounded the United States Botanic Garden this week, as the newly renovated conservatory flung open its doors on Tuesday to a public hungry for the healing power of plants."[19]

More than a million visitors annually enjoy the living plants, exhibits, workshops, lectures, and courses offered at the conservatory. Kindergarteners are shepherded from gallery to gallery with their clipboards and pencils on treasure hunts, checking off each special plant as they find it, and other schoolchildren attend the annual Hands-On Plant Science program. Adults of all ages continue to learn about the great diversity of these ecologies on display, all enjoying the tranquility of this special place in the heart of the city.

Who Did It?

The Department of Justice did not release its Amerithrax Investigative Summary until February 19, 2010. This report described a seven-year task force investigation involving the coordinated efforts of the FBI, the Department of Justice, and the US Postal Inspection Service to determine the source of the anthrax used in the 2001 attacks. According to the department's report, "By 2007, investigators conclusively determined that a single spore-batch created and maintained by Dr. Bruce E. Ivins at the United States Army Medical Research Institute of Infectious Diseases was the parent material for the letter spores."[20]

The handwritten note accompanying the anthrax was intended to throw investigators off Ivins's trail while sowing religious and political dissension. Finally, in 2008, an indictment was sought, "charging Dr. Ivins with Use of a Weapon of Mass Destruction. . . . Aware of the FBI investigation and the prospect of being indicted, Dr. Ivins took an overdose of over-the-counter medications on or about July 26, 2008 and died on July 29, 2008."[21]

The fallout from the anthrax attacks continues to reverberate among security and infectious disease professionals. This attack on Capitol Hill had an enormous impact on the design, configuration, and complexity of the Capitol Visitor Center's mechanical and filtration systems. Intensive design reviews by federal experts dictated major changes for the center, significantly affecting schedule and cost in our effort to ensure Capitol Hill life-safety and security in the face of new bioterrorism risks.

Immediate Visitor Center Security and Life-Safety Changes

The 9/11 and anthrax attacks led to reviews and evaluations of construction codes nationwide. On Capitol Hill we performed in-depth security and life-safety reviews of our already completed construction drawings.

MORE LIFE-SAFETY RISKS: COVID-19 AND CONGRESS

In order to respond to a range of possible biohazard and other life-safety risks in the future, Capitol officials can effectively move forward only with the support of Congress. According to the *Washington Post*, that support was missing when the COVID-19 pandemic hit Capitol Hill, since testing was not "mandatory for lawmakers and staff."[22]

When many employees of the Capitol Police, staff members of the Architect of the Capitol, and its contractors tested positive for COVID-19, J. Brett Blanton, 12th Architect of the Capitol, required that his employees wear masks. But without a comprehensive mask requirement for everyone on the Hill, along with mandatory and frequent testing, the best efforts of the architect were clearly not sufficient to stop the spread of the virus. Representative Susan Wild (D-PA) told the *Washington Post* that during the January 6 insurrection, she was evacuated along with three hundred to four hundred others to a "crowded" location. "About half the people in the room are not wearing masks, even though they've been offered surgical masks," Wild said. "They've refused to wear them. . . . We weren't even allowed to get together with our families for Thanksgiving and Christmas, and now we're in a room with people who are flaunting the rules."[23]

"If you were to design a way of quickly spreading COVID-19 throughout the country," the *Post* article continued, "Capitol Hill could be the ideal scenario. . . . Many members of Congress still do not regularly wear masks. Then they go home, usually without being tested on arrival at the Capitol or at departure. . . . Congress can act swiftly to mitigate health threats, just as members and staff were quickly protected after letters containing anthrax were mailed to congressional offices in 2001."

In 2022, after two years of the epidemic, the Omicron variant of the virus led to a new infection peak. The *New York Times* reported, "Just when it seemed the atmosphere on Capitol Hill could not get worse, Omicron came to town. At least 129 House members and senators have announced a coronavirus infection since the outset of the pandemic, nearly a quarter of the lawmakers in Congress." But still, despite two representatives dying after contracting COVID, lawmakers on the right still refuse to wear masks as others fear for their health. The House sergeant at arms, William J. Walker, said that during House floor votes, "I see people—members, staff—without masks. I'll walk up to them and ask them to put the mask on. Some just walk away from me."[24] It is impossible for those who serve the Congress on Capitol Hill to help control the spread of the COVID pandemic or any future infectious disease or biological threat without congressional cooperation and mutual concern for one another's well-being.

After our reviews with government security groups, we relocated mechanical room air intakes from stone structures designed for the East Front lawn to a more secure location. This kicked off a series of meetings and presentations with House and Senate leadership to explain the need for these changes and the requirement to take more space in the Capitol. Only with their agreement could we begin to redesign the air shafts, heating, ventilating, and air conditioning systems, which were all major revisions to our construction documents.

Of concern to a number of senators were their private hideaway offices in the Capitol. On November 20, 2002, *Roll Call* reported that "at least ten Senators will be forced to vacate their hideaways on the Capitol's East Front in the coming months to make way for the ongoing construction of the 580,000-square-foot visitor center."[25]

Senate and House leadership worked with us as we determined the amount of Capitol space necessary for connections between buildings. We fully supported the efforts of the US Capitol Police, the Defense Threat Reduction Agency, and other external federal security authorities as they called for significant project changes to further strengthen security and life-safety measures. Senate Sergeant at Arms Terrance W. Gainer, who was chief of Capitol Police for four years during the course of the project, was quoted in the *Washington Post* in March 2007: "The design morphed with the evolving threats."

Gainer continued to wonder what someone would want to do ten years from now and how prepared we would be for that. "How would an enemy penetrate?" he asked, and "What would he bring in? How would he attack? We played each one of those scenarios out. We were unmerciful in our demands and requests. . . . Any threat that was coming up, we wanted to make sure that we could counter. . . . I think we added to the time and cost, much to the chagrin of the architect."[26]

While significant threat scenarios were played out by the Capitol Police in 2004 and 2005, they did not include plans to counter the threat of thousands of insurrectionists attacking the Capitol from all sides. Nor did they include plans to assure a streamlined approval process for timely mutual assistance between the Capitol Police and its law enforcement partners. It appears that the separation of powers between the executive and legislative branches of government led to a time-consuming chain of approval on January 6, 2021, before necessary executive branch assistance could be dispatched with authorization to access Capitol grounds.

In the wake of the 2021 insurrection, House Speaker Nancy Pelosi established Task Force 1-6 to identify "actions or decisions that could be taken immediately or in the near term to improve the security of the Capitol, Members and staff." One of the task force's findings was there were too few trained Capitol Police intelligence officers as liaison to the Joint Terrorism Task Force and other law enforcement organizations to receive and analyze threats.[27] Two years after the insurrection, former Capitol Police chief Steven A. Sund was quoted as writing, "'The security and information sharing policies and mandates put in place after September 11 failed miserably on January 6,' warning that it could easily happen again and that 'The biggest intelligence failure was within my department.'"[28] If more trained analysts had been in place during visitor center planning, it is likely that additional security changes would have been required, not only for the center, but for the Capitol itself and the wider Capitol Hill complex.

Congress's Future Space Needs Become Immediate

At the time of the 9/11 and anthrax attacks, we were preparing to release the visitor center construction drawings for competitive bids. The scope of work for the future House and Senate expansion spaces included only the outer shell consisting of concrete foundations, walls and the roof formed by the plaza above. But both chambers recognized that post 9/11 security changes created an opportunity to add large amounts of finished space to the project, not for visitor center functions, but for congressional use. Appropriating funds for these major additions during normal times would have been politically risky, but in the context of the security emergency, these major scope additions were added to the visitor center project with little controversy.

What had been "future" expansion space became an immediate need when Congress directed me to expand the project to include the complete design and build-out of eighty-five thousand square feet of space for the House of Representatives and

Figure 8.7. Skylight and circular stairs in both Senate and House expansion spaces. Courtesy of Michael McCann

another eighty-five thousand square feet for the Senate. A further complication of this major change was that these new spaces were not to be designed for standard office usage but rather as flexible meeting rooms for both chambers, including a two-story-high House hearing room, which all carried a more restrictive public assembly code classification. Accommodating this in an underground high-security building required the addition of more complex life-safety, exiting, and electromechanical provisions.

We went back to the drawing boards to design what are essentially two new eighty-five-thousand-square-foot buildings with all the planning, design, approvals, and construction this required. When these expansion areas are considered, along with the Congressional Auditorium and its meeting rooms, circulation areas, and support areas, half of the project now consisted of areas dedicated to House and Senate use, rather than visitor-related areas. This ninth expansion of the Capitol could just as appro-

Figure 8.8. House expansion two-story hearing room. Courtesy of Michael McCann

priately be renamed the House and Senate Meeting Center instead of the Capitol Visitor Center.

Construction Methodology: Design-Bid-Build

The Government Accountability Office had reported that experiences on previous Capitol Hill projects demonstrated that in order to minimize conflict among multiple subcontractors, it was best to prepare and bid a single set of construction drawings. With this design-bid-build single general contractor method, we could carefully control the Capitol Visitor Center's smooth integration into the Capitol building. We could also minimize disruptions to Congress's ongoing daily work and more

efficiently manage security and day-to-day congressional oversight.

By the time of the 9/11 attack, project changes and extended review periods had already caused a seven-month delay. We now had no time to revise the full set of drawings yet again, and still put it out for bids in time to meet the deadline of the next presidential inaugural in 2005. We were forced to do exactly what the GAO report had warned against—split our single-phased design-bid-build process into two separate construction projects.

Our excavation and foundation drawings were almost complete on September 11, and we now repackaged and bid that scope of work as a new first phase, Sequence 1. Our goal was to begin excavation and foundation construction while incorporating new post-9/11 security requirements throughout the evolving building design. We would then separately bid the electromechanical and architectural finishes as a second phase, Sequence 2.

Our newly compressed schedule called for the first contractor to complete its foundation work just as we awarded the second contract in order to minimize on-site construction conflicts. Coordinating the work of several contractors on the same site at the same time was enormously challenging because it involved preventing them from interfering with and delaying one another.

Unfortunately, the Washington, DC, region had many major construction projects under way at this time. This complicated the bidding process, since few qualified construction workers were available. Our constricted schedule also meant that few general contractors were willing to bid, and those who did would not commit to the tight schedule.

We worked with the Congress during the same period to determine what programmatic uses they wanted housed in the House and Senate's new expansion spaces. We then designed those spaces, prepared construction documents, and bid the two eighty-five-thousand-square-foot additions. This became a third set of construction documents that had to be completed at the same time as the overall project since fire, life-safety, communications, and security systems had to be interconnected throughout the greatly expanded building. Yet each part of the project had to be released for competitive bid at different times and built under three separate contracts. Our plan to initiate a conventional design and construction project was dead. Each of the potential problems the 1981 GAO report identified as risks with multiphase projects now began to play out in real time.

Stringent Capitol Police background checks further constricted the already limited pool of qualified workers available in all necessary construction trades. Many were denied clearances due to past infractions, including driving while intoxicated and even marital disputes. A construction management firm was needed to help monitor and coordinate

these multiple contractors since my agency did not have sufficient staff to add these major projects to our existing Capitol Hill workload. I retained the General Services Administration to run the selection process since I anticipated that members of Congress might challenge the results of this process if their home state constituent firms were not selected. GSA's involvement assured we could successfully withstand such objections.

GSA recommended Gilbane, Inc., of Providence, Rhode Island, with Paul J. Choquette Jr., its president, as our key contact person. Senators did question this award, demanding proof that the process had been fair. GSA's assistance, along with agency's documentation, made the selection easy to support.

Cutting the Baby in Thirds

We competitively awarded the first-phase excavation and foundation contract, Sequence 1, to Centex Corporation. Centex began work during the second-wettest year in the region's history, causing

Figure 8.9. Wild ducks at CVC construction site. Courtesy of Architect of the Capitol

major ponding on the dense, almost impermeable clay, making excavation and dump truck access extremely difficult.

The flooding attracted waterfowl, and as a bit of comic relief, a duck was found nesting in one of the dumpsters at the foot of the Capitol excavation. Someone notified the US Fish and Wildlife Service, and a representative was sent to cordon off the area with yellow warning tape and instructions to not disturb the wild duck and her nest until after the eggs hatched. We protected them as directed, even though that caused another month's work delay in that section of the site.

Removal of Another
Appropriations Obstructionist

In April 2003 our project manager, Joe Sacco, received an email from Tom Forhan of Congressman Obey's office, asking, "What would termination costs be if the project was simply canceled, at least a rough estimate?" Sacco developed an order-of-magnitude estimate of costs to restore the site to its original condition:

$50 million to fill in the hole in the East Front and contract termination

$1.5 million to restore the historic Olmsted site elements

$20 million for site restoration of Capitol grounds

$10 million to restore the Capitol's East Front

$5 million for miscellaneous utility connections and demobilization

We submitted this rough analysis, totaling approximately $90 million, to Obey's office. We received no reply or follow-up questions, nor were we directed to fill in the hole.[31]

With respect to the House's new expansion space, Congressman Obey's personal preference was to build additional office space rather than meeting rooms, a two-story-high hearing room, and other major spaces called for by House leadership. Other Democratic leaders had joined Republicans in approving this program, but Obey had not participated in the decision-making process. Insisting on changes that could no longer be accommodated, he again delayed approvals and the release of appropriated funds at several critical junctures.

On May 4, 2005, *Roll Call* reported that "House Appropriations ranking member Rep. David Obey acknowledged Tuesday that he has staged a three-week block on the approval of plans for the House office space that will flank the Capitol Visitor Center, disparaging schematics that he claims failed to provide sufficient 'work space' for lawmakers and their staffs."[32]

That same day Obey was quoted in *CQ Today*: "If appropriators wanted him to stop blocking funds for work on the House section of the Capitol Visitor Center, they 'are going to have to take me out of the loop.' . . . Consider him out. . . . The fiscal 2005 war supplemental . . . now includes language taking ranking members out of the loop."[33]

Over the course of the Capitol's evolution, a wide range of divergent congressional opinions have impacted the work of its architects. With the visitor center, an editorial in *Roll Call* pointed out that "there have been roughly two dozen significant changes that have layered additional costs and delays on the project," and many of these were due to increased security or other requirements imposed by Congress. The editorial concluded with "advice to Members of Congress: By all means, provide proper management of your agency chiefs. But allow them to do their jobs without meddling, or else the jobs will never be done properly."[34]

Notes

1. Shaffer, interview with J. Dennis Hastert, courtesy of the National Park Service, Flight 93 National Memorial, Oral History 743.

2. Shaffer, interview with Nellie Neumann, courtesy of the National Park Service, Flight 93 National Memorial, Oral History 722.

3. Shaffer, interview with Wilson "Bill" Livingood, courtesy of the National Park Service, Flight 93 National Memorial, Oral History 739.

4. Shaffer, interview with J. Dennis Hastert.

5. Alan M. Hantman, personal transcription of voice recording heard at Flight 93 Memorial Visitor center.

6. "9/11 Response," District of Columbia National Guard Newsletter, September 2001.

7. Moynihan, *Freedom Without Fortresses*, 6.

8. Rosalyn Hantman, personal recollections of meeting at Anacostia High School.

9. Barbara Boxer, "The Issues: Homeland Security," Wayback Machine, September 23, 2004–December 2, 2009, http://Boxer.senate.gov/issues/hsec.cfm.

10. Barbara Boxer, "Barbara Boxer: DHS Was a Mistake. I Regret Voting for It," *Washington Post*, July 25, 2020.

11. Note enclosed with envelope of anthrax delivered to office of Senator Tom Daschle, October 15, 2001.

12. United States Senate Committee on Finance, "Grassley Learns Anthrax Clean-Up Tops $23 Million So Far, EPA Says Final Cost Unknown," press release, March 6, 2002.

13. Government Accountability Office Investigative Report, June 4, 2003.

14. "Thomas Jefferson to Benjamin Rush, 17 August 1811," *Founders Online*, National Archives, https://founders.archives.gov/documents/Jefferson/03-04-02-0085.

15. US Senate, *Congressional Record*, October 25, 2001.

16. US Senate.

17. "Reopening Public Facilities after a Biological Attack," National Academy of Sciences, Board on Life Sciences, 2005.

18. Ellen Gamerman, "Senate Workers Return to Hart Building," *Baltimore Sun*, January 23, 2002.

19. Anne Raver, "DC's Other, Calmer Hothouse," *New York Times*, December 13, 2001

20. US Department of Justice, "Amerithrax Investigative Summary," February 19, 2010.

21. US Department of Justice.

22. Kendra Barkoff Lamy and Doug Heye, "Congress Needs to Make Coronavirus Testing Mandatory for Lawmakers and Staff," *Washington Post*, October 3, 2020.

23. Pauline Villegas, Rachel Chasan, and Hannah Knowles, "Storming the Capitol Was Textbook Potential Coronavirus Superspreader, Experts Say," *Washington Post*, January 8, 2021.

24. Jonathan Weisman, "As Omicron Spreads, the Mood on Capitol Hill Turns Even Grumpier," *New York Times*, January 13, 2022.

25. Mark Preston, "Visitor Center Affecting Senate Hideaways," *Roll Call*, November 20, 2002.

26. Michael E. Ruane and Joe Stephens, "Capitol Visitor Center Debut Again Delayed," *Washington Post*, March 9, 2007.

27. Task Force 1-6, "Capitol Security Review: Assessment," March 5, 2021.

28. Steven A. Sund, *Courage under Fire*, quoted in Carol D. Leonnig, *Washington Post*, January 1, 2023.

29. Theresa Agovino, "9/11 Ten Years Later: Reimagining the Skyscraper, How Safety Needs Transformed the Business of Building in NY," *Crain's New York Business*, May 9–15, 2011.

30. Agovino.

31. Notes of Joseph Sacco, CVC Project Manager, April 2003.

32. Jennifer Yachin, "Obey Blocking CVC Plan," *Roll Call*, May 4, 2005.

33. David Clark, *CQ Today*, May 4, 2005.

34. "Obey's Victory," *Roll Call*, August 14, 2006.

NINE

Construction, Sandstone, and Catafalques

Construction Risks and Warnings

What method should be selected to minimize risk in constructing the visitor center's seventy-foot-deep reinforced concrete foundation walls while also avoiding any damage to the Capitol's 225-year-old foundation just a few feet away? The contractor selected for excavation and construction of the wall, Centex Corporation, and its consulting firm, Nicholson Construction Company, chose a distinctive slurry-wall process that used a clamshell bucket to remove earth one bite at a time.

I knew this solution would best protect the Capitol's foundations, but that did not prevent my recurrent dreams of the majestic Capitol building, seemingly balanced at the top of a gray concrete cliff of a wall, from shifting, teetering, and then slowly sliding into the excavated void. That horrific image had been painted by representatives of the Government Accountability Office at a Senate Appropriations hearing. GAO always qualified their reports and projections by raising every possible negative occurrence, despite the fact that they had participated in the meetings that reached the decisions they now warned Congress about.

To assure the Capitol's structural integrity and prevent their warnings from becoming reality, we placed vibration and movement detectors at many points along the length of the existing Capitol building. These instruments let us monitor any movement during construction so we could detect problems and address them immediately. We also photographed and catalogued every existing crack in the Capitol structure to assure none could be attributed to our new construction.

A delicate construction ballet began when the clamshell bucket was lowered between pairs of temporary guide walls at each twenty-foot-long foundation segment. As the bucket removed soil, the resulting trench was filled with a thick, muddy mixture called slurry to maintain the trench's unsupported earth walls to prevent their caving in. A seventy-foot-long reinforcing steel cage was then lowered into the trench and concrete was poured in to form each segment of the concrete foundation wall.

As concrete began filling each section of trench, the lighter slurry mixture rose to the top, where it was collected and reused. This process continued as twenty-foot-wide, seventy-foot-deep sections were cast with each pour, forming a series of dashes. Sections between dashes were excavated and filled with the next concrete pour until we formed a continuous perimeter foundation wall. With the wall completed, the team could begin excavating earth within the footprint of the visitor center.

As each twelve-foot-deep layer of soil was excavated, steel rods were drilled through each newly exposed wall section (fig. 9.1). These 120-foot-long tie-back rods extended beneath the existing Capitol foundations and acted like three-inch-diameter screws, holding the new wall in place by resisting the pressure exerted by the building's weight and preventing any weakening of the Capitol's foundations. This was a months-long process, and as more and more earth was trucked away, we closely monitored the work that ultimately exposed the new wall

Figure 9.1. New foundation wall. At each twenty-foot-wide section of wall (defined by the vertical joints) three rows of foundation wall tiebacks were drilled beneath the Capitol's foundations to prevent any building movement. Courtesy of Architect of the Capitol

to a depth of fifty feet. The stone and plaster Capitol walls showed no signs of movement for the entire duration of the excavation and foundation construction process.

Trucks loading up with excavated earth required more than sixty thousand round trips, and security required that, before each dump truck was allowed to come on-site, it was screened several blocks away by Capitol Police and given a maximum of three minutes to reach the entry gate to assure it presented no risk.

Sequence 2 Competitive Bidding

Our revised construction schedule included three separate six-week approval periods over the course of the work. Unfortunately, these four months of oversight committee reviews consumed a total of eight months. When prospective Sequence 2 bidders learned of our constricted schedule, only two were willing to invest the time and expense to prepare competitive bids. One was already working on the excavation and reinforced concrete build-

Figure 9.2. Excavation and perimeter wall construction. Courtesy of Architect of the Capitol

ing shell, Centex Corporation. Other potential bidders believed Centex had too much of a bidding advantage and bowed out, except for Manhattan Construction.

On the $150 million scope of work, the Centex bid came in higher by $3 million. Even though it would have been easier to have Centex as the single contractor working on-site, I awarded Sequence 2 to Manhattan, the lower bidder. While I believed significant savings in the areas of site mobilization, staging of the work, and contractor conflict avoidance could more than offset the $3 million bid difference, Congress would not have accepted my awarding the contract to the higher of two qualified bidders.

Unfortunately, heavy rains, flooding, and other site factors delayed Centex's completion of the first phase, resulting in a multimillion-dollar delay charge from Manhattan, quickly confirming my concerns about potential site conflicts. These delays, in addition to the extensive post-9/11 additions of the new House and Senate expansion areas, made it impossible to complete construction of the visitor center in time for the 2005 presidential inaugural. To avoid even more site conflicts between contractors, we competitively bid the newly designed House and Senate expansions and assigned the winning bidder, Grunley Construction Corporation, to work under Manhattan's overall coordination.

The Capitol Preservation Commission finally acknowledged these schedule realities and allowed us to prioritize the completion of the roof and plaza area closest to the Capitol so that a newly inaugurated president could stand on the rotunda steps in 2005 and watch the troops pass in review.

To save time and accomplish this new priority, we switched the column design in this area from less costly poured-in-place reinforced concrete to three-story-high steel box columns. They were fabricated

Figure 9.3. Roof construction begun with three-story-high unsupported steel box columns. Courtesy of Architect of the Capitol

off-site and strengthened to rise the full three-story height of the center's plaza level roof without the intermediate floor slabs that normally provided stability. Under this form of top-down construction, floor slabs would be built later. Much of the follow-on work could now be performed under protection of a roof, shielding Capitol building occupants from dirt and noise. Structural columns and slabs farther from the Capitol were later built of more cost-effective, but labor-intensive, poured-in-place reinforced concrete.

This section of roof and plaza surface was completed in time to support troops passing in review at President George W. Bush's second inaugural. This out-of-sequence, top-down roofing change had consequences for the rest of the construction schedule and budget. The visitor center opening date was ultimately set for December 2, 2008, to coincide with the 135th anniversary of the completion of the *Statue of Freedom* and to conveniently avoid political sen-

sitivities leading up to the November elections one month earlier.

Chief Justice Roberts: Architecture Is Substantive

Across First Street Northeast at the Supreme Court, I was building a good working relationship with Associate Justice Anthony Kennedy. That would continue through the major Supreme Court Building renovation and systems modernization we initiated before the Senate Judiciary Committee. The court had been in its current home for seventy years without major work. I testified, "As you know, this project is required to address significant life-safety issues, enhance security for occupants and visitors, and to replace obsolete building systems."[1]

My budget request for $113,500,000 in support of the court's fiscal year 2002 budget submission

Figure 9.4. Roof construction at face of Capitol in preparation for George W. Bush's inauguration. Courtesy of Architect of the Capitol

Figure 9.5. George W. Bush's presidential inaugural with troops passing in review, 2005. Courtesy of Architect of the Capitol

was based on preliminary design drawings for this renovation and improvement project. We defined the project scope in enough detail to develop an order-of-magnitude budget, but appropriators still requested that we commission an "independent peer review of the project to objectively evaluate whether the scope and cost were valid."[2] The review concluded that the scope was valid, the costs reasonable, and that the project should not be delayed.

Although it is one of three constitutionally created branches of government, until 1935 the Supreme Court had not occupied a dedicated home of its own since its inception in 1790. The court had little choice since our nation's founders entrusted all budget appropriation powers to the Congress, and none to the justices. For more than 150 years the court had been a virtual vagabond. It met at the Merchants' Exchange Building in New York City, in Philadelphia's city hall, and in a series of US Capitol building locations provided by the Congress. All of these transitory spaces lacked adequate accommodations for the court.

Not until 1929 did Chief Justice William Howard Taft, who had been president sixteen years earlier, convince Congress to appropriate funds to construct a building the court could call home and physically separate it from the Congress. A trapezoidal lot was allocated on First Street Northeast, directly across from the Capitol, and Taft selected Cass Gilbert as the project's architect. Nationally known for his 1913 design of New York's Woolworth Building, a sixty-story terra-cotta-clad Gothic Revival structure, then the tallest building in the world, Gilbert also designed the statehouses of Minnesota, Arkansas, and West Virginia.

Cass Gilbert's Design: Lots of Marble

For the US Supreme Court, Gilbert designed an imposing Greco-Roman neoclassical temple establishing the court's high place among the larger buildings on Capitol Hill. To achieve a sense of quality, permanence, and dignity, Gilbert spent $3 million of its $9.4 million budget on a variety of rich marbles from the United States and around the world. The Corinthian building exterior is of white Vermont marble, while the four open courtyards are faced with crystalline flaked white Georgia marble. Sweeping marble surfaces also faced major interior spaces, which presented serious acoustic problems.

Figure 9.6. US Supreme Court Building. Courtesy of Architect of the Capitol

The magnificent forty-four-foot-high Supreme Court Chamber is lined with ivory vein marble from Alicante, Spain. Its twenty-four ivory buff and golden columns of Old Convent Quarry Siena marble are from Liguria, Italy. To obtain and assure the quality of this special Italian marble, Gilbert met during this pre–World War II era with the fascist Italian strongman Benito Mussolini. These beautiful Ionic columns majestically define all sides of the chamber, but behind the four columns at the front of the room, the marble wall is hidden from view by sumptuous red velvet gold-trimmed draperies. Heavy draperies are also hung between each pair of columns along the other walls.

These draperies are necessary to dampen the sound of voices reverberating throughout the chamber, making it difficult to follow oral arguments of the Supreme Court Bar attorneys. Those red velvet draperies, along with the thick square-patterned red and gold carpeting and upholstered mahogany pews and chairs, help dampen the reverberant sound. High above the bench, looking down on the proceedings, is a seven-foot-high, forty-foot-long sculpted marble frieze depicting representations of the Majesty of Law and the Power of Government. Moses carrying the tablets of the Ten Commandments stands among the eighteen "Great Law-Givers of History" represented on the frieze. He looks down from the southern wall, while the Prophet Mohammed looks down from the northern wall holding the Koran and a scimitar. An imposing lineup for any attorney presenting their case.

The court has historically been fiscally conservative and adverse to requesting budget increases from the Congress. Therefore, in order to develop complete confidence in the cost and scope of our proposal, which far exceeded any prior budget request, the court brought in an outside group of reviewers that independently validated our conclusions. The appropriators then authorized us to move forward with the project.

During the ongoing design process I worked with the court's three-member building committee chaired by Associate Justice Sandra Day O'Connor,

along with Kennedy and Associate Justice David Souter. Each was fully engaged in all aspects of the project, including understanding the multiple phases the project would go through in this fully-occupied and noise-averse building. Each of our presentations was clearly reasoned to withstand any in-depth questioning or concerns this panel of justices, who took nothing for granted, might express. The design process culminated in 2003 with Chief Justice William Rehnquist's remarks at a ground-breaking ceremony, during which he said, "Until this building opened, the Court did not have a home of its own. From 1801 to 1935 it occupied cramped quarters across the street in the Capitol, very much at the sufferance of Congress, and most justices worked out of their homes. Having its own building was of great symbolic importance to the Court. . . . After seventy years it is overdue for a renovation."[3]

The justices and I discussed the possibility of building a tunnel to connect the court to the Capitol Visitor Center, as we were doing for the Library of Congress. They were emphatically against compromising the court's hard-won physical separation from the Congress. Rehnquist's sensitivity to this requirement for separation has continued under his successor, Chief Justice John Roberts. In an April 2010 speech at the Indiana University School of Law, Roberts discussed the rejection of the proposed connecting tunnel: "Do you really think the Supreme Court would occupy the place it does today if it was still in the basement of the Capitol? . . . Architecture is substantive."[4]

In both the renovation of Cass Gilbert's masterpiece and in the resolution of the Great Hall acoustics problem, we maintained the architectural integrity of the Court's wonderfully substantive home.

Beneath the Crypt: Caskets and Catafalques

On June 5, 2004, as construction progressed at both the visitor center and the Supreme Court, former president Ronald Reagan died in California at the age of ninety-three. The casket was first displayed at the Ronald Reagan Presidential Library in Simi Valley, California, before it was flown on a US Air Force 747 to Andrews Air Force Base outside of Washington, DC. From there the former president would lie in state in the Capitol Rotunda and then be transferred to the Washington National Cathedral for a state funeral service. The Lincoln Catafalque, the velvet-draped bier constructed in 1865 to hold the assassinated president's casket in the Capitol Rotunda, would be called into service once again.

Before the visitor center was built, the catafalque could only be viewed by the few visitors intrepid enough to seek its resting place beneath the Capitol crypt. Visitors walked a convoluted path down a long flight of stairs, turning to an out-of-the-way corridor, passing a mailroom, a women's restroom, and climbing back up another flight of stairs. Only then, at the end of a bare corridor, could they peer through a locked, spear-pointed gate into the unadorned barrel-vaulted chamber originally planned as President George Washington's tomb. Since Washington's will stipulated that he be buried at his home in Mount Vernon, Virginia, that vacant constricted space became home to Lincoln's historic bier.

Ronald Reagan and a Unique Casket

On June 9, 2004, the catafalque was awakened from its rest and borne into the rotunda, pressed once again into the service of our country. The Military District of Washington was historically responsible for administering state funerals, with the last full lying-in-state ceremony several decades earlier, in 1973, for President Lyndon B. Johnson. Now, in a post-9/11 world, the Reagan state funeral was the first one designated as a National Special Security Event, and the US Secret Service was, therefore, in charge of security. Dozens of world leaders were to travel to Washington to pay their respects, and that could be a tempting target for would-be terrorists.

The Military District's funeral coordinator, Thomas Groppel, informed me that Reagan's casket presented some unusual challenges. It weighed far more than prior caskets because the president's widow, former First Lady Nancy Reagan, had directed that the walnut coffin be lined with marble, increasing its weight to eight hundred pounds.

The first concern was for the Lincoln Catafalque itself, which my agency maintained and protected. The Military District manager asked me to confirm that the rough pine boards that had been hastily nailed together in 1865 could carry a load greater than it had ever borne in its 139-year history. Importantly, we also had to assure that during the ceremony the pallbearers could safely carry the casket up the monumental stairs of the Capitol's West Front, into the Capitol Rotunda, and gently lower it onto the catafalque.

Several members of my staff joined me at the catafalque then resting at the center of the rotunda. Our team tilted the catafalque onto two side legs and held it securely, angled some eighteen inches above its nine-inch-high fabric-wrapped base. The musty scent of history enveloped me as I knelt down, peering into the darkness beneath the black velvet–draped bier. The plain-sawn pieces of this table-like structure stirred thoughts of the laborers who built this catafalque under the intense pressure of Lincoln's assassination. As I inspected their generations-old handiwork, I was struck by the meaning of the task we had before us on that twenty-first-century evening. Each of us wanted the ceremonies the next day to proceed flawlessly, and for our nation to honor not only the fortieth president but also the democracy he had served.

Nothing about the catafalque's construction was complicated. No rot, no rust, nor any cracked boards were evident in this simple structure with its solid four-inch-by-four-inch wood corner posts. Our team eased it gently down onto the platform base, extending some twelve inches beyond the catafalque on all sides. I was comfortable informing Groppel that the historic bier should handle the casket's weight without difficulty.

The pallbearers were drawn from all five branches of the armed forces. The Joint Services Honor Guard was charged with transferring the 800-pound casket

Figure 9.7. Lincoln Catafalque without its base. Courtesy of Architect of the Capitol

from a hearse near the White House ellipse to a caisson, an 86-year-old converted transport wagon for a 75-millimeter cannon.[5] It was to be drawn by six matched horses from the Third US Infantry Regiment, the Old Guard, based in Fort Meyers, Virginia. The three horses on the left would be ridden by soldiers in blue ceremonial uniform, those on the right saddled but riderless.

The casket was to travel down Constitution Avenue to the sound of muffled drums, accompanied by Reagan family members, an honor guard, and multiple military units. Following behind the caisson would be Sergeant York, a black riderless horse bearing a sheathed sword attached to an empty saddle. At the request of Nancy Reagan, President Reagan's brown riding boots were to be placed in the stirrups, reversed to indicate that he would never ride again.

The forty-five-minute procession was to deliver the caisson to the base of the stairway on the west-facing side of the Capitol and was met by a twenty-one-gun salute fired from three howitzers amid the strains of "Hail to the Chief." There the problems would begin.

In earlier years, funeral corteges arrived at the East Front of the Capitol at the much shorter central stairway leading directly into the rotunda. But visitor center construction forced the switch to the West Front, a far more difficult ascent. Three separate eight-person teams of pallbearers were assigned to carry the casket over successive segments of the route. The first was to slide the flag-draped casket from the caisson and, with measured steps, carry it up the first two flights of Olmsted's grand stairway. Each of the eight pallbearers would bear a one-hundred-pound share of the eight-hundred-pound burden in a controlled, coordinated, and respectful manner.

As they ascended the stairs, all team members had to adjust the height of their handholds, raising the back end of the casket to keep it level. The second team of eight armed forces pallbearers were to relieve them at the landing halfway up the staircase and carry the casket for the remaining flights, then up a series of ramps to the Capitol door, where a third team would relieve them and carry the casket into the Capitol and up an internal flight of still steeper stairs into the Capitol Rotunda.

The last leg of this journey was to the center of the rotunda, to the foot of the waiting Lincoln Catafalque. The bearers would next turn sideways and smoothly lift the casket high enough to clear the catafalque, step onto the nine-inch base of the historic bier, sidestep in unison across the length of the base, center the casket, and gently lower it down.

The Rehearsal

On the night before the formal ceremony, a full Capitol Rotunda dress rehearsal was held, with members of my team assisting in setting up concentric circles of stanchions and stands for the media. The first team of pallbearers successfully carried the fully weighted test casket up the first two flights of the stairway and lowered it onto a rolling casket trolley so that the next team could relieve them. The second team successfully brought the casket to the door of the Capitol, where it was again placed on a rolling casket trolley for the third team to assume the task. This team brought the casket into the Capitol, up the last steep flight of stairs, and to the foot of the catafalque at the center of the rotunda.

As we all stood watching, the pallbearers were unable to step onto the surrounding base while lifting the eight-hundred-pound test coffin high enough to clear the catafalque. These brawny service members were physically drained. They just couldn't do it. That last nine-inch-high step was the final straw.

We were just hours from the start of the formal ceremony that would be televised around the world. The only acceptable solution was to reduce the height of the base to an almost negligible level to allow the pallbearers to keep the casket at the same carrying height and smoothly clear the catafalque as they stepped onto the base and sidestepped across it. Overnight, our carpenters built a new rectangular donut-shaped base only two inches high. It was wrapped in black fabric and delivered to the rotunda. The old nine-inch base was removed, and the new two-inch base was installed around the catafalque. The new assembly looked perfectly fine, and since the ceremony was imminent, we had to trust that this solved the problem.

Figure 9.8. Installing new low base on catafalque. Courtesy of Alan M. Hantman

The Ceremony

That June afternoon, the formal funeral procession proceeded slowly up Constitution Avenue to the cadence of a constant drum roll, solemnly delivering the casket to the foot of the Capitol's western stairs at 7:00 p.m. To a twenty-one-gun salute and repeated strains of "Hail to the Chief," the first team of white-gloved pallbearers lifted the casket from the caisson and, preceded by a three-person American Flag Guard, carried it to the midpoint of the monumental stairway, where they placed it on a casket trolley.

The second team of pallbearers relieved the first, climbed the rest of the stairway, and was met there by former First Lady Nancy Reagan, somberly dressed in black with large circular eyeglasses and a simple gold necklace. She reached out to touch the flag-draped casket as it passed in front of her and followed closely behind, her left hand on the arm of her escort, US Army Major General Galen B. Jackman, commander of the Military District of Washington. A petite yet forceful woman walking alongside a tall, imposing general in formal military dress and white gloves.

This team brought the casket up the final set of ramps to the Capitol's west-facing door, followed by Mrs. Reagan and her escort. The third team of armed forces pallbearers lifted the casket from a second trolley at the Capitol door and carried it up the final internal stairway and into the rotunda to the sound of a continuous drumroll.

Members of the Reagan family, the Congress, and the Supreme Court and dignitaries from around the world filled the rotunda. Standing among the throng, I held my breath as the third team approached the catafalque, halted, and turned inward to adjust their handholds. The first pair of pallbearers stepped up. One pallbearer had some difficulty disentangling his

Figure 9.9. First of three teams of armed forces pallbearers on western stairway leading to President Reagan's lying-in-state ceremony. Courtesy of Architect of the Capitol

Figure 9.10. Rotunda aerial view of third team of pallbearers approaching Lincoln Catafalque. Courtesy of Architect of the Capitol

feet from the draped fabric but quickly recovered, adjusting his stance and hold on the casket. The rest of the pallbearers stepped smoothly onto the new lower base, sidestepped across the fabric surface, centered the casket on the catafalque, and gently lowered it into place.

I smiled in relief as George Washington gazed down on the scene from Constantino Brumidi's *Apotheosis* 180 feet above the rotunda floor.

The pallbearers stood at attention as House Chaplain Daniel Coughlin delivered the invocation. A new five-person honor guard marched to their positions surrounding the casket and rested the butts of their ceremonial rifles on the rotunda floor. Only then did the pallbearers turn to step off the base and march out of the rotunda.

The president pro tempore of the Senate, Ted Stevens of Alaska, was the first to offer a eulogy, followed by House Speaker Dennis Hastert. They both referred to Reagan's famous image of a shining city on a hill. Vice President Dick Cheney spoke of "the vision and the will of Ronald Reagan that gave hope to the oppressed, shamed the oppressors and ended an evil empire. . . . My fellow Americans, here lies a graceful and gallant man."[6]

The stress and relief of the moment seemed to greatly expand the already voluminous rotunda chamber. With the assistance of a member of the honor guard, each speaker laid a wreath at the casket. Cheney then escorted the former First Lady to stand beside the coffin of her husband of fifty-two years. At the conclusion of thirty-four hours of public view-

Figure 9.11. Casket leaving Capitol on way to service at Washington National Cathedral. Courtesy of Architect of the Capitol

itors can view this historic artifact as it stands ready for each new assignment.

God and the Congress

While the physical construction of the visitor center proceeded, planning was under way to develop educational programs about congressional history, the legislative process, and the mechanics of our representative democracy. Many references to God and religion were slated to become part of our planned exhibit documents, including speeches by President Abraham Lincoln, an 1800s-era Bible used during Senate oath-of-office ceremonies, a photo of a historic Christmas tree, and at least a dozen and a half more. These multiple religious references were insufficient for a number of congressional members and religious revisionist historians.

In September 2004 the script for the orientation film was circulated to members of the Capitol Preservation Commission. It was developed by the film production organization Donna Lawrence Productions, which had won top awards in almost every national and international festival for special format and documentary productions and had produced the orientation film for the National Constitution Center in Philadelphia.

The twelve-minute film, developed with our Content Working Group of experts, was to be shown before tours of the Capitol building. According to Lawrence's report about the draft script, their goals were to help visitors "gain an appreciation for representative democracy as reflected in the workings of the Congress; recognize the challenge of creating one out of the many; gain a human view of the Congress and how real people get real things done; realize that what happens here matters in our day-to-day lives; experience an emotional connection to the Capitol building as the physical center of our representative democracy; and feel a renewed sense of the critical role we all play in this process."[7]

Responses from Capitol Preservation Commission members to the first draft included reasonable

ing, the military honor guard lifted the casket from the catafalque and, to a muffled drum roll, carried it back toward the National Mall. A twenty-one-gun salute rang out, and the remaining two pallbearer teams took turns ceremoniously carrying the casket down the Olmsted monumental stairway, carefully placing it in a hearse for the drive to the state funeral service at the Washington National Cathedral.

The catafalque was returned to its barrel-vaulted niche beneath the Capitol crypt, where it rested until December 30, 2006, when it was once again called to duty for the lying-in-state ceremony of President Gerald R. Ford Jr. With the completion of the Capitol Visitor Center in 2008, the catafalque found a new niche in Exhibition Hall, where millions of vis-

suggestions that the film should introduce the Capitol building earlier and should focus more strongly on the country's founding principles. Donna Lawrence Productions incorporated these changes, but we still did not have final approval. We were unaware that demands for many additional changes were yet to come.

Whose Version of History?

When he served as House majority whip, Representative Tom DeLay (R-TX), a member of the Capitol Preservation Commission, shared the draft orientation film script with David Barton, who had been vice chair of the Texas Republican Party and was known as a Christian nationalist and a revisionist historian. In Barton's 1989 book *The Myth of Separation: What Is the Correct Relationship between Church and State*, published by an organization he founded, WallBuilders Press, he attempts to prove that the separation of church and state is a myth.[8]

Barton submitted an eighteen-page response to the script, which members of our design team reviewed. They were able to respond to some concerns, but not all. For example, Barton did not object to the Capitol being referred to as "a temple of liberty," but he did object to the sentence, "The soundtrack gives voice to this secular temple," calling it "egregiously and factually untrue." He wanted "secular temple" deleted and requested that the film incorporate the prayer chapel, the sculpture of Moses, and the inscription over the Speaker's rostrum, along with additional listings and images of faith, family, and churches. He asked that all references to "representative democracy" or "democratic" processes, principles, or society be deleted and replaced with the phrase "constitutional republic."[9]

One line in the script stated, "We learn that as the country was born and evolved out of an ongoing struggle, so too with this great building," Barton suggested that "evolved" be replaced with "grew." According to him, "No one will object to the country 'growing' but many will object to the country 'evolving'—just as many object to the Constitution 'evolving' through any means other than the will of the people. The point can be made without the use of any evocative language."[10]

Prolonged discussions resulted in months of delay as we awaited the necessary approvals to begin film production. Several modifications were made: among them, changing "secular temple" to "magnificent temple." The Senate quickly authorized moving ahead, and after a further delay Speaker Dennis Hastert finally sent a letter authorizing me to proceed with production.

Unfortunately, a call from the Speaker's office soon directed me to destroy Hastert's letter of approval and consult with DeLay's office to satisfy Barton's ongoing concerns with film content.

The Speaker had been supportive of the visitor center project, so this change of heart requires some explanation. In 1994 Congressman Dennis Hastert managed Tom DeLay's successful run for House majority whip against Newt Gingrich's candidate, Bob Walker (R-PA). Hastert was then appointed chief deputy whip. An article in the *Texas Observer* stated, "and when Gingrich collapsed in 1998, DeLay engineered the elevation of Hastert to his current post as Speaker of the House. They remain close allies, and DeLay is often described as a Wizard of Oz–like figure behind the colorless Hastert."[11] In October 2004, when DeLay was rebuked by the House Committee on Standards of Official Conduct, Hastert, now Speaker, showed his support by not reappointing the committee chair.

Barton's influence with DeLay was far greater than the clout of any member of the Capitol Visitor Center team. Jeff Trandahl, the clerk of the House and a strong project proponent, assured me he would talk with Tim Berry, DeLay's chief of staff, to resolve the Barton issues. Through a series of negotiating sessions, Trandahl ultimately paved the way for the orientation film production to finally move ahead.

In the Future, More Tinkering with History?

Debates about whose version of history and whose "facts" will be used to inform future generations of Capitol visitors will likely never end. Religious, cultural, and political battles on Capitol Hill will never cease to have an impact on the Capitol and its visitor center, presenting new challenges to those entrusted with its responsible stewardship. I believe that calls for additional changes of a religious nature will be successful, because few members of Congress will take the political risk of debating God and religion on the floor of the Senate or House of Representatives.

Barton will likely continue to be heard in future political campaigns, as he was in the 2016 presidential election process, as described in a *New York Times* op-ed by Katherine Stewart, a journalist who writes about issues related to separation of church and state: "At the rightmost edge of the Christian conservative movement, there are those who dream of turning the United States into a Christian republic subject to 'biblical laws.' In the unlikely figure of Donald J. Trump, they hope to have found their greatest champion yet. He wasn't 'our preferred candidate,' the Christian nationalist David Barton said in June, but he could be 'God's candidate.'"[13]

Considering Congress's diverse political, cultural, and religious perspectives, it was inevitable that the visitor center's educational programs would flex and shift as we faced the challenge of seeking an impossible consensus. Yet even as political pressure was used to influence the content of our programs, the compromises reached did not fundamentally alter the work of our team of experts.

On November 28, 2008, *Washington Post* senior editor Marc Fisher posted on the publication's blog under the headline "DC's New Underground Jewel":

> As a demonstration of how to blend education and entertainment without insulting the intelligence of the citizenry, the Visitor Center is a smash hit—Here . . . are the stories of how a bill becomes law, what members of Congress really do, how the Capitol came to be, how Washington the city evolved, and who the great men of our nation have been, as seen in their own hand . . . (the exhibit design is by Ralph Appelbaum, the Michael Jordan of the museum world). . . . Watch short films that tell the story of each side of Congress while checking out live video of that day's session. . . . Stroll along a series of models to see how the Capitol Hill neighborhood developed. . . . Watch kids become totally entranced by the centerpiece of the main exhibit, a please-touch architecturally-correct model of the Capitol dome. . . . Even more important, the Visitor Center sends a signal . . . that meaty content can still succeed in the effort to educate citizens who grow up with only the slightest whiff of civics in their schooling.[14]

After fifteen years, Exhibition Hall was redesigned and reopened in 2022 to incorporate a kid-friendly classroom and several new exhibits, but it does not include any mention of the insurrection of January 6th, 2021.

Capitol Sandstone, Slavery, and a Court Injunction

George Washington understood the importance of stately architecture and set the precedent for all subsequent increments of Capitol growth when he laid the cornerstone of the Capitol on September 18, 1793, in a formal Masonic ceremony. Five days later, the city's commissioners agreed to Washington's suggestion that the Capitol be faced with freestone to "heighten the sense of permanence and grandeur." In his book about the history of the Capitol, William Allen writes, "The sandstone (also called freestone) quarries around Aquia Creek, Virginia, . . . produced a fine-grained brownish stone that did not contain bedding layers and could therefore be worked 'freely' in any direction. . . . Sturdy, flat bottomed boats called scows were used to bring the stone to the federal city, where a wharf was built at the foot of New Jersey Avenue to receive the cargo destined for the Capitol."[15]

The quarry, purchased by Pierre L'Enfant in 1791, was on Wigginton's Island, now called Government Island in Stafford County, Virginia. Enslaved African Americans, their labor leased out by their owners, worked this quarry to supply stone and then to construct the Capitol and the White House. The important role played by slaves had been little recognized by history, but an effort to begin to rectify this was discussed in a joint House and Senate press release in 2005 announcing the establishment of a special task force

> to Study the History and Contributions of Slave Laborers in the Construction of the US Capitol. This task force is the result of legislation passed previously and will make recommendations to the Speaker of the House of Representatives and the President pro tempore of the Senate for appropriate recognition of the efforts of these slave laborers. "It is our hope that the work of the task force will shed light on this part of our history, the building of our greatest symbol of democracy. The time to recognize this work is long overdue and we look forward to the recommendations of the task force," the Congressional Leadership said.[16]

I asked William C. Allen to draft the study. In his introduction, he wrote:

In every colony north and south, from the seventeenth century on, the building trades drew upon slave labor to augment the available supply of free workmen. . . . When the Capitol was begun in the 1790s, slave labor had a well-established record in the building trades. . . . In years past, the labor of everyday workmen of all races and ethnicities was not considered a subject worthy of scholarly notice. The issue of slavery in particular was an embarrassing topic that did not sit well with squeamish writers.[17]

Allen's review of this history indicates that a new respect has belatedly been accorded to "lower-class laborers and slaves [who] . . . worked along-side of free blacks and whites in the areas of carpentry, masonry, carting, rafting, roofing, plastering, glazing, and painting." Furthermore, "documents that made such scholarship possible have never been lost, have never been 'discovered,' and have in fact been available to the public for generations."[18]

A ten-page appendix to this task force report lists slave labor payments made, primarily in the 1790s, specifically for work at the Capitol. The National Archives house financial records and "the names of local residents who rented their slaves to the commissioners for various purposes asso-ciated with construction activities. Remuneration was $60 a year (raised to $70 in 1797)." Among the many residents listed is Thomas Law, who "is remembered as a wealthy developer whose wife was Martha Washington's granddaughter. Not here of course are many of the names of slaves who actually performed the labor that helped build the nation's Capitol."[19]

There was no experienced labor for stonecutting and carving in a region that used wood and brick for construction. Washington's decision to face the Capitol in stone created a serious labor problem for commissioners who ended up bringing a number of experienced masons from a Masonic Lodge in Edinburgh, Scotland. To find local laborers for stone quarrying, one firm advertised in the *Virginia Herald*: "Wanted to hire, for the next year, to work on the FREE-STONE QUARRIES lately occupied by the Public, on Aquia Creek, Sixty strong, active NEGRO MEN, for whom good wages will be given—They shall be well used and well fed."[20]

Recommendations of Slave Labor Task Force

Stone quarrying was a backbreaking task that required the use of pickaxes and iron wedges to split stone, which was then lifted onto wooden sleds hauled down to flat-bottomed scows and poled forty miles upriver to the New Jersey Avenue wharf. There the stones were dressed into usable blocks, largely by slaves, and then moved inland by wagon. The Architect of the Capitol Agency provided one of those rectangular blocks, a 318-pound stone measuring 15 by 21 by 14 inches, for display at the Smithsonian's National Museum of African American History and Culture on the National Mall. The quarry on Government Island is now listed on the National Register of Historic Places and serves as a county park.

The Slave Labor Task Force developed a resolution presented by Henry C. Johnson (D-GA) at a House hearing on July 7, 2009: "Mr. Johnson of Georgia. Mr. Speaker, I move to suspend the rules and agree to the concurrent resolution (H. Con. Res. 135) directing the Architect of the Capitol to place a marker in Emancipation Hall in the Capitol Visitor Center which acknowledges the role that slave labor placed in the construction of the United States Capitol, and for other purposes." The resolution stated:

> Whereas enslaved African-Americans provided labor essential to the construction of the United States Capitol;
>
> Whereas the report of the Architect of the Capitol entitled "History of Slave Laborers in the Construction of the United States Capitol" documents the role of slave labor in the construction of the United States Capitol; . . .
>
> Whereas recognition of the contributions of enslaved African-Americans brings to all Americans an understanding of the continuing evolution of our representative democracy; and
>
> Whereas a marker dedicated to the enslaved African-Americans who helped to build the Capitol will reflect the charge of the Capitol Visitor Center to teach visitors about Congress and its development: Now, therefore, be it Resolved by the House of Representatives (the Senate concurring),

> The Architect of the Capitol, subject to the approval of the Committee on House Administration of the House of Representatives, and the Committee on Rules and Administration of the Senate, shall design, procure, and place in a prominent location in Emancipation Hall in the Capitol Visitor Center a marker which acknowledges the role that slave labor played in the construction of the United States Capitol.[21]

During the debate following the resolution, John Lewis declared:

> Slavery is part of our nation's history of which we are not proud. However, we should not run or hide from it. . . . The history of the Capitol, like the history of our nation, should be complete. . . . Mr. Speaker, with this resolution, this untold story will now be told. . . . Thanks to the work of the Slave Labor Task Force, we will now honor those slaves who built our temple of freedom. . . . This physical and permanent marker will pay tribute to the blood, sweat and toils of the African-American slaves who helped build this magnificent building and ensure that their story is told and never forgotten.[22]

Three years later, Lewis issued a press release announcing the unveiling in Emancipation Hall by House and Senate leadership of a marker commemorating slave laborers of the US Capitol. A bronze plaque was installed on the northern wall of Emancipation Hall, acknowledging the efforts of all who worked on the Capitol building. A block of Aquia Creek sandstone from the Capitol's original East Front portico is displayed below the plaque with the quarrier's chisel marks clearly evident:

> THIS SANDSTONE WAS ORIGINALLY PART OF THE UNITED STATES CAPITOL'S EAST FRONT, CONSTRUCTED IN 1824–1826. IT WAS QUARRIED BY LABORERS, INCLUDING ENSLAVED AFRICAN AMERICANS, AND COMMEMORATES THEIR IMPORTANT ROLE IN BUILDING THE CAPITOL.

Figure 9.12. Marker commemorating enslaved laborers who helped build the US Capitol. Courtesy of Jeffrey Schwarz Photography

a national reconciliation and education. In addition to the stone marker in Emancipation Hall, he supported the task force's recommendation to train Capitol guides to properly interpret experiences of African Americans as slave laborers and to create online exhibits and educational materials about slave labor in the Capitol.

Façade Deterioration and Interior Sandstone

The freestone used to build the Capitol was easier than marble to quarry, shape, and use during initial construction, but its softness made it subject to severe weathering. As the stone deteriorated over time, past architects of the Capitol replaced it with marble, except for the western façade, which was repaired or replaced with Indiana limestone. In the mid-1950s, the sandstone east-central façade became so heavily deteriorated that it led to the design of a thirty-two-foot deep eastern expansion replicating the scale and detail of the deteriorated sandstone, but built with far more durable marble, providing Congress with more office space. A part of the historic sandstone wall can still be seen as an interior wall at the crypt entrance when entering from the visitor center, as well as at other locations.

The rotunda's circular interior wall was built with the same sandstone, but since these walls were originally intended to be painted, stone blocks in a wide range of variegated tones were accepted and laid up without concern for color consistency. This is evident in the rotunda today, where two or three different tones of sandstone can be seen within any section of this interior wall. It looks uncoordinated because it is.

Once this stone was set and sufficiently dried, it received its first coat of paint in 1827, and prior to 1905 many additional layers of paint and whitewash were applied. The Capitol superintendent then stripped the walls down to their base stone, mistakenly believing that a restoration was needed to return them to their original unpainted condition. The rotunda walls have remained unpainted ever

On the four-hundredth anniversary of the introduction of African slavery to the English colonies in 1619, and fourteen years after the formation of the Task Force on Slavery, Congress marked the anniversary in September 2019 with an Emancipation Hall ceremony. This ceremony completed the circle initiated in 2007 with James Billington's effort to have the name of the visitor center's Great Hall changed, which led to a congressional debate resulting in a change more profound and meaningful than he had ever intended. Emancipation Hall now serves as the beating heart of the Capitol Visitor Center, graciously welcoming millions of people each year, inviting them to learn about the Congress, the formative years of our country, and the memorial to those who helped build the Capitol.

Congressman John Lewis died ten months later, on July 17, 2020. Lewis was consistent in his call for

Figure 9.13. Unpainted rotunda walls showing uncoordinated range of sandstone colors. Courtesy of Jeffrey Schwarz Photography

since, presenting us with the challenge of finding a sandstone source for the Capitol Visitor Center that was consistent with the range of color and quality of the original variegated stone.

The original quarries at Aquia Creek, forty miles down the Potomac River, were unable to provide the volume of fine-grained brownish stone needed to yield the 147,000 square feet of finished sandstone required for our project. Manhattan Construction Company of Fairfax, Virginia, our general contractor for this second phase of construction, subcontracted the procurement, fabrication and installation of all stonework to a single firm, Boatman and Magnani, Inc., of Capitol Heights, Maryland. This centralized control was set up to create single-source responsibility for the entire stone process, and hopefully a seamless outcome. Boatman, working with our associate architect CRTKL, searched for quarries throughout several states that might yield sandstone compatible with that of the rotunda.

Two potential quarries were found in Pennsylvania, both hundreds of miles away. Each quarry sent sample sandstone slabs to the rotunda for us to compare quality and color. We selected a fine quality sandstone from Annandale Stone of Boyers, Pennsylvania, which had the capacity to produce the volume of stone needed. Boatman issued a purchase order with them to furnish all raw stone slabs for the project and with Quarra Stone Company of Madison, Wisconsin, to fabricate it.

Unfortunately, relationships throughout the chain of stone provision, fabrication, and installation soon became fractured among Manhattan, our general contractor; Boatman, our installer; Quarra, the stone fabricator; and the Annandale quarry.

The Federal Court Injunction

A judge in the US District Court for the Western District of Pennsylvania, as reported by the Special

Master appointed by the court, issued an "Injunction Order [which] precipitated the restructuring of the contractual arrangement for the procurement and fabrication of the sandstone for the project."[23]

This injunction, based on a suit initiated by Quarra Stone Company, was not a good foundation on which to build a productive working relationship, and it led to problems with slab deliveries from Annandale to Quarra, and also to Quarra's lagging deliveries of fabricated stone for installation on-site. This then delayed Boatman's installation work, resulting in costly change orders from all the contractors who had to wait for the stone installation to perform their part of the work.

During monthly public hearings I kept Senate appropriators informed of the number of truckloads of stone needed along with those actually shipped by Quarra. Delays continued to build, and appropriators wondered why we couldn't force our general contractor and its subcontractors to produce and ship sufficient truckloads of finished material to meet our schedule. Our hands were tied. Effective control was in the hands of a federal judge in the Western District of Pennsylvania.

Thomas Jefferson and Construction of the Capitol's South Wing

We were not the first to encounter schedule delays and cost increases on major US Capitol expansion projects. President Thomas Jefferson and architect Benjamin Henry Latrobe encountered similar problems during construction of the Capitol's south wing from 1803 to 1808. We would experience still more problems with the construction of the Capitol Visitor Center two hundred years later. In March 1803 funds were appropriated for the expansion because the House of Representatives had added thirty-eight new members and required more space. Jefferson offered Latrobe a temporary position to complete the project and mandated that construction begin in April. To meet that deadline, Latrobe had to order stone immediately, since it is a long-lead construction material.

In Latrobe's February 20, 1804, negative report to Congress about building progress, Allen writes Latrobe blamed "the slow progress on wet weather, which flooded the freestone quarry, and the lack of workmen."[24] Delayed stone deliveries and congressional opposition sounded uncomfortably familiar to me. Allen continues that, in his 1806 annual report, Latrobe attempted to explain the problems he encountered:

> Difficulty with stone delivery was cited as the principal cause of disappointment, although "every encouragement was offered to the quarries to make extraordinary exertions." . . . And while he had already been granted two appropriations for completing the south wing, Latrobe asked for more money to finish the work in 1807. . . . Latrobe had promised the president the wing would be ready for the House by December 1, 1806, and now found that promise impossible to keep.[25]

It is clear that high levels of congressional opposition have remained consistent over the years for many important projects, and that promises to presidents made by senators or architects sometimes don't work out.

A Sandstone Jigsaw Puzzle

Two centuries later, while trying to create a stone pattern compatible with the rotunda's wide range of sandstone colors, we wrestled with how to create a harmonious whole out of thousands of such variegated sandstone pieces. The solution started at the quarry with our contract documents clearly specifying a range of sandstone colors that would be acceptable. The quarried blocks and sawn slabs that did not fit within this range were rejected.

Many identically sized, finished sandstone pieces were needed for the expansive walls of Emancipation Hall and throughout the visitor center. Guided by a stone matrix prepared by CRTKL's Janice Adams, field coordinator Tim Hutcheson laid these finished

Figure 9.14. New sandstone wall in Emancipation Hall. Courtesy of Jeffrey Schwarz Photography

slabs out on the floor, arranging them as they were delivered. This prevented an unbalanced overall pattern by creating arrangements that avoided a preponderance of darker or lighter slabs in any one area. While the pattern may appear to be random, it was sensitively studied and carefully worked.

Despite the lawsuits, the new sandstone was beautifully laid up by our stone installers, Boatman and Magnani. It is richly varied in tone and texture, imbuing this newest Capitol extension with a sense of tradition and permanence. As visitors ride escalators from this new underground building into the Capitol, the virtually seamless light-filled transition appears natural and thoroughly compatible with the historic stonework of the crypt and rotunda, becoming part of the Capitol's harmonious whole.

Notes

1. Statement of Alan M. Hantman, Fiscal Year 2002 Appropriation Request, before the US House of Representatives, Committee on Appropriations, Subcommittee on Commerce, Justice, State, the Judiciary, March 29, 2001.
2. Transcript of Fiscal Year 2002 Appropriation Request, before the US House of Representatives, Committee on Appropriations, Subcommittee on Commerce, Justice, State, the Judiciary, March 29, 2001.
3. Chief Justice William Rehnquist, Prepared Remarks at Groundbreaking Ceremony, Modernization of the Supreme Court Building, June 17, 2003.
4. Chief Justice John Roberts, Speech at Indiana University School of Law, April 2010, quoted in "Chief Justice Roberts on Home Turf in Indiana," *BLT: The Blog of Legal Times*, April 8, 2010.
5. Department of Defense, June 7, 2004.
6. William Branigin, *Washington Post*, June 9, 2004.
7. Donna Lawrence, Approved Final Treatment, Orientation Film, United States Capitol Visitor Center, Donna Lawrence Productions, 1 2.15.04, 1.

8. David Barton, *The Myth of Separation: What Is the Correct Relationship between Church and State* (Aledo, TX: WallBuilders Press, 1989).

9. David Barton to Tom DeLay, Critique of Capitol Visitor Center Orientation Film, 2006.

10. Barton to DeLay.

11. Robert Dreyfuss, "DeLay Incorporated," *Texas Observer*, February 4, 2000.

12. Stephanie Simon, "Historian Remains Key Ally of Right," *Politico*, September 8, 2013.

13. Katherine Stewart, "Betsy DeVos and God's Plan for Schools," *New York Times*, December 13, 2016.

14. Marc Fisher, "DC's New Underground Jewel: Best in a Decade," *Washington Post* blog, November 28, 2008.

15. Allen, *History of the United States Capitol*, 25.

16. "Special Task Force to Study the History and Contributions of Slave Laborers in the Construction of the US Capitol," Joint House and Senate Leadership Press Release, May 27, 2005.

17. Allen, *History of Slave Laborers*.

18. Allen, 9, 2.

19. Allen, 18.

20. *Virginia Herald*, December 22, 1794, quoted in Jane Henderson Conner, "Government Island: Its Forgotten History and Interesting Stone," unpublished manuscript, 1980.

21. "Providing for Design of Slave Labor Marker in Capitol Visitor Center," July 7, 2009, *Congressional Record*, vol. 155, no. 100.

22. "Providing for Design of Slave Labor Marker."

23. John J. Dingess, Esquire, Record before the Special Master, March 22, 2006. The judge had entered a referral order creating a special master to make recommendations covering almost two years of court-related actions in Civil Action No. 03-1276, before the Honorable Joy Flowers Conti: Quarra Stone Company, LLC, plaintiff vs. Samuel W. Tiche, d/b/a Annandale Sandstone, Boatman & Magnani, Inc., and Manhattan Construction Co., Defendants.

24. Allen, *History of the United States Capitol*, 54.

25. "Report of the Surveyor of the public buildings of the United States, at Washington," November 26, 1806, communicated to Congress on December 15, 1806, quoted in Allen, 67.

TEN

Tying It Together

A Critical Capitol Transition Area

In the course of the Capitol's two-hundred-year evolution, each new increment of growth has been designed with respect for the existing building, to preserve it as a cohesive whole. We too worked to assure that the visitor center design would create a seamless and dignified transition for visitors as they entered the Capitol. Key to this were the creation of an intuitive procession of escalators, elevators, and interconnecting stairs as they rise smoothly from the underground center into the Capitol's East Front; the incorporation of daylight and outside views to keep guests oriented; and the provision of quality building materials compatible with the historic Capitol.

Parking has always been an important issue on Capitol Hill, and the 1960s East Front expansion was designed to permit direct access into the Capitol building from a future five-hundred-car garage beneath the East Plaza. The 1993 truck bomb attack in the underground garage at New York's World Trade Center spotlighted now obvious parking security risks. The Capitol garage was never constructed.

Fortunately, the proposed entry area was built at the perfect transition point to provide direct entry to the Capitol for millions of annual visitors. Our major design challenge was in working within the limitations of the closely spaced concrete piers supporting the central portico above. This forced us to arrange the stairs, escalators, and elevators into narrow side-by-side circulation streams, much like the teeth of a comb. While this transition was

physically possible, the configuration was constricted and would not be as welcoming or seamless a link into the historic Capitol we considered important.

Tight Excavation and Micro-Piles

As we began construction work in this sensitive area, we found the working clearances adjacent to the Capitol's foundations too tight for standard pile-driving equipment, which would create risk to the Capitol itself. A structural review dictated that more compact equipment was needed to auger-drill smaller-diameter, more closely spaced micro-piles. Importantly, the review also found that by removing the two central concrete piers we could open up this constricted area to create a single, clear pathway for both stairs and escalators, a much more gracious way to transition between the visitor center and Capitol.

Before removing the piers, the weight of the rotunda steps and portico first had to be transferred to a pair of massive, specially fabricated thirty-eight-foot-long, seven-and-a-half-ton steel beams. I marveled at the precision of the steel workers as they delicately maneuvered the beams through the carriageway opening into this confined space, without damaging existing stonework.

With the piers removed, the stairs and escalators could rise cleanly through the old carriageway area into the Capitol, with the arched carriageway opening bringing natural light into this dramatic new entrance. As visitors ascend into the Capitol, these glazed archways provide views of the stately House

Figure 10.1. Removal of two central piers creating a stair and escalator transition area into the Capitol. Courtesy of Architect of the Capitol

Figure 10.2. Steel workers installing new support beam at the old carriageway entrance. Courtesy of Architect of the Capitol

Figure 10.3. Glazing the old carriageway opening. Courtesy of Architect of the Capitol

Figure 10.4. Open stair and escalator transition connecting Capitol building and visitor center. Courtesy of Alan M. Hantman

and Senate wings, orienting them to their Capitol destination while eliminating any sense of being in a confined underground space, a midcourse design change that greatly improved the arrival experience.

This entryway to the Capitol frames the visitor center on the west, while on the eastern side, vis-itors are welcomed with full views of the Capitol Dome as they traverse stairways and gently curving entry ramps that usher them down to the center's entrances eighteen feet below East Capitol Street.

During our early design stages, newspaper crit-ics proclaimed that it would not be possible for an underground building to achieve a true sense of openness. Our design team proved them wrong by creating an open and light-filled building, appreciated by all who use it. As architect Daniel Libeskind said: "In a strange way, architecture is really an unfinished thing, because even though the building is finished, it takes on a new life. It becomes part of a new dynamic: how people will occupy it, use it, think about it."[1]

To reinforce the sense of continuity with the historic building, we designed decorative stone floors and bronze doors, railings and grills that gave the public spaces a sense of appropriateness and permanence. We then populated these spaces with statues from the National Statuary Hall Collection to create a sense of scale and continuity.

National Statuary Hall: A King and an Astronaut

In 1857, when the House of Representatives moved into its new and larger chamber, it had not yet decided how to use the old House Chamber. According to House historian records, "The old Hall of the House, empty and deserted, remains an unappropriated waste, and as it now appears—draped in cobwebs, and carpeted with dust, tobacco, and apple pomace (from apple vendors)—a conspicuous nuisance."[2]

Representative Justin Morrill of Vermont proposed that the hall be made into an artistic showplace, and legislation signed into law by President Abraham Lincoln in 1864 provided that

> the President is hereby authorized to invite each and all States to provide and furnish statues, in marble or bronze, not exceeding two in number for each State, of deceased persons who have been citizens thereof, and illustrious for their historic renown or for distinguished civic or military services such as each state may deem to be worthy of this national commemoration; and when so furnished, the same shall be placed in

the Old Hall of the House of Representative, in the Capitol of the United States.[3]

King Kamehameha I and the Resolution

I welcomed a delegation from the Association of Hawaiian Civic Clubs who wore multicolored muumuus, native Hawaiian cloaks, and business suits as they presented me with a copy of their resolution of October 29, 2005, "Urging the US Architect of the Capitol to Relocate the Statue of King Kamehameha I to a More Prominent Position in National Statuary Hall and Insure the Dissemination of Accurate Historic Information About King Kamehameha I."[4]

The delegation also presented a copy of the resolution to Senators Daniel Inouye (D-HI) and Daniel Akaka and Congressmen Neil Abercrombie (D-HI) and Ed Case (D-HI), hoping to build support to move the fifteen-thousand-pound statue. Members of Hawai'i's Royal Benevolent Societies, the Office of Hawaiian Affairs, the Hawai'i State Society of Washington, and a number of other organizations were unhappy about the king's current Statuary Hall location.

Once Hawai'i became a state in 1959, it was entitled to place two statues in the Capitol. In 1969 Hawai'i presented its King Kamehameha I statue to the Congress. It was cast from molds taken from an 1879 statue by sculptor Thomas R. Gould, which stands in Kohala, the king's birthplace, on the island of Hawai'i.

The Architect of the Capitol website describes the statue:

> Kamehameha in his regal garb, including a helmet of rare feathers attached to woven plant fibers. The gilded cloak is based on one that Kamehameha's subjects made for the king by weaving yellow feathers of native birds into a fine mesh net. The spear in his left hand symbolizes the ability to defend oneself and one's nation. It is also a reminder that Kamehameha ended the wars among the Hawaiian people. His right hand

Over the past 150 years, all fifty states have selected two distinguished citizens to be honored with a statue in the Capitol. The first was in 1870 of Nathanael Greene, a Revolutionary War general from Rhode Island. In July 2020, in the wake of George Floyd's murder, the House voted to banish from the Capitol all statues of Confederate figures or those who supported White supremacist causes. In 2020 Senate Majority Leader Mitch McConnell did not take up the bill and declared it "an attempt to 'airbrush the Capitol.'"[5]

A year later, on June 29, 2021, the House again passed a bill with a bipartisan vote of 285–120 mandating that any such statue in the Statuary Hall Collection be removed from public display and sent back to its state of origin at the state's cost or be delivered to the Smithsonian Institution by the Architect of the Capitol. This would affect a dozen statues, including one of Jefferson Davis, the president of the Confederate States of America, and the bust of Chief Justice Roger B. Taney, who wrote the majority *Dred Scott v. Sandford* opinion in 1857, which found that Black people were not citizens of the United States under the Constitution.

The bill, passed by a Democratic House majority in June 2021, was not voted on in the Senate. The bicameral bill was reintroduced on February 28, 2023, but as of this writing has not been acted upon. A growing number of states have voluntarily recalled their statues and replaced them with other notable citizens: Arkansas replaced its statue of Confederate sympathizer Uriah Milton Rose and White supremacist James Paul Clarke with those of musician Johnny Cash and civil rights activist Daisy Bates, and Virginia removed its statue of Robert E. Lee in 2020, replacing it with one of civil rights leader Barbara Johns in 2023. Florida replaced its statue of Confederate General Edmund Kirby Smith in 2018 with one of Mary McLeod Bethune, a civil rights activist and presidential adviser, on July 13, 2022.

is extended in a gesture of aloha, the traditional spirit of friendly greeting.[6]

The statue of Kamehameha, which is just shy of ten feet tall with a three-foot-six-inch-high solid granite base, was the largest in the National Statuary Hall Collection. Because of its great weight, a structural analysis was required to determine which areas of the floor could safely support its fifteen thousand pounds. The king was placed against a wall in Statuary Hall, behind a row of other statues. On June 11 each year a delegation from Hawai'i holds a lei draping ceremony to celebrate the Hawaiian state holiday of Kamehameha I Day. The delegation was upset that this constricted location did not allow the celebrants to honor the king's memory with the full respect and visibility it deserved.

Selecting Visitor Center Statues

At the time of the delegation's visit, our agency's curator, Barbara Wolanin, was developing a list of statues that could potentially be moved from the Capitol's collection to the visitor center. Statuary Hall and several overflow corridors had become too crowded, and the Joint Committee on the Library and the Capitol Preservation Commission decided to relocate some of the collection. I enthusiastically supported this initiative since this would help create a sense of continuity between the two structures.

Some members of Congress carried this concept too far by calling for studies to identify places in the visitor center for fifty new statues so that each state could donate a third statue. Such a proposal would have created crowding in every corner of the visitor center and done nothing to reduce Capitol overcrowding.

Few states volunteered to have one of their statues moved out of the Capitol. The premier locations were in National Statuary Hall, the Hall of Columns on the House side of the Capitol, and in the crypt. Other statues are located in the northern and southern wings of the Capitol. One option was to relocate the most recent statues added to the collection, effectively grandparenting in statues from the original thirteen colonies. Five of the most recent additions were those I had the honor of recommending for acceptance into the collection. Four statues represent Native Americans, including two women, and all honor individuals who impacted the history of western states:

Sarah Winnemucca, a defender of human rights, author, and educator, was "a member of the Paiute tribe born in what would later become the state of Nevada."[7]

Po' Pay was the leader of the Pueblo Revolt of 1680 against Spanish conquerors, the first American Revolution. He was from the San Juan Pueblo, in what is now the state of Nevada.[8]

Sakakawea of the Shoshone and Hidatsa tribes in what was to become the state of North Dakota, is shown with her infant son strapped to her back. "Her indomitable spirit was a deciding factor in the success of Lewis and Clark's . . . expedition."[9]

Chief Washakie, of the Shoshone tribe, is one of the most respected leaders in Native American history. He negotiated the Fort Bridger Treaty of 1868 with the Army leading to the establishment of a three-million-acre reservation for his people in Wyoming's Wind River country.[10]

In 1997 Colorado decided to honor astronaut John "Jack" Swigert Jr. with a statue that would be its second donation to the National Statuary Hall Collection. Swigert excelled first as an Air Force combat pilot during the Korean War and then as the command module pilot aboard the Apollo 13 mission. His actions were critical to safely returning the

Figure 10.5. Statue of John L. Swigert Jr., Colorado. Courtesy of Jeffrey Schwarz Photography

crew of the aborted mission back to Earth. In 1982 Swigert was elected to Colorado's sixth congressional district but tragically died before assuming office.

Until this time, all of the statues in the collection were a natural stone color or were finished with a solid bronze tone (except for gold leaf accents on the statue of King Kamehameha I). Colorado's statue of Swigert was designed with the bronze, white, red, blue, and yellow colors that accurately depicted the spacesuit he wore. Our curator was concerned that visitors were constantly touching and rubbing the statues, wearing off their finishes over time. She recommended that instead we propose that the statue have a monochromatic finish rather than multiple

STATUES MOVED TO THE VISITOR CENTER

All these additions to the National Statuary Hall Collection were moved into the visitor center, as was a new statue of Helen Keller as a young girl. Her statue was accepted into the collection in 2009, when Alabama recalled its 1908 statue of politician Jabez Lamar Monroe Curry under the 2000 law permitting states to recall prior donations and replace them with representations of other notable citizens.

Kansas governor George Washington Glick's statue was recalled under the same 2000 law, and replaced in 2003 by a bronze statue of General Dwight D. Eisenhower, which now stands in the Capitol Rotunda. Additional states have also initiated such replacements, including Nebraska, which replaced the statue of William Jennings Bryan in 2019 with Chief Standing Bear of the Ponca tribe and plans to replace that of Oliver P. Morton with one of author Willa Cather. In addition, a statue of Frederick Douglass was donated in 2013 when an act of Congress permitted the District of Columbia to provide a single statue. Since the District of Columbia is not a state, this piece stands in a place of honor in Emancipation Hall as part of Congress's art collection.

colors, which would be easier to maintain. I agreed with her recommendation.

Senator Ben Nighthorse Campbell and Colorado state representatives, however, disagreed, and the delegation successfully prevailed on the Joint Committee on the Library, my oversight body for the reception and location of statues, to allow the artists, George and Mark Lundeen, to complete the bronze statue as they wished.

A Sensitive Underground Location

Twenty-four statues were moved into the visitor center, and King Kamehameha I was among them. The Hawaiian delegation was quite willing to have the statue moved out of its back-row spot in National Statuary Hall, but since Kamehameha I was a king and respect was to be paid to his status, no one could be permitted to walk above the head of his statue.

We were challenged to find a satisfactory solution to the delegation's concerns since the visitor center is underground, with the East Plaza's constant pedestrian ebb and flow directly above. We sat-

isfied the Association of Hawaiian Civic Clubs, however, with our recommendation that Kamehameha be placed beneath the corner of a skylight and its surrounding fountain in the northeastern section of Emancipation Hall.

The king in all his majesty now stands in a prominent and respectful location in Emancipation Hall, and the lei draping ceremony on King Kamehameha I Day each year is celebrated with sunlight streaming in through the expansive skylight above. The footprint of the fountain prevents anyone from walking above the king's head (fig. 10.6).

Extending the Garden

Other long-delayed Capitol Hill projects moved ahead at the same time as the visitor center. In 1991 Congress passed legislation to finance a new national garden by establishing the National Fund for the United States Botanic Garden. This was a not-for-profit public-private partnership administered by the Architect of the Capitol under the oversight of the Joint Committee on the Library. This three-

Figure 10.6. Statue of King Kamehameha beneath the visitor center north skylight. Courtesy of Jeffrey Schwarz Photography

acre outdoor garden completed the block bounded by Maryland Avenue, First Street Southwest, and Independence Avenue and increased the Botanic Garden's capacity to display the plants and trees that naturally grow in the mid-Atlantic region and explain their importance to the environment.

The fund began ramping up its $12 million fundraising effort under Board of Trustees Chair Teresa Heinz. In 2004, during the National Garden's final design and construction phases, in order to avoid any hint of political bias, Heinz stepped down as chair when her husband John Kerry ran for president. The Teresa and H. John Heinz III Foundation was a major founding sponsor of the National Garden.

The garden was designed by associate landscape architect EDAW Inc. of Alexandria, Virginia (which included design concepts from a 1993 design competition), with associate architect Tobey + Davis. The fund ultimately raised $11.5 million in contributions from nationwide garden clubs, individuals, and garden-related corporations including Ames True Temper, HGTV, Lowe's Home Improvement, and Scotts.

At the ground-breaking ceremony, I concluded my remarks by thanking those involved in this public-private partnership and quoted an old Chi-

Figure 10.7. Leone Reeder (fund president), First Lady Laura Bush, and Jim Hagedorn, a major donor, cutting the National Garden dedication ribbon. Courtesy of Architect of the Capitol

nese proverb, "The best time to plant a tree is fifty years ago. The second-best time is now." We were there that day to plant seeds for the future and celebrate continuity with the past.

Honorary trustees included First Lady Laura Bush along with six former First Ladies: Barbara Bush, Rosalynn Carter, Hillary Clinton, Betty Ford, Lady Bird Johnson, and Nancy Reagan. We constructed a colorful mosaic-lined water garden near the entrance, dedicating it to the First Ladies of the United States. On a clear fall day in September 2006, Laura Bush graciously took part in the formal National Garden ribbon cutting ceremony.

Major displays include a formal rose garden with hundreds of varieties of historical and modern roses, a showcase garden displaying native flora of the mid-Atlantic region in natural settings, a butterfly garden featuring scented and nectar producing plants that attract adult butterflies, and a wetland created with rainwater that is captured and recirculated on-site.

The National Garden became an integral part of the US Botanic Garden under the stewardship of the architect. At the heart of the combined indoor and outdoor gardens are hundreds of annual public programs. The fund's successful private fundraising initiative had made it possible to expand and complement this national treasure, first conceived of more than two hundred years ago.

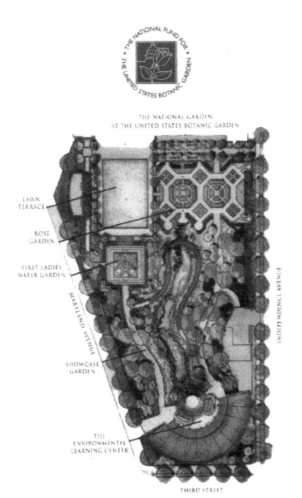

Figure 10.8. Design plan of the National Garden. Courtesy of SmithGroup Landscape Architects

Restoring Olmsted's Landscape Structures

We were in the process of restoring Olmsted's landscape structures, in addition to preserving hundreds of trees and restoring important Olmsted view corridors, as heavy visitor center construction was concluding and interior construction work progressed. The original fountain planters flanking the East Capitol Street entrance to the plaza, shown in his 1874 masterplan, required significant restoration work.

The piping on the oval bronze fountains on the upper level had deteriorated, and the red granite structures were primarily used as planters. This pair of water features was originally designed to create a fine rainbow mist framing the view of the Capitol Dome for those entering the grounds from East Capitol Street, with concealed lighting maintaining the rainbow during evening hours. Unfortunately, when long lines of people waiting to enter the Capitol stood between the fountains and the wind came up, they got soaked, a problem we had to address.

We removed the fountain planters, rebuilt their complex piping, and reinstalled them when the redesigned plaza was prepared to receive them. The water jets in the bronze basins are now monitored by anemometers to lower water pressure under windy conditions, protecting visitors from blowing spray.

Figure 10.9. View of dome and conservatory from the National Garden. Courtesy of Architect of the Capitol

Figure 10.10.
Reinstalling Olmsted's
bronze fountain basins.
Courtesy of Architect
of the Capitol

Figure 10.11. Adjusting Olmsted fountain spray heads. Courtesy of Architect of the Capitol

Figure 10.12. Reinstalling Olmsted lanterns. Courtesy of Architect of the Capitol

Olmsted's creations once again function as fountain planters or purely as planters, depending on the season. We also removed, restored, and reinstalled Olmsted's six fourteen-foot-tall red granite piers, topped with bronze and glass lanterns, that stand adjacent to the fountains.

We used the same red stone that had been selected for the fountains and lanterns to create two ADA-compliant elevator structures that blend in with the family of Olmsted's richly detailed historic structures. Maintaining Olmsted's dictum of not obstructing views of the Capitol building, no other new aboveground elements were added to the East Plaza. By mounting high-intensity lighting fixtures on these structures, we now could uniformly illuminate the east side of the Capitol Dome. This lighting blends seamlessly with the other three quadrants of the dome, lit by fixtures mounted on the Capitol building roof. The dome is also automatically lit from dusk to dawn each day by an astronomical time

Figure 10.13. ADA-compliant visitor center elevators. Courtesy of Architect of the Capitol

clock in the Capitol basement and can be seen as the same uniformly glowing landmark from all points of the compass.

Olmsted's elegant ironwork shelter, originally built for a north–south streetcar line, had also deteriorated badly over time. We disassembled it and brought it to a remote site, where it was fully restored. We then reinstalled the shelter at the same historic location, where it can grace the grounds for the next hundred years, its wrought iron benches providing a well-shaded respite on hot summer days.

The Washington, DC, chapter of the American Institute of Architects presented our project and our landscape architects, Sasaki Company, with its Landscape Architecture Award of Excellence.

The Fire Marshal

In the immediate aftermath of the 9/11 and anthrax attacks, Fire Marshal Kenneth Lauziere instituted greatly enhanced criteria for the design and testing of the visitor center's fire and life-safety systems. He insisted upon major revisions to protocols he had

helped develop, changes that complicated already completed designs and required revisions to systems already installed. It soon became clear that his criteria also conflicted with the Capitol Police's critical security concerns.

Lauziere knew he would be responsible if those systems malfunctioned, and he would not issue the certificate of occupancy required to open the visitor center until all of his concerns were resolved. I was committed to providing all necessary fire and life-safety systems for the Capitol Visitor Center and testing them to assure each performed as designed, but most project experts, including our electrical consultants and fire science and engineering consultants, believed these changes were unwarranted, went well beyond code requirements, and would result in major project delays and cost increases.

The National Fire Protection Association was the only appropriate authority to review Lauziere's new demands and provide authoritative recommendations. I asked the association to organize a blue-ribbon panel of experts to review our fire and life-safety protection issues to determine whether our original design was sound and, if necessary, offer viable alternatives to the fire marshal's heavily revised design and testing criteria. The fire marshal agreed to take part in this process only if he could select panel members.

The Government Accountability Office representative, Bernie Unger, effectively quashed the panel concept by testifying that although Lauziere's requirements exceeded code criteria and were not called for in the construction documents, these requirements were not unreasonable and should be allowed to proceed. Years later, Unger told me that he rejected my efforts to create a National Fire Protection Association review panel because he believed it would delay the project and further increase costs. He never anticipated that the fire marshal's new requirements would delay the project by a year and add millions of dollars to costs.

During this complex process, many expressed frustration during both House and Senate Appropriations hearings, and this was fully covered in the press. In February 2006, *Roll Call* reported:

> When building a 580,000-square-foot underground addition to a structure that is by all accounts one of the top terrorist targets in the United States, testing the fire and safety systems is a bit harder than just making sure a few smoke detectors are working.... The complicated fire-protection and safety features in all three sections of the CVC "not only have to perform well individually, but their operation has to be integrated," the Government Accountability Office noted in its testimony. "If the CVC team encounters any significant problems with their functioning, either individually or together, the project could be seriously delayed."[11]

Lauziere continued to develop his testing plan before he finally submitted it at a hearing before the House Appropriations Subcommittee. In August 2007, *Roll Call* reported:

> Bernard Unger, the CVC project manager, said at one point during Tuesday's hearing that given

the complexity of the fire marshal's plan, he considers it more likely the testing process would take eleven months or perhaps a year. . . . Some Members have questioned the AOC on why testing the system is expected to take so long. A year ago, Hantman told Senate appropriators that the CVC "is virtually the nation's beta test site for the very comprehensive security and fire- and life-safety systems that are being installed."[12]

The complexity is due to the center's underground location, the more stringent fire and life-safety requirements a place of public assembly requires, and the high level of security required at the seat of our federal government. The functions of these separate yet interconnected systems can sometimes conflict.

Security versus Fire and Life Safety

Fire and life-safety systems operate to detect and extinguish fires and provide alarms and mass communication systems to alert occupants to risks. They also enable safe evacuation of a building through fire-resistant spaces and doors designed to give people adequate time to safely exit. The risks range from fire, gas leaks, storms and floods, structural problems, and other security threats. Conflicts arise when external security threats dictate that it is safer to shelter in place rather than evacuate. Life-safety systems are programmed to release all doors for emergency egress, but this also leaves the doors open for outside intruders to enter. It was controlling for this possibility that required such time-consuming and complex coordination between systems.

These testing protocols continued to evolve, delaying the visitor center completion and frustrating the Congress, including its appropriators. At a February 2008 House Appropriations hearing, *Roll Call* reported, "Fire and life-safety testing at the Capitol Visitor Center remains the biggest potential threat to the facility's scheduled November opening, officials overseeing the project told appropriators on Thursday. 'I never thought fire alarm testing would make my heart pound at night, but it does,'" said Debbie Wasserman Schultz (D-FL), chair of the Appropriations Subcommittee on the Legislative Branch.[13] Senate appropriator Bob Bennett repeatedly expressed his frustration directly to the fire marshal but was unable to get him to accelerate his testing schedule. The issue of conflicting systems was finally resolved once the fire marshall's schedule ran its course and significant related costs were added to the project budget.

Task Force 1-6: Ongoing Security Issues in 2021

It seems ironic that after all the intensive effort to redesign the fire and life-safety systems to promote safe egress, the most grievous risk to the Capitol and the Congress came years later from insurrectionists smashing their way into the Capitol to disrupt the counting of the electoral votes following the 2020 presidential election. The thin blue line of unprepared and poorly led Capitol Police was unable to defend against the mob of thousands on January 6, 2021.

The January 6 insurrection is a harrowing example of the conflict between security and fire and life-safety systems, presenting a danger to both the police and the Capitol's occupants. Because of the sensitivity of the counting of electoral votes, no alarms were sounded to interrupt the process, and members remained in the House and Senate chambers unaware that insurrectionists had broken through doors and windows and were advancing their way. If alarms had been sounded, members and staff might have rushed from the chambers directly into the path of rioters while trying to exit the Capitol. This same kind of conflict had been at the core of the intense debate over the design and testing program for the security and life-safety systems that delayed the visitor center.

Speaker Nancy Pelosi's Task Force 1-6 was composed of "professionals with law enforcement, legal, personal protection, intelligence, operational, and Congressional experience." It was led by retired lieutenant general Russel L. Honoré, with a mission to provide a nonpartisan six-week assessment of how to improve Capitol security operations and infrastructure physical security. The task force's review began by stressing the obvious challenge discussed at several points in this volume regarding "the inherent tension between public access and physical security. Any security measure that reduces physical access to the Capitol makes it less accessible to the public it serves."[14]

Capitol Security Operations

Task Force 1-6's assessment urged an increase in staff, training, analytic tools, standardization of its intelligence processes, and "close collaboration across the intelligence and law enforcement communities to obtain early warning and gain collective understanding."[15]

These recommendations are necessary to shift the Capitol Police to a threat-based operations model, where a member of intelligence staff becomes part of the police command center, providing threat briefings on a daily basis to inform decision-making. This coordination had also clearly been missing at the command center back on 9/11, when briefings to members of Congress consisted of information gleaned from televised reporting rather than from the larger intelligence community.

Other important report recommendations included adding 854 authorized positions to the department, creating ongoing individual and team training programs, civil disturbance training, leader development programs, and a dedicated quick reaction force for response to crises anywhere in the district, and reestablishing the mounted unit for crowd control (which was disbanded in 2005 in a politically misguided cost-saving measure). The task force also considered it important to give the Capitol Police chief "authority to request external law enforcement and National Guard support without Capitol Police Board preapproval in extraordinary emergency circumstances."[16]

As a former member of the Police Board, I agree that the chief must have such authority, since in reviewing the issues of the January 6 crisis, it appears that the sergeants at arms were overly sensitive to the political optics of both the president's rally and early insurrectionist threats online. They therefore failed to respond quickly enough to the chief's request for authority to mobilize the Capitol Police and seek National Guard assistance, both in advance of and during the January 6, 2021, insurrection.

Physical Security Infrastructure

The task force also focused on perimeter security fencing considerations since thousands of people had pushed through flimsy bicycle rack barriers set up to protect the Capitol perimeter. For the short term, their recommendations included the use of ten-foot-high mobile fencing that can be erected and taken down quickly. Temporary protective fencing is an option we all supported on the Police Board, but I always objected to the concept, supported by the sergeants at arms, of permanent fencing or obstacles, that I believed would make the Capitol appear to be fortified against our own citizens.

As an alternative method for securing the Capitol and House and Senate office buildings for the long term, while still maintaining public accessibility, the task force recommended construction of a retractable fencing system as part of "a fully integrated system of obstacles, cameras, sensors, and alarms."[17] The concept of a fully integrated system certainly makes sense, as long as the obstacles are not visually intrusive and the system is actively monitored on-site by appropriate numbers of Capitol Police. If the appearance of a visibly fortified Capitol can be avoided by building a fully retractable system that can be efficiently maintained and operated, then this could be a viable resolution to the conflict between security and accessibility by providing both at our Temple of Liberty. Two months after Task Force 1-6's Capitol Security Review, the *Washington Post* reported, on May 20, that the House passed a bill that includes "$529.7 million for security improvements, including $250 million to harden the Capitol complex for retractable or mobile fencing, bulletproof doors and windows, new entrance vestibules, and cameras."[18]

The Speaker's Elevator and Personal Threats

During the course of construction, our project team experienced a number of conflicts with Speaker Hastert's office that added to overall project cost and schedule. Hastert's chief of staff, Scott Palmer, was more powerful than most House members. During the construction of the Capitol interface area, Palmer summoned me to his office in the Speaker's Capitol suite.

The two-hundred-year-old Capitol was never designed to accommodate millions of annual visitors. Changes in floor levels between the Capitol's many additions and its narrow winding steps made it particularly challenging for visitors with disabilities. To resolve this problem, the visitor center project included two new twenty-five-passenger elevators to take visitors from the top floor of the new underground building to each of three major floors of the Capitol. We were also in the process of enlarging two existing elevators at the center of the Capitol to make them wheelchair accessible and code compliant.

Renovation of the existing elevators was under way during the 2005 peak spring and summer tourist season, and they were not slated to be fully operational for many months. Capitol guides were ushering visitors with disabilities to the Speaker's personal elevator, occasionally tying it up when the Speaker and his staff needed it. Speaking for Hastert, Palmer insisted that this infringement be stopped.

Our project team, along with Capitol Police and tour guide management, explored the possible use of alternative elevators and corridors, but Palmer rejected all options. He directed that the elevators under construction be completed expeditiously to avoid inconveniencing the Speaker any longer. Palmer appeared to have little interest in the needs of disabled visitors, and his directive was crystal clear. Failure would not be tolerated, and my job was on the line.

When we brought this directive to a staff meeting of the Capitol Preservation Commission, Senate representatives chose not to comment on the Speaker's new requirement or how it would affect our project's schedule and costs. I had little choice but to direct the contractor to renovate the existing elevator immediately, right at the center of this heavy construction zone. Once it was renovated, we then constructed a corridor-tunnel within the work zone, complete with lighting, sprinklers, and carpeting, to protect visitors as they accessed the newly compliant elevator.

Meeting the Speaker's demand took management time away from the visitor center proper and further delayed final stonework and other finishes in that East Front portion of the project. After several months of expensive construction workarounds, I requested permission from the Speaker's office to remove the temporary visitor tunnel. Palmer refused since disabled visitors would once again have to use the Speaker's elevator. This out-of-sequence elevator rebuilding was ultimately completed at an increased cost of almost five hundred thousand dollars plus related project delays. This is but one example of multiple changes dictated for personal convenience or political hubris that impacted the project, wasting taxpayer money.

It could have been worse. Strong support of the visitor center project by the Speaker's senior staffer, Ted Van Der Meid, was critical to avoiding other obstacles to project progress. The Hill quoted Ray LaHood (R-IL) saying of Van Der Meid, "He has a lot of influence. . . . He does everything that [Palmer] does not want to do."[19]

Van Der Meid was counsel for the Speaker, director of his floor operations, and in charge of oversight of the Capitol Visitor Center and House officers, including Jeff Trandahl, clerk of the House. Trandahl attended the weekly commission staff meetings on behalf of the Speaker and helped resolve outstanding issues to keep the project moving. Van Der Meid worked positively with Trandahl, and they were both concerned with security, aesthetics, and progress. Most senior staffers avoided associating their names with any decision, and it was often difficult reaching consensus on a wide range of design and construction issues. Van Der Meid's assistance was critical, but even he could not reverse poor decisions when Speaker Hastert or Scott Palmer demanded their way.

The Great Hall Morphs into Emancipation Hall

Early in the project, the Capitol Preservation Commission determined that the visitor center's major spaces would be given generic names rather than be dedicated to notable individuals or members of Congress. This impeded early fundraising efforts since naming rights requested by potential donors could not be granted. When we began working on interior finishes, I was directed to name the center's main

---

ERASING HASTERT'S PRESENCE

When the US Capitol Visitor Center was opened to the public, Speaker Hastert's voice could be heard in the twelve-minute pre-tour orientation film declaring as he loudly rapped his gavel, "The House will be in order!" The film remained unchanged for years until his conviction and imprisonment, when it was then altered to replace his voice with a less controversial one calling the House to order. His portrait as Speaker was removed and placed in storage.

space the Great Hall and contract for its signage. I had objected to the name years earlier, pointing out that there was already a Great Hall in the library's Jefferson Building, in the Supreme Court Building, and in various other federal buildings in DC. I didn't think "Great Hall" was distinctive enough to identify the heart of the visitor center. I urged that it be recognized as a central gathering space for all, much like a village commons, and offered the name Rosalyn had suggested, the Capitol Commons, but I was told the decision was final.

In January 2007, as construction was approaching its final stages and my ten-year term as architect was drawing to a close, I invited Jim Billington, Librarian of Congress, and his wife, Marjorie, to tour the nearly completed visitor center with Rosalyn and me. As we entered the building, I mentioned that the center's central space had been named the Great Hall.

Billington's face turned beet red. He was beside himself saying that this could not be, the Library of Congress already had a Great Hall, that he should have been made aware of this "disaster." His anger increased when I reminded him that his representatives had been fully involved on visitor center advisory panels all along, and also that I agreed with him and had been overruled when I recommended another name. Marjorie Billington apologized for his anger and attempted to calm him down, to no avail.

This marked the beginning of Billington's campaign to convince members of Congress to change the name. Congressman Zach Wamp (R-TN), ranking member of the Legislative Branch Appropriations Subcommittee, became the major champion of his cause, and he enlisted Congressman Jesse Jackson Jr. (D-IL) along the way.

Abraham Lincoln Sways the Congress

"Abraham Lincoln was injected into an otherwise staid budget discussion by the House Appropriations Committee this week," the *Washington Post* reported on June 15, 2007,

when Reps Zach Wamp (R-TN) and Jesse L. Jackson Jr. (D-IL) argued that the main entry hall of the planned Capitol Visitor Center should be named to honor the slaves who built the Capitol. The two lawmakers convinced the panel to toss out plans to call the 20,000-square-foot hall 'the Great Hall' and instead name it "Emancipation Hall." This despite the fact that $250,000 in signs saying "Great Hall" had already been purchased. Wamp was quoted as saying, "I didn't think this up, I felt it. It's the right thing to do." Nothing in the Capitol refers to the slaves who toiled there and that it didn't matter that Great Hall had already been chosen by the Architect of the Capitol. "It doesn't mean you should keep a mistake," he said.[20]

Although I agree one should not "keep a mistake," this was an example of calling out the architect rather than his congressional colleagues who directed the architect to permanently retain what had only been a placeholder name. This directive does not exist in writing because, like many other directives, it was given verbally. In my agency's June 2005 report "History of Slave Laborers in the Construction of the United States Capitol," we presented evidence that the enslaved, rented out by their owners, had played a significant role in the construction of the Capitol.

The *Post* article went on to say that "Jackson dismissed objections by other lawmakers by making a dramatic case for the name change. 'Emancipation is the great, enduring theme of our nation's still unfolding story,' he said. 'Without emancipation, our house divided would not have stood. . . . We would never have had, in the words of Abraham Lincoln, "a new birth of freedom."'"[21]

The History of Slave Laborers at the Capitol

Most members of Congress understood that little could be gained by objecting to the "Emancipation Hall" name change. The resulting bill designating the

Great Hall of the Visitor Center as Emancipation Hall was accompanied by a minority report from the Committee on Transportation and Infrastructure's Representative John L. Mica, who wrote,

> I have concerns about renaming the Great Hall of the Capitol Visitor Center. Throughout the history of the Capitol, none of the monumental spaces, such as the House and Senate chambers or the rotunda, have been named after specific individuals or events in history. Instead these great spaces of the Capitol have long been called by their functional names. By doing so, all people regardless of race, ethnic heritage, culture or human travails are equally recognized. . . . The Great Hall of the Capitol Visitor Center will become a monumental space with its own unique history; and just as those spaces have not been named, I believe the Great Hall should be reserved and left to honor all Americans.[22]

Mica proposed instead that the 16,500-square-foot, museum-quality exhibition hall be named Emancipation Hall. Space would be provided for the Eman-cipation Proclamation, and, according to his report, "permanent exhibits on the Constitution and the post–Civil War amendments proposed by Congress and ratified by the states to abolish slavery, to guarantee equal protection under the law, and to ensure the right to vote. . . . This beautiful hall will have strong historical and contextual links to emancipation."[23]

Alternatively, Mica suggested naming the congressional auditorium Emancipation Hall because leaders would discuss issues that would serve to promote human freedom and our commitment to the Declaration of Independence and Constitution. Senator Wayne Allard (R-CO) pointed out that others who worked on the Capitol in centuries past also deserved recognition, including those from Scotland. There was little additional opposition, and new signs were ordered and fabricated to replace those already erected.

Wamp and Jackson, with the assistance of Abraham Lincoln, turned the issue into a politically sensitive recommendation Congress could not refuse. The two congressmen were invited to the White House in December 2007 by President Bush for the private signing ceremony of HR 3315. They had

Figure 10.14. Integration of visitor center entrance and East Plaza into Olmsted's landscape. Courtesy of Architect of the Capitol

June 2010

not originally conceived of the name change, but they pursued Billington's initiative and reaped the political benefit. Billington's lobbying efforts had protected the exclusivity of his own Great Hall, but I doubt he had anticipated the significant, emotionally fraught dispute that ensued.

The real winners of this debate are the millions of Americans who can safely visit their Capitol annually by entering through monumental Emancipation Hall, including the descendants of the enslaved Black Americans now memorialized there. Hopefully the name Emancipation Hall will remind people of the sacrifices made generations ago and the need for our country to remain, as Congressman Jesse Jackson Jr. argued, "a beacon of freedom and democracy around the world."[24]

Since its 2008 dedication, this ninth and largest expansion of the US Capitol has been fully integrated into the fabric of Capitol Hill life, providing necessary meeting and expansion spaces for the House and Senate, while safely welcoming visitors to the people's house to learn about and observe the workings of the Congress. Bringing this long-delayed dream to fruition was a magnificent challenge.

ONGOING DOME RESTORATION PROJECT

Even as the visitor center was being completed, the funding requested back in 2000 to repair the Capitol Dome was still not forthcoming. When my term ended in 2007, my chief operating officer, Stephen Ayers, became acting architect and was confirmed as the 11th Architect of the Capitol three years later. In 2012 he testified before Congress, as the New York Times reported, "To the myriad indignities suffered by Congress . . . add this: the Capitol's roof is leaking, and there is no money to fix it. . . . While Senate appropriators have voted to repair the dome, which has not undergone major renovations for 50 years, their House counterparts say there is not money right now. . . . 'The dome needs comprehensive rehabilitation,' said Stephen T. Ayers. . . . 'It's a public safety issue.'"[25]

Arguments remained the same, a reprise of the report on the dome's leaks fifteen years earlier. Ayers had to continue pleading the dome's case to the Congress, but I doubt he retrieved my rust-filled coffee can from the archives for his presentation. He received funding to repair the screening walls at the base of the dome, but he needed another $61 million to restore the main exterior work. When funding was ultimately appropriated, the final phase began, and Hoffman Architects was again recalled to help implement the work.

The same paint removal techniques used during my tenure were used again on the interior of the dome, along with the lock and stitch and stainless steel strapping techniques proposed in our master plan. The suspended donut netting was also used again for rotunda protection, and alternative color palettes were tested on the coffered dome to determine which appeared best from the rotunda floor below.

We finally celebrated this last phase of the quarter-century-long dome restoration odyssey, initiated by the 9th Architect of the Capitol, advanced by the 10th Architect, and concluded as promised by the 11th Architect, Stephen Ayers, in time for the January 20, 2017, presidential inauguration. I trust that major dome work will not be necessary for decades into the future. Whomever the Architect of the Capitol is at that time, they will need a stout heart and much patience.

Notes

1. Libeskind quoted in Dushkes, *The Architect Says*, 138. (Libeskind is known best as the master plan architect for the New York World Trade Center reconstruction after 9/11).
2. "The Creation of National Statuary Hall," Office of the Historian.
3. "About the National Statuary Hall Collection," Architect of the Capitol. aoc.gov.
4. Resolution of October 29, 2005, Association of Hawaiian Civic Clubs.
5. Catie Edmondson, "House Votes to Remove Confederate Statues from US Capitol," www.nytimes.com/2020/07/22/us/politics/confederate-statues-us-capitol.html.
6. National Statuary Hall Collection, King Kamehameha I, https://www.aoc.gov/explore-capitol-campus/art/about-national-statuary-hall-collection.
7. "Sarah Winnemucca Statue," Architect of the Capitol, aoc.gov.
8. "Po'pay Statue," Architect of the Capitol, aoc.gov.
9. "Sakakawea Statue," Architect of the Capitol, aoc.gov.
10. "Chief Washakie Statue," Architect of the Capitol, aoc.gov.
11. John McArdle, "CVC Watch," *Roll Call*, February 21, 2006.
12. John McArdle, "Emergency Systems Likely to Delay CVC," *Roll Call*, August 1, 2007.
13. Legislative Branch House Appropriations Hearing, *Roll Call*, February, 2008.
14. Task Force 1-6, "Capitol Security Review," March 5, 2021, 1, 2.
15. Task Force 1-6, 2–3.
16. Task Force 1-6, 3.
17. Task Force 1-6, 9.
18. Spencer S. Hsu, "Jan. 6 Riot Caused $1.5 Million in Damage to Capitol—and US Prosecutors Want Defendants to Pay," *Washington Post*, June 3, 2021.
19. Representative Ray LaHood quoted in Jonathan Kaplan, "Ted Van Der Meid: The Institutionalist," *The Hill*, October 20, 2005.
20. Lyndsey Layton, "A Name Change to Honor Slaves Who Built Capitol," *Washington Post*, June 15, 2007.
21. Layton.
22. Congressman John Mica, minority report, House Resolution 3315, To provide that the Great Hall of the Capitol Visitor Center shall be known as Emancipation Hall, 110th Congress, 2007–2008.
23. Mica.
24. Layton, "Name Change."
25. Jennifer Steinhauer, "Capitol Dome Is Imperiled by 1,300 Cracks and Partisan Rift," *New York Times*, August 24, 2012.

ELEVEN

Perspective and Appreciation

Visitor Center Dedication Ceremony

At noon on December 2, 1863, at the height of the Civil War, "the fifth and final section" of the nineteen-foot-tall *Statue of Freedom* was raised to the top of the Capitol Dome and bolted into place.[1] On December 2, 2008, 145 years later to the day, the original plaster cast of Thomas Crawford's *Freedom* proudly stood as the focal point of Emancipation Hall overseeing the Capitol Visitor Center's formal dedication. The Capitol Police Honor Guard marched into the hall and presented the colors.

As the US Marine Corps Band played, George Washington and the spirits of those who labored since 1793 to bring his far-reaching vision to fruition in stone, brick, and iron seemed to be present, joining with the thousand souls gathered there in placing their hands over their hearts and singing "The Star-Spangled Banner."

House Chaplain Daniel Coughlin delivered the invocation:

> Bless all who have worked to bring this multilayered dream to reality. Grant joy to your people as we dedicate the [Capitol] Visitor Center. . . . Planted underground may this seed, now cracked open, bring forth new life to Capitol Hill, where religious and national traditions are enshrined by history; where crafted architecture opens ever-new dimensions to the meaning of freedom in Your people.[2]

These words were in keeping with the person I knew Chaplain Coughlin to be. I had confided in him and sought his calming presence as congressional pressures rose in the midst of project changes, additions, and cost increases. We walked the project together while it was under construction, and he understood the magnitude of the work, the tremendous effort our teams of workers invested in its success. When he blessed all who worked to "bring this multilayered dream to reality," when he spoke of "crafted architecture open[ing] ever-new dimensions to the meaning of freedom," he was speaking to those workers, those professionals who invested so much in this creation. He was also speaking to me.

Speaker of the House Nancy Pelosi presided over the ceremonies, welcoming and thanking politicians and dignitaries for attending, including former Senate majority leader Tom Daschle, a strong supporter of the center and our agency's historic preservation initiatives. Pelosi's party was just emerging from House minority status, years that effectively lasted through the life of the entire design and construction process.

I understood that in the charged atmosphere on Capitol Hill following the string of hearings questioning our project's post-9/11 progress and cost, it was politically difficult to publicly acknowledge those who had come to celebrate the culmination of their years of service dedicated to planning, designing, and constructing the center, its educational exhibits, the Congressional Auditorium, and all

Figure 11.1. Visitor center dedication ceremony. Courtesy of Architect of the Capitol

the House and Senate meeting rooms and support spaces Congress added to the project.

Coughlin's gentle words rang that day from the walls of Emancipation Hall in appreciation of the thousands of professionals, contractors, and skilled workers who had brought to fruition the stately center now being dedicated. This was in keeping with my foreword to William Allen's book about the Capitol's construction history: "In reading about the history of the Capitol, I am struck by the fact that for more than 200 years it has been a work in progress. Construction of the building that George Washington approved was begun in 1793 but was soon altered by an architectural metamorphosis dictated by changing circumstance, fashion, and fortune. Furthermore, as the nation grew so did the Congress and the Capitol. Change and growth seem to be the threads that bind the Capitol's history together."[3]

In the Company of My Predecessors

The portraits of Benjamin Latrobe and Thomas Ustick Walter, the 2nd and 4th Architects of the Capitol, graced the walls of my Capitol building office, gazing back at me on the long evenings I spent in their company. They had persevered in their times by maintaining their visions as each contributed to the Capitol's centuries-long stewardship even while dealing with shifting levels of congressional support. As I faced my own opportunities and challenges, I often reflected on their experiences, as well as those of my other predecessors, seeking clues to their success.

They designed and constructed additions to the Capitol over the course of two centuries, sensitively building on one another's work, transforming it into the symbol of America we see today. Their portraits spoke to me of formidable problems, some of which are written into the historical record and others known only to them.

"Even before the first stone was laid, the Capitol was a lightning rod of controversy," historian William Allen wrote.

Every step in its evolution has been scrutinized under the political microscope by those insistent upon exposing misdeeds—whether they are real, perceived or imaginary. This is the nature of public works in America. . . . The prominence of the Nation's Capitol continually magnified the scrutiny, and those in charge of its design and construction have had a notoriously tough time enduring the minute examination of congressional watchdogs, the press, and the public. This situation has been part of the Capitol's story from the beginning and will probably play a conspicuous role forever.[4]

Under strong congressional pressure these stewards revised, restored, and expanded the Capitol Hill complex. "One of the Capitol's most celebrated architects was also one of its most severely criticized," Allen wrote. "Benjamin Henry Latrobe [serving 1803–17] was routinely condemned in Congress for spending more than his appropriation and for taking too long to complete his work."[5]

In 1851 Thomas U. Walter also encountered a divided Congress when he was selected to triple the Capitol's size after congressional resistance to the expansion failed. Senator Isaac Walker of Wisconsin argued before his colleagues in what is now the Old Senate Chamber, "I believe that [the Capitol Extension] will destroy the architectural beauty of the Capitol altogether—that it will make it . . . an architectural monstrosity. . . . It will incur an enormous expenditure which . . . is chiefly to be incurred for the benefit of private individuals."

Allen noted,

supporters of the project were again thwarted by temporary roadblocks to further appropriations set up by those who still did not think the Capitol needed to be larger. Senator Solon Borland

Figure 11.2. The first ten architects of the Capitol. Courtesy of Architect of the Capitol

of Arkansas was a leader of the opposition. . . . History has rendered its verdict on Senator Borland's position. Not only have the new wings allowed the Capitol to function into the twenty-first century, they have given the building an imposing grandeur that the old structure lacked. The enlargement magnified the Capitol's presence over the city of Washington and gave it the bearing of a truly great building.[6]

The ongoing story of building, rebuilding, and repairing the Capitol is threaded through the core of our nation's history, having a critical impact on the stewardship role of its architects. Congress, in its deliberations, dictated which of the building's physical issues would be addressed in a timely fashion and which would languish for decades. Despite these political battles, the Capitol's designers and builders succeeded in blending two hundred years of growth and change into a cohesive, visual whole. We strove

to follow in their footsteps with the support of key members of Congress. My most steadfast mentor was Senator John Warner.

Senator John Warner: Civility

My relationship with Senator John Warner began in 1996, as we sat before a warming fireplace in his Capitol building conference room discussing my candidacy. It was a sign of the man that he didn't conduct the interview from behind an imposing desk or at a formal conference room table. He appreciated my enthusiasm and stressed the importance of protecting our heritage on Capitol Hill.

At the time I certainly didn't fully understand the workings of Congress, but over the years the senator was there to offer guidance as I encountered thorny challenges. I valued our talks, and in the final weeks of my tenure, we spoke again. While reflecting on

Figure 11.3. Senator John W. Warner and Alan M. Hantman. Courtesy of Architect of the Capitol

my legacy in designing and constructing this major Capitol addition, Warner shared some of his experiences in championing the design and construction of the Vietnam Veterans Memorial Wall some twenty-five years earlier. The winning design, to be built on the National Mall, was selected from among 1,421 competition submissions. The submission selected was created by a previously unknown twenty-one-year-old architecture undergraduate student at Yale, Maya Lin.

Lin's design visualized a V-shaped wall eight inches high at each end that, as described by the US Commission of Fine Arts, sloped into the earth as two 247-foot-long wings that "grew in height until they met at its ten-foot-high apex—like a 'wound that is closing and healing.'"[7] The design met fierce objections from many veterans, members of Congress, and the press. It was ridiculed and referred to as a ditch or gash in the earth, but Warner and other key congressional supporters were determined to see the construction through to completion, as was described in the *Washingtonian* in February 2007:

> In the 25 years since that day's dedication of the Vietnam Veterans Memorial (November 13, 1982), millions have come to see what is now a landmark. They read the names of the 58,256 dead and missing on the wall. They stare at their reflections in the polished black granite. Few can resist touching it. . . . The fight was bitter, fueled by emotions that had as much to do with the war as they did with the memorial itself. There were death threats, racial slurs, and broken friendships. Memories of that time still spark pain and anger.[8]

Warner smiled as he remembered those battles. He was proud of the power of Maya Lin's design, the perseverance of its supporters, and the compromise of adding a bronze statue by Frederick Hart, *The Three Soldiers*, which finally won over naysayers and turned this memorial into one of the most consequential sites in Washington, DC.

Warner assured me that the visitor center would, in time, be recognized and accepted as an integral part of the fabric of Washington, DC, an expansion that honored all that came before. His message was particularly welcome as we sat together discussing the final stages of construction, including the push and pull of congressional concerns and oversight and the necessity of placing the ongoing drama into the longer-term perspective warranted by this historic project. Warner's decades of public service provided him with this long-view political perspective, one I had not fully developed during my ten years at the Capitol.

As chair of the Senate Rules and Administration Committee, Warner was the first member of Congress to welcome me as architect, and the last to thank me and bid me farewell ten years later.

Congressional Support

Senate Democratic Leader Harry Reid (D-NV) supported the visitor center project and the day-to-day work of my agency from his powerful leadership position. He graciously joined Senator Warner and hundreds of our employees at my farewell gathering to express appreciation for my agency's service to the Congress. Later, as Senate majority leader, he entered his statement made on the floor of the Senate into the *Congressional Record*: "I had the good fortune earlier today, to have the first visit in a long time to the new Capitol Visitor Center. . . . I congratulate the office of the Architect of the Capitol. They did a wonderful job. . . . It is a facility of which we can all be proud. . . . People can come here safely and securely."[9]

Senator Bob Bennett also shared his personal observations on the process and ultimate opening of the center: "People are always opposed to what's in their best interests. So just go ahead and do it, and they'll appreciate it down the road when it's done. Some of my colleagues who were a bit grumpy about the project are now saying, 'Did you see the Visitor Center? It's spectacular!'"[10]

Congressman John Mica had been a staunch champion of the project from its conception by my predecessor, George White. During my tenure, Mica's commitment never flagged. In newspaper articles, the most supportive voice was often Mica's. He invested significant political capital championing the project with his House of Representatives colleagues.

Our agency's stewardship was only possible with the active support of these and other members of Congress, members who were willing to champion our work. In the House, these champions included Representatives Ray LaHood, Jerry Lewis, Carolyn Maloney (D-NY), Clerk Jeff Trandahl, and Counsel to the Speaker Ted Van Der Meid. In the Senate, these champions included Senate Majority Leaders Tom Daschle and Trent Lott and Senator Thad Cochran (R-MS), and I thank them all for their vision and essential support in the best interests of the Congress.

The Architect of the Capitol Team

I am enormously proud of our team of 2,300 dedicated Architect of the Capitol employees who I was honored to serve with as conscientious stewards of the national treasures on Capitol Hill. On behalf of Congress and the American people, they protected, maintained, and upgraded the Capitol and its grounds, Supreme Court, Library of Congress, and congressional office buildings. Staff members worked largely behind the scenes in each Capitol Hill building, providing quality service, day and night, in support of the Congress.

It is the current AOC agency employees who restored the Capitol after the insurrection of January 6, 2021, by replacing or repairing smashed windows, doors, and broken furniture, overseeing the restoration of statues, paintings, and the presidential inaugural platform, cleaning and restoring ransacked offices, corridors, and House and Senate chambers of residue from fire extinguishers, sprayed tear gas, and human waste. The *Washington Post* reported that a "security funding bill passed by the House included $40 million for the Architect of the Capitol for direct attack-related costs," along with "another $529.7 [million] . . . for security improvements."[11] Much important new work remains for the Architect of the Capitol Agency in the wake of the insurrection.

The departments of architecture, engineering, and construction will, I know, commit themselves to this mission, just as they did during my tenure for the design and construction of the Capitol Visitor Center, the modernization of the Supreme Court, the renovation and expansion of the Botanic Garden Conservatory, the construction of the National Garden, the perimeter security program, the Capitol Power Plant's West Refrigeration Plant expansion, the first phase of the Capitol Dome restoration, and hundreds of other projects, large and small, across the Capitol Hill campus. Achieving any level of success in our stewardship role would have been impossible without the full commitment of this diverse and highly motivated team and its leaders.

Capitol Visitor Center Team

As I walked the site during construction, speaking with skilled artisans in all trades, they often expressed their pride and personal commitment to this Capitol expansion project. For a great many this was the pinnacle of their careers, as it was for mine. Whenever one visits the center, the quality of construction work by craftspeople across dozens of construction specialties becomes evident. This impressive work has been celebrated by industry peers, as highlighted by the Washington Building Congress for recognition in their Craftsmanship Awards Program. An Architect of the Capitol press release listed the awards:

> For professional workmanship throughout the facility by individuals who are "creative, precise, and possess the special skills associated with quality craftsmanship." These features include the six skylights which allow natural light into the CVC; the custom light fixtures located

throughout the CVC and expansion spaces that complement the existing fixtures in the Capitol Building; the installation of major hardscape features such as stairs and seat walls, as well as the re-installation of historic elements such as fountains and lanterns on the East Front; and the installation of monumental interior wall stone and marble, and ornamental staircases, doors and other hardware.

The technical skills of the teams responsible for electrical and fire alarm systems installation, and plaster work were honored with Craftsmanship Awards and . . . the CVC project also received the "Hall of Fame Award" for the masonry work done throughout the facility.[12]

Construction industry recognition was well earned by the dedicated craftspeople who understood the importance of investing their best efforts on a project of such historic dimensions.

I too honor the accomplishments of the thousands with whom I was privileged to serve on the visitor center team, those who invested their skills and creative professionalism in designing and building this largest expansion of the Capitol in its centuries-long history. People from many firms worked tirelessly to blend our creation into the historic Capitol and grounds. I thank you all on behalf of Congress and the millions of Capitol visitors who, for generations to come, will be safely and respectfully welcomed through its new front door.

Center Recognition

After a visitor center tour, Rebecca W. Rimel, president of the Pew Charitable Trusts, which spearheaded the original $100 million private fundraising effort, wrote then acting architect Stephen Ayers that the Capitol Visitor Center is "a spectacular facility worthy of the great building it will support."[13]

In 2008 contemporaneous press reports recognized the importance of our project and its impact on Capitol Hill. Marc Fisher, *Washington Post*

senior editor, wrote on his blog on February 28, 2008, that

> as a station on the classic Washington tourist circuit, as a contemporary museum of American civics and government . . . the Visitor Center is a smash hit—the best addition to the District's tourism portfolio since the FDR Memorial in 1997 and the Holocaust Museum in 1993. Contrary to early concerns that the Visitor Center was being built to siphon tourists away from the Capitol Building itself, the exhibition space is designed to funnel you into the real thing. . . . The result is an aesthetic boost to the Capitol campus.[14]

A *Roll Call* editorial headline on December 1, 2008, the day before the center's dedication, read "A Beautiful Facility That Is Worthy of the Capitol." According to the editorial, "Essentially, [Hantman] built a second Capitol, a 580,000-square-foot underground structure with a footprint larger than that of the Capitol itself. . . . It honors the original."[15]

After his tour of the center just before its dedication, the 2008 American Institute of Architects national president Marshall Parnell observed:

> Congress is the people's house, and the new center truly makes sure that the people have a place in the Capitol. That, in essence, is the goal of civic architecture—to connect the highest aspirations of our society to the people who comprise that society. The Architect of the Capitol, who led this process, has served the Congress and the country in a way that would make their predecessors proud. I hope the millions of Americans and visitors from around the globe recognize that the greatness of our country is not only the strength of our civic institutions, but also in the civic architecture that makes these institutions accessible to the people.[16]

As the great American architect Frank Lloyd Wright said, "Noble life demands a noble architecture for noble uses of noble men. . . . Maybe we can show government how to operate better as a result of better architecture."[17]

We can keep hoping.

Commemorating the Capitol Visitor Center's Tenth Anniversary

Senator Warner was correct. Like the Vietnam Memorial, the center hosted more than twenty-one million visitors in its first decade. In 2018 I proudly attended a ceremony celebrating ten years of the center's service to the Congress and the American people, hosted in the Congressional Auditorium by the 11th Architect of the Capitol, Stephen Ayers.

During its first ten years, the center hosted more than 6,000 events, supported 38 congressional ceremonies in Emancipation Hall, provided 320,000 group tours, and produced millions of brochures and other educational materials. More than a thousand historical documents and artifacts had been displayed in Exhibition Hall through 19 exhibit rotations, and more than 3 million visitors had been served in the Capitol Café .[18]

The visitor center was intended to accommodate this volume of visitors, meeting activity, and much more. These statistics demonstrate that the design and quality of the center's public and congressional spaces have supported Congress's needs while broadening the Capitol's ability to involve, inspire, and inform visitors about the legislative process and the central role it plays in our nation's democracy. Since its formal opening in 2008, the center has become an integral part of the life of the Congress and is recognized as the Capitol's front door for its visitors.

Lessons Learned: History Will Repeat Itself

Scenes of constant drama play out within the US Capitol building. Leading roles often shift with new elections as past decisions fade out of focus, and the politics of the day continue to shape the Capitol's physical reality. My list of lessons learned was topped by the recognition that the Hill's everchanging population represents a microcosm of our vast country's population. A full gamut of political philosophies lives and thrives within the Capitol complex, with members ranging from competent ethical stewards who take the long view in the best interests of our democracy to those who seek power primarily in the service of self.

I often testified at witness tables, judged by panels of lawmakers, several of whom had broken or seriously bent the law as they tried to once again prevail in their ever-present next election. For many, the concept of the citizen legislator has given way to the norm of lifetime political careers for those who serve twenty, thirty, or more years and then move on to become K Street lobbyists, taking advantage of the earning power their government connections provide.

Another lesson learned was that government reports may recommend assigning responsibility to a single general contractor, but Congress will probably dictate major changes that will cause delays resulting in having to split a single project into multiple subprojects. Major construction work will also have to run the gauntlet of delayed funding, reviews, and approvals at each phase, with evolving security criteria compelling further changes.[19]

The Capitol Visitor Center is a prime example of this. Initially designed to serve millions of guests, it grew and morphed to the point that half its total area is dedicated to congressional meeting and support space that will rarely be seen by the visiting public. In reality, it is a minor miracle that the center was actually brought to fruition as a stately, high-quality extension of the Capitol. Without congressional champions, this would not have been possible.

Notes for My Successors

I highlight lessons learned for my successors, beginning with the reality that our Capitol must be designed to stand the test of time using materials compatible with George Washington's original vision of a stately national Capitol. I repeat the concern voiced by Senator Kay Bailey Hutchison at my confirmation hearing when she criticized newly built Capitol meeting rooms: "They are worthy of any Holiday Inn in America, but not worthy of the United States Congress. . . . Our generation has a responsibility to maintain the quality that our forefathers and foremothers gave us."[20]

With 535 members of Congress, some will push for quick solutions to complex problems without sufficient understanding of security and life-safety needs and the imperative to continue welcoming visitors, even as the Capitol remains a target of enemies both foreign and domestic. Some members will delegate much of their power to unelected staff, who are often unqualified party loyalists, making respon-

sible stewardship increasingly difficult to achieve. But future architects of the Capitol must remain true to their oath of office and their professional standards despite pressures to compromise them.

I recommend that future architects seek the best design professionals to serve on peer review panels to critique projects and think out of the box as alternative, and possibly better, solutions are examined. Most important, as projects move forward and problems and roadblocks inevitably surface, it's important to keep the project team working positively together and not give in to members who call for you to select scapegoats to blame.

I also share guidance offered me by my predecessor George White: "Much controversy and criticism will come your way, and you have to take it without

Figure 11.4. Night view of the Doorway to Democracy. Courtesy of Architect of the Capitol

publicly pushing back. You need to develop a thick skin." Finally, in order to accomplish anything of significance, it is critical to build relationships with constructive members of both chambers who are willing to champion the work of the agency.

The position of Architect of the Capitol presents magnificent challenges. Despite the difficulties confronted, when walking the Capitol's corridors at night, I found that a historical presence radiated from its walls as I followed in the footsteps of my predecessors, of generations of representatives, senators, and presidents, of those who shaped our centuries-long flow of democracy. A sense of continuity flowed from those years as I heard my solitary footsteps echo from those same walls and gracefully arched ceilings. I was honored and humbled by the responsibilities of walking those corridors as an officer of Congress, as I hope future architects will be, contributing as best they can to the ongoing chronicle of the Capitol, the worldwide symbol of our nation.

Notes

1. Allen, *History of the United States Capitol*, 325.
2. Daniel Coughlin, invocation at Capitol Visitor Center dedication ceremony, December 2, 2008.
3. Hantman, foreword, in Allen, *History of the United States Capitol*, xiii.
4. Allen, *Controversies in the Construction History*.
5. Allen, 4.
6. Allen, 4–5.
7. US Commission of Fine Arts, "A Century of Design, 1910–2010," exhibit panels, 2010.
8. Denise Kersten Wells, "The Vietnam Memorial's History: Twenty-Five Years Ago, the Vietnam Veteran Memorial Divided Washington. Today It's an Emotional Touchstone," *Washingtonian*, November 1, 2007.
9. US Senate, Proceedings and Debates of the 110th Congress, Second Session, April 14, 2008, *Congressional Record*.
10. Hantman, personal notes, phone call from Senator Bennett, November 19, 2008.
11. Hsu, "Jan. 6 Riot."
12. "AOC's Capitol Visitor Center Project Recognized by Washington Building Congress, 2008 Craftsmanship Awards," AOC Press Release, April 15, 2008.
13. Rebecca W. Rimel, president of the Pew Charitable Trusts, letter to Acting Architect of the Capitol Stephen T. Ayers, AIA, September 17, 2007.
14. Fisher, "DC's New Underground Jewel."
15. "A Beautiful Facility That Is Worthy of the Capitol," *Roll Call*, December 1, 2008.
16. "Marshall Parnell, 2008 AIA President," AOC Press Release, December 9, 2008.
17. Frank Lloyd Wright, quotefancy.com, quotes 48 and 116.
18. "US Capitol Visitor Center, 10th Anniversary, Commemorating 10 Years of Service to Congress and Visitors," Architect of the Capitol brochure, November 29, 2018.
19. Comptroller General, "Conventional Design and Construction Methods."
20. Juliet Eilperin, "Senators Ask New Architect to Nix Cars on East Front, Hantman Becomes Tenth to Hold Post," *Roll Call*, January 30, 1997.

ACKNOWLEDGMENTS

Under the Dome adds another link to the centuries-long chain of Capitol history, an evolutionary process overseen by those who committed their professional energies and talents to our magnificent challenge. This chronicle would never have been written without the consistent support, constructive criticism and keen insights that my life partner, Rosalyn Frank Hantman, brought to seemingly endless creative and editing cycles. Rosalyn's perseverance helped bring the manuscript to a point where we could seek to pry open the doors of the publishing world.

The resources of our daughter Julie Hantman led us to Georgetown historian Adam Rothman and through him to our publisher, Al Bertrand, director of Georgetown University Press. Tours of the Capitol, its new visitor center, and working meetings soon turned into a constructive relationship and an agreement to retain an editor to help reorganize and refine the manuscript.

Finding an experienced professional capable of diving together into this complex process of refining the chronological flow of the manuscript became another challenge that Julie resolved by initiating a search which led to editor extraordinaire Henry Ferris. Raising perceptive and challenging questions, Henry's talents as a strong and focused guide, together with Rosalyn's critical eye, helped me refine *Under the Dome*. Al Bertrand's review and presentation of the manuscript to Georgetown University's faculty editorial board led to its enthusiastic endorsement and the decision to publish.

Al Bertrand and his Georgetown editorial, production, and marketing support teams, including Rachel McCarthy, Elizabeth Sheridan, Virginia Bryant, Francys Reed, Leila Sebastian, and their consultants (Billie Smith-Haffener and Erin Kirk), worked on copy editing, book design, marketing, and the plethora of details necessary to bring the production process to fruition. Their support made it happen, and I thank them for their commitment and professionalism.

A critical part of this process included multiple reviews by historian William C. Allen, now historian emeritus of the Architect of the Capitol Agency, whose *History of the United States Capitol*, the definitive Capitol chronicle, was a major source of inspiration for *Under the Dome*. I thank him for his unstinting support and thoroughness in assuring the manuscript's historical accuracy.

Through the long process, a host of relatives and friends provided inspiration and support, including my daughters Allyson, Deborah, and Julie, their partners Howard, Steve, and Jeff, and grandchildren Adele, Audrey, Justin, Charlotte, Lucy, and Lila. Howard Goldberg and Glenn Ostrager provided wise and practical legal counsel, while Jeff Schwarz provided not only professional level photographic support but also image preparation and enhancement to facilitate their publication. I thank them all for being there throughout this challenging process.

The Architect of the Capitol Agency Team

The core of my ten years as head of the Architect of the Capitol Agency and the work described in *Under the Dome* was built upon the talents and dedicated service of the 2,300 agency members. It is they who performed the work and met the myriad challenges faced daily on Capitol Hill in support of the Congress and the national treasures entrusted to our care. We lived this history together. While it is impossible to list all the members of the Architect of the Capitol Agency deserving recognition, I gratefully acknowledge their contributions and recognize the following leaders and support staff for their integrity and commitment to excellence.

Susan Adams
Bruce Arthur
Stephen Ayers
Scott Birkhead
Tom Carroll
Margaret Cox
Cal Durgan
Ken Eads
Carlos Elias
Matthew Evans
David Ferguson
Tom Fontana
Herb Franklin
Anna Franz
Sharon Gang
Bob Gleich
Chris Goldman
Dan Hanlon
Kevin Hildebrand
Bob Hixon
Arlen Holmes
Doug Jacobs
Jim Krapp
Peter Kushner
Karen Livingston
Timothy Macdonald
Eva Malecki
Michael Marinaccio
Glenn Marshall
Peter May
Quinton McCall
Art McIntye
Dick McSeveny
Yvonne Messick

Robin Morey
Kevin Mulshine
Steve Payne
Robert Pennington
Amita Poole
Lynda Poole
Christopher Potter
Stuart Pregnall
Bonnie Pritchett
Luis Rosario
Bryan Roth
Kristen Schmehl
Martha Sewell
Holly Shimizu
Danielle Sigmon
Gregory Simmons
Cynthia Snyder
Lawrence Stoffel
Garland Strawderman
Hector Suarez
Deborah Thomas
Frank Tiscione
Rebecca Tiscione
Michael Turnbull
Chuck Tyler
Peggy Tyler
Elliot Wagner
John Weber
William Weidemeyer
Don White
Bernard Wilson
Barbara Wolanin
Marilyn Wong-Wittmer

Capitol Visitor Center Design Team

Our team of architectural, engineering, and construction professionals was extraordinarily succesful in continuing the Capitol's centuries-long architectural metamorphosis by creating a center that now supports the expanded needs of the Senate and the House and graciously welcomes visitors from around the country and the world to our Capitol while providing them with an opportunity to learn about the Congress.

It is my honor to recognize and express my great appreciation and admiration to the thousands who invested their skills and creative professionalism over the years to designing and building the Capitol Visitor Center. These firms and individuals represent all those whoworked tirelessly on behalf of generations yet to come, under very challenging conditions, to sensitively meld the center with the historic United States Capitol building.

Architecture and Engineering

Architects of the Capitol
George White, 9th Architect of the Capitol
Stephen Ayers, 11th Architect of the Capitol

Architect of the Capitol Agency
Susan Adams
Bruce Arthur
Carol Beebe
Scott Birkhead
Nadine Bradley
Drew Coulsen
Cal Durgin
Ken Eads
Carlos Elias
Matthew Evans
Tom Fontana
Robert Hixon
Douglas Jacobs
Peter Kushner
Gary Lee
Peter May
Nam Pham
Amita N. Poole
Melissa Prophet
Joe Sacco
Martha Sewell
Joe Shelton

Peer Advisory Panel
Edward L. Barnes
David Childs

Henry M. (Harry) Cobb
Tom Johnson
Robert Peck

Associate Architect and Engineer: CRTKL Associates, Inc., Baltimore, Maryland, and Washington, DC
Harold L. Adams
Janice Adams
Jay Becker
Steve Buck
Dawn Butler
Michael Considine
Serge Dillenseger
D. Rodman Henderer
Neal Hudson
Tim Hutcheson
Ann Kemble
James Kitco
Robert Knight
Matthew Loeffeler
Brad Mahon
Andrea Mains
Mike McQueen
Diane Phelan
Kiril Pivovarov
Matt Rohr
Dick Sapio
Darren Shumatte
Dean Speelman

Rick Stewart
Richard Storck
Kaan Tanali
Goodluck Tembunkiart
David V. Thompson
Darren Vican
Aimee Woodall
Heidi Zielstorff

Structural Engineering and Blast Analysis: Weidlinger and Associates, New York, and Cambridge, Massachusetts
John Bonita
Abdol Hagh
Mehrdad Mirzakashani
Todd Rittenhouse
Bob Smilowitz

Mechanical Engineering and Plumbing: James Posey Associates, Inc., Baltimore, Maryland
Tim Cech
Karl Gumnick
Carl Hossfeld
Rich Lang
Mike Lippy
Kevin McCarthy
Denny White

Fire Science and Engineering: Hughes Associates, Inc., Baltimore, Maryland
Ajay Prasad
Brian Rhodes
Eric Rosenbaum

Civil Engineering: David Volkert and Associates, Alexandria, Virginia
James R. Spencer
Cesar Vargas
Fred White
Earl Wilkens

Lighting: H. M. Brandston Partnership Inc., New York
Scott Mathews
Burr Rutledge

Waterproofing: Gale Associates, Baltimore, Maryland
T. Stephen Kisielnicki
Ed Madden

Commissioning: Sebesta Blumberg and Associates, Inc., Arlington, Virginia
Oleska Breslawec
Crystall Merlino

Hardware: ECSI, Erbshloe Consulting Services, Haymarket, Virginia

Landscape Design, Arboricultural, and Associated Services

Landscape, Hardscape Architects: Sasaki Associates, Watertown, Massachusetts
Neil Dean
Alan Ward
Lori Ellis

Tree Protection: The Care of Trees, Gaithersburg, Maryland
Chris Cowles

Tree Maintenance: Davey Tree Expert Co.
Heather A. White

Trees: National Shade LP, Houston, Texas

Irrigation: Irrigation Consultant Services, Conyers, Georgia

Water Features: Robert Scott Water Features

Fountains: Wesco Fountains, Inc., Venice, Florida

ADA, Pedestrian and Vehicular Movement, Vertical Transportation, and Environmental

ADA Accessibility: Code Access, Birmingham, Alabama

    James Scott

Vertical Transportation: John A. Van Deusen and Associates, Inc., Livingston, New Jersey

    Hakan Tanyeri

Pedestrian Movement: Parsons, Brinkerhoff, Quale and Douglas, Inc.

    Gregory Benz

    Bruce Douglas

Visitor Count: Randi Korn and Associates, Inc., Alexandria, Virginia

    Jean Kalata

Traffic and Bus Management: Robert L. Morris, Inc., Bethesda, Maryland

    Robert Morris

Environmental: Greenhorne and O'Mara, Inc.

    Joan Glynn

    Robert J. Handy Jr.

    Ross Vorhees

Subsurface Utilities: Accurate Locating Inc., Hanover, Maryland

    Van Singer

Archaeology: John Milner Associates, Inc., Alexandria, Virginia

    Kerri Culhane

    Donna Seifert

Exhibits, Audiovisual, Theaters, Food Service

Exhibits: Ralph Appelbaum Associates, Inc., New York

    Ralph Appelbaum

    Kevin Crotty

    Dinah Lofgren

    Christopher Micelli

    Marianne Schuit

    Deborah Wolff

Film Production and Orientation Theater Production: Donna Lawrence Productions, Louisville, Kentucky

    Larry Christensen

    Donna Lawrence

Theater, Auditorium, and Audiovisual: Auerbach and Associates, New York and San Francisco

    Charles Cosler

    Paul Garrity

    Daniel Mei

    Steve Pollock

Boyce Nemec Designs, Connecticut

    Andrew Smith

Acoustical Engineering: Cerami and Associates, Inc., New York

    Victoria Cerami

    Patricia Scanlon

Food Services: Cini-Little International, Inc.

    William V. Eaton

    Leslie Krewatch

    Tim O'Mara

    Ray Petit

Culinary Advisers: Ellicott City, Maryland

    Michael Pantano

Signage, Graphics, Models, and Renderings

Signage and Graphic Design: Douglas Gallagher

Renderer: Michael McCann Associates, Inc., Toronto
  Michael McCann

Howard Associates, New York and Ohio
  Dick Howard
  Tom McCartney

Scale Models: Scale Models Unlimited, Menlo Park, California
  Lisa Gemmiti
  Matthew Kellett
  Ron Marian

Construction Management and Estimating

Construction Management: Gilbane Company, Inc., Providence, Rhode Island, and Washington, DC
  Paul Choquette
  Lynn Class
  Andy Furor
  Bruce Hoffman
  Mark Luria
  Jennifer May
  Kelly Mullin
  John Rota
  Flip Salyer
  Marvin Shenkler
  Mike Soderman
  Mark Thifault
  Keith Valdez
  Gary Wright

Cost Estimator: Atkins HF&G (formerly Hanscomb, Inc.), Alexandria, Virginia
  Reza Amirkhalili
  Ian Jones

Financial Feasibility: Ernst & Young, LLP
  Andy Anderson
  Michael Buckley
  Pam Dubois

General Contractors and Subcontractors

Sequence 1 General Contractor: Centex Corporation Inc., Fairfax, Virginia
  Jim Carr
  Keith Dugan
  Will Fishback
  Bob Frew
  Rebecca Nordby
  Charlie Oh
  Alex Palacios
  David Selzer
  Steve Smithgall
  John Tarpey
  Robert Van Cleave

Sequence 1 Foundation Wall Subcontractor: Nicholson Construction Co., Pittsburgh

Sequence 1 Excavation: Cherry Hill Construction, Jessup, Maryland

Sequence 2 General Contractor: Manhattan Construction Co., Virginia
  Nabeel Aboulhosn
  Ted Baker
  Joan Barone
  Mark Baxter
  Jon Clark
  Chuck Detwiler
  Dale Harlow

Rob Howk
Ryan Helland
Jerry Lefever
Vincent Maldonado
Derick Scott
David Uffelman

Sequence 2 Mechanical Contractor: John M. Kirlin, LLC

Sequence 2 Stonework: Boatman and Magnani, Capitol Heights, Maryland

Sequence 2 Quarry: Annandale Sandstone Quarries, Inc., Boyers, Pennsylvania

Sequence 2 Stone Fabricator: Quarra Stone Company, Madison, Wisconsin

Sequence 2 Subcontractor, House and Senate Expansion Space: Grunley Construction Company, Inc.
Kenneth M. Grunley
William M. Six

To all these companies and individuals and the thousands of additional unnamed professionals, skilled artisans, and construction workers who contributed to this, the largest addition to the US Capitol in more than 230 years, I thank you on behalf of Congress and the millions of visitors who are safely and respectfully welcomed to their Capitol each year through its new front door.

It has been my honor to work with you.

SELECTED BIBLIOGRAPHY

Books, Pamphlets and Documents

Aikman, Lonnelle. *We, the People: The Story of the United States Capitol.* Washington, DC: US Capitol Historical Society, 2011.

Allen, William C. *Controversies in the Construction History of the United States Capitol Complex.* Washington, DC: Architect of the Capitol, 2007.

———. *The Dome of the United States Capitol: An Architectural History.* Washington, DC: Government Printing Office, 1992.

———. *History of Slave Laborers in the Construction of the United States Capitol.* Washington, DC: Architect of the Capitol, 2005.

———. *History of the United States Capitol: A Chronicle of Design, Construction and Politics.* Prepared under the direction of the Architect of the Capitol. Senate Document 106-29, 106th Congress, 2nd session. Washington, DC: US Government Printing Office, 2001.

———. *"In the Greatest Solemn Dignity": The Capitol's Four Cornerstones.* Washington, DC: Government Printing Office, 1995.

———. *The United States Capitol: A Brief Architectural History.* Washington, DC: Government Printing Office, 1990.

Beveridge, Charles E., and Paul Rochelcau. *Frederick Law Olmsted: Designing the American Landscape.* Edited by David Larkin. New York: Rizzoli, 1995.

Brown, Glenn. *Glenn Brown's History of the United States Capitol: Annotated Edition in Commemoration of the Bicentennial of the United States Capitol.* Annotated by William W. Bushong. Washington, DC: US Government Printing Office, 2000.

Bushong, William B. *Uncle Sam's Architects: Builders of the Capitol.* Washington, DC: United States Capitol Historical Society, 1994.

Dushkes, Laura S., comp. and ed. *The Architect Says: Quotes, Quips and Words of Wisdom.* Princeton, NJ: Princeton University Press, 2012.

Fallen, Anne Catherine. *A Botanic Garden for the Nation: The United States Botanic Garden.* Washington, DC: US Government Printing Office, 2007.

Lott, Trent. *Herding Cats: A Life in Politics.* New York: ReganBooks, 2005.

Meigs, Montgomery C. *Capitol Builder: The Shorthand Journals of Montgomery C. Meigs, 1853–1859, 1861.* Edited by Wendy Wolf. Washington, DC: US Government Printing Office, 2001.

Moynihan, Daniel Patrick. *Freedom Without Fortresses: Shaping the New Secure Environment.* Symposium Proceedings, National Building Museum, Washington, DC, November 27, 2001.

Ralph Appelbaum Associates. "Preliminary Interpretive Principles and Themes." Report to the Capitol Visitor Center Working Group, Washington, DC, June 2001.

Scott, Pamela, and Antoinette J. Lee. *Buildings of the District of Columbia.* New York: Oxford University Press, 1993.

Shaffer, Kathie. Interview with J. Dennis Hastert. Oral History Transcripts, Flight 93 National Memorial, FLNI OH 743 Hastert, J. Dennis,

March 20, 2013. Transcribed by Charlotte R. Jones. Shanksville, PA: National Park Service, 2013.

———. Interview with Nellie Neuman. Oral History Transcripts, Flight 93 National Memorial, FLNI OH 722 Neumann, Nellie, February 13, 2012. Transcribed by Shirly Sowerbrower. Shanksville, PA: National Park Service, 2012.

———. Interview with Wilson "Bill" Livingood. Oral History Transcripts, Flight 93 National Memorial, FLNI OH 739 Livingood, Wilson Bill, March 1, 2012. Transcribed by Kathie Shaffer. Shanksville, PA: National Park Service, 2012.

US Architect of the Capitol. "Revalidation Report: United States Capitol Visitor Center." Washington, DC, 1999.

US Comptroller General. "Conventional Design and Construction Methods Are More Applicable for Capitol Hill Construction Projects." Government Accountability Office, Washington, DC, 1981.

White, George M. *Under the Capitol Dome*. Washington, DC: American Institute of Architects, 1997.

———. "United States Capitol Visitor Center: Final Design Report." Architect of the Capitol, Washington, DC, November 10, 1995.

Newspapers, Cable News, Websites

AOC.gov Website and *Shoptalk* Newsletter
Baltimore Sun
The BLT: The Blog of Legal Times
Congressional Quarterly
CNN
Crain's New York Business
District of Columbia National Guard Newsletter
Haskell News (Oklahoma)
The Hill
New York Times
Politico
Richmond Times-Dispatch
Roll Call
Texas Observer
USA Today
US News and World Report
Washingtonian
The Washington Post

IMAGE CREDITS

Figure 7.7. Architect of the Capitol
Figure 7.8. Architect of the Capitol
Figure 7.9. Jeffrey Schwarz Photography
Figure 7.10. Alan M. Hantman

Figure 8.1. National Park Service, Flight 93 National Memorial
Figure 8.2. Alan M. Hantman
Figure 8.3. National Park Service, Flight 93 National Memorial
Figure 8.4. Architect of the Capitol
Figure 8.5. Architect of the Capitol
Figure 8.6. Architect of the Capitol
Figure 8.7. Michael McCann
Figure 8.8. Michael McCann
Figure 8.9. Architect of the Capitol

Figure 9.1. Architect of the Capitol
Figure 9.2. Architect of the Capitol
Figure 9.3. Architect of the Capitol
Figure 9.4. Architect of the Capitol
Figure 9.5. Architect of the Capitol
Figure 9.6. Architect of the Capitol
Figure 9.7. Architect of the Capitol
Figure 9.8. Alan M. Hantman
Figure 9.9. Architect of the Capitol

Figure 9.10. Architect of the Capitol
Figure 9.11. Architect of the Capitol
Figure 9.12. Jeffrey Schwarz Photography
Figure 9.13. Jeffrey Schwarz Photography
Figure 9.14. Jeffrey Schwarz Photography

Figure 10.1. Architect of the Capitol
Figure 10.2. Architect of the Capitol
Figure 10.3. Architect of the Capitol
Figure 10.4. Alan M. Hantman
Figure 10.5. Jeffrey Schwarz Photography
Figure 10.6. Jeffrey Schwarz Photography
Figure 10.7. Architect of the Capitol
Figure 10.8. SmithGroup Landscape Architects
Figure 10.9. Architect of the Capitol
Figure 10.10. Architect of the Capitol
Figure 10.11. Architect of the Capitol
Figure 10.12. Architect of the Capitol
Figure 10.13. Architect of the Capitol
Figure 10.14. Architect of the Capitol

Figure 11.1. Architect of the Capitol
Figure 11.2. Architect of the Capitol
Figure 11.3. Architect of the Capitol
Figure 11.4. Architect of the Capitol

INDEX

ABOUT THE AUTHOR

Alan M. Hantman was appointed 10th Architect of the Capitol by President Bill Clinton and was the first to be confirmed by the US Senate, serving from 1997–2007. With a staff of 2,300 he was entrusted with the operation and stewardship of the national treasures on Capitol Hill including the Capitol, Supreme Court, Library of Congress, House and Senate Office Buildings, historic artwork, and Capitol grounds. Hantman was responsible for the design and construction of the 580,000-square-foot US Capitol visitor and meeting center, which increased the Capitol by 70 percent, the largest increment of growth in its history.

Hantman previously served as vice president of architecture, planning, and historic preservation at Rockefeller Center, was certified by the National Council of Architectural Registration Boards, and was elected to fellowship in the American Institute of Architects.